Acclaim for *Hypocrite in a Pouffy White Dress*

"A deliriously, levitatingly funny memoir . . . The thread of tough humor working its way through this memoir serves to backlight moments of exquisite realization . . . and startling, genuine epiphanies."
—*Kirkus Reviews* (starred review)

"Gilman's wise-cracking, raw narrative . . . is reminiscent of David Sedaris's writing and will draw a similar audience. Hilarious, assured, and moving, these are wildly entertaining stories that readers will share instantly with friends."
—*Booklist*

"*Hypocrite in a Pouffy White Dress* is hip and hilarious."
—Susan Shapiro, author of *Five Men Who Broke My Heart*

"This is not so much a sequel to as an enlargement of *Kiss My Tiara*; Susan Gilman's voice is somehow both representative of a generation and unmistakably her own. A book to savor silently that makes you laugh out loud."
—Nicholas Delbanco, author of *The Vagabonds* and *Old Scores*

"Amusing, entertaining, and laugh-out-loud funny."
—Cheryl Peck, author of *Fat Girls and Lawn Chairs*

"If David Sedaris married most of the cast of *The Breakfast Club*, the resulting child just might be Susan Jane Gilman. She channels the voices of her inner geek, freak, hipster, and princess with razor sharp wit and no small measure of grace. If you have a friend who came of age any time between *Carrie* and *Clueless* and you don't buy them this book, then face it—you aren't a very good friend."
—Joshilyn Jackson, author of *Gods in Alabama*

Also by Susan Jane Gilman

Kiss My Tiara

hypocrite
in a
pouffy white dress

TALES OF GROWING UP
GROOVY AND CLUELESS

SUSAN JANE GILMAN

WARNER BOOKS

NEW YORK   BOSTON

Material in *Hypocrite in a Pouffy White Dress* originally appeared in an article by Susan Jane Gilman entitled "Power Pouf" in the June 2001 issue of *Real Simple* magazine.

The chapter "Mick Jagger Wants Me" by Susan Jane Gilman originally appeared in a slightly different form in the Fall 1994 issue (Vol. 20/2&3) of *Ploughshares* under the title "Meeting Mick Jagger." That version of the essay was awarded an Avery Hopwood Literary Award by the University of Michigan prior to its publication.

Warner Books

Time Warner Book Group
1271 Avenue of the Americas, New York, NY 10020
Visit our Web site at www.twbookmark.com

Printed in the United States of America

First Printing: January 2005

10   9   8   7   6   5   4   3   2

Library of Congress Cataloging-in-Publication Data

Gilman, Susan Jane.
    Hypocrite in a pouffy white dress : tales of growing up groovy and clueless / Susan Jane Gilman.
        p.   cm.
    ISBN 0-446-67949-6
    1. Gilman, Susan Jane—Childhood and youth. 2. Girls—New York (State)—New York—Biography. 3. Young women—New York (State)—New York—Biography. 4. New York (N.Y.)—Biography. 5. Geneva (Switzerland)—Biography. I. Title.
    CT275.G4295A3 2004
    974.7'1043'092—dc22   2004006637

Book design and text composition by Stratford Publishing Services

Cover design by Brigid Pearson

For my family

Acknowledgments

THIS BOOK WOULD have been impossible to write without my mother, Ellen. Not only did she obviously give birth to me, but she has taught me the supreme value of imagination and creativity. Likewise, this book would have been equally impossible to write without my father, David. Not only did he, too, have a role in my birth, but he has continually inspired me to live courageously and not take myself too seriously.

My husband, the Amazing Bob Stefanski, deserves his own acknowledgments page for his steadfast support, love, patience, and availability as a sounding board, as well as for giving me the adventure of a lifetime.

Countless thanks are due my editor, Amy Einhorn, for her continually amazing work, commitment, optimism, and high tea at Fortnum & Mason, as well as to my agent, Irene Skolnick, for her eternal hand-holding and clear understanding of what is truly important.

I would also like to thank Dollie and Paul Llanso, and Irit and Yitzik Lev for their friendship and sharing their "space" with me; Susie Walker for bringing me home to her garden; Maureen McSherry for agreeing to read whatever I sent her; Jackie and Ken Davidson for keeping me sane; and Cathline James and Roy Langstaff for their endless support.

My thanks as well to Kitt Rasmussen. To Anyzette and Jacques Lebet: *Merci beaucoup pour tout.* I'd also like to acknowledge Eric Messinger simply because he deserves it.

Yet above all, I must express my undying gratitude to my phenomenal brother, John, who has been along for the entire ride, both literally and literarily. I could not have done this without his support, dedication, sound judgment, and killer sense of humor. Kid, you've been incredible. I am blessed to have you as my brother; I cannot thank you enough. This one, above all, is for you.

Contents

Author's Soapbox

THIS IS A BOOK about growing up ambitious and engaging in some spectacularly imbecilic behavior. Although I was taught never to let the truth get in the way of a good story, the tales here are true—or, at least, I've recounted them as honestly as I can remember them. In some cases, names and details of people and places have been altered to protect the guilty and innocent alike.

I've written this book, in part, because it seems that all of us could use a good laugh these days. Yet I've also written it because so many of the stories women are currently telling are all about getting a man. Or about getting over a man. Or about getting laid. Or about not getting laid. Or about not getting laid and not getting a man, but deciding we're okay with it.

Having spent criminal amounts of time sleeping with inappropriate men myself, then bragging about it, I love hearing about other people's romantic and sexual ineptitude as much as the next person. Yet ultimately, there's so much more to women's lives that's worthy of attention and ridicule. Hence, this collection. While a few stories do involve a boy, a bra, and a booty call, mostly their focus is elsewhere—on other passions and delusions that we all experience in one form or another.

It's my hope that these "coming of age" stories will make readers laugh, and prove once and for all that a girl doesn't need a guy in her life in order to act like a complete idiot. Certainly I, at least, never have.

—*Susan Jane Gilman*

PART I

Grape Juice and Humiliation

Chapter 1

Nudie Hippie Kiddie Star

WHEN I WAS LITTLE, I was so girlie and ambitious, I was practically a drag queen. I wanted to be everything at once: a prima ballerina, an actress, a model, a famous artist, a nurse, an Ice Capades dancer, and Batgirl. I spent inordinate amounts of time waltzing around our living room with a doily on my head, imagining in great detail my promenade down the runway as the new Miss America, during which time I would also happen to receive a Nobel Prize for coloring.

The one thing I did not want to be was a hippie.

"For Chrissake, you're not a hippie," said my mother, fanning incense around our living room with the sleeves of her dashiki. "You're four years old. You run around in a tutu. You eat TV dinners and complain when the food doesn't look exactly like it does on the packages. Hippies don't do that," she said. "Hippies don't make a big production out of eating their Tater Tots.

"Come to think of it, hippies don't torture their little brother by trying to sell him the silverware, either," she added. "If I were you, I'd worry less about being a hippie and more about being an extortionist."

But even by age four, I was aware of my family's intrinsic grooviness, and it worried me no end. Like most little kids—or anyone, for that matter—I suffered from contradictory desires. While I wanted to be the biggest, brightest star in the universe, I also wanted to be exactly like everybody else.

And so, I was enormously relieved when my parents announced we were going away to Silver Lake for the summer. From what I understood of the world, "going away" was what normal Americans did. It was 1969, and my family was living in a subsidized housing project in Upper Manhattan, in a neighborhood whose only claim to fame at the time was that its crime and gang warfare had been sufficient enough to inspire the hit Broadway musical *West Side Story*.

At Silver Lake, not only would we be taking a real summer vacation, but, according to my mother, there was even the slight possibility I'd get to be in a movie. Apparently, she knew a filmmaker there named Alice Furnald, who had been casting around for kids.

To call Silver Lake a resort would be an exaggeration. It was a summer colony founded by Socialists, people either too exhausted from manual labor or too unfamiliar with it to care much about landscaping. Small bungalows had simply been built on plots of land, then left to recede back into the woods around them. Dirt roads led to the eponymous lake, which shimmered, mirrorlike, at the start of each summer before deteriorating into a green porridge of algae by late August. The community's one concession to civilization was "the Barn," an old red farm building used as a recreation center. Otherwise, Mother Nature had been pretty much left to "do her thing" as the colonists liked to say.

For a kid, Silver Lake presented infinite ways to inflict yourself on this natural world, and my new friends quickly schooled me in a range of distinctly un-girlie pleasures. Our parents might have been sitting cross-legged on the grass nodding along to the Youngbloods—*"C'mon people now! Smile on your brother"*—but we had ants to incinerate and decapitate, worms to smush, frogs to stalk, fireflies to take hostage, caterpillars to outwit, slugs to poke at with a stick, berries to pulverize with a rock, and dead moles to dig up in the garden and fling around the kitchen moments before lunch. We discovered that if we scraped reddish soil from the side of a mound by the lake, then mixed it with water, we got a terrifically sloppy, maroon-colored mess. It stained our clothes and the teenagers called it "bloody muddy," so of course we were determined to play with it as much as possible. It was like the caviar of mud.

Better yet was the four o'clock arrival of the ice cream man. I suspect the London Blitz generated less hysteria and mayhem. As soon as we heard the bells on the Good Humor truck jiggling up the road, every single kid under the age of twelve went insane. "Ice cream!" we shrieked. Dashing out of the water, we raced over to our parents, snatched money out of their hands before they could finish saying *and get a Creamsicle for your father, please,* then zoomed up the hill barefoot and screaming. It wasn't so much the ice cream man arriving as the ice cream messiah.

In Silver Lake, I romped through my days in a state of semi-delirium, fully at home in the world, happy in my skin. Twirling and somersaulting in the sunlit lake, I was an Olympic gold medalist, I was the queen of water ballet, I was a weightless, shining goddess with nose plugs and a lime green Danskin bathing suit that kept falling off my shoulders and riding up my butt. I spent my days yelling, "Mom, Mom, Mom! Look at this! Look at this!" then doggie-paddling around the kiddie pen like a maniac.

Yet like most idyllic things, Silver Lake seemed to exist in this state only to serve as a backdrop for some pending and inevitable craziness.

And that's where Alice Furnald and her movie camera came in.

Alice Furnald was known in the colony as an *artiste* with a capital "A." While other mothers walked around in flip-flops and rubbery bathing suits, Alice wore ruffled pencil skirts and platform shoes and white peasant blouses knotted snuggly between her breasts. Whenever she chewed gum—which was pretty much all of the time—everything on her jiggled. I called her "The Chiquita Banana Lady," and I meant this as a compliment: who didn't want to look adorable with a pile of fruit on her head?

One night, Alice called a meeting at the Barn. "As you might know," she announced, "I'm planning to shoot a film here in Silver Lake." Its title was going to be *Camp*, she said. If she meant this ironically, she seemed unaware of it.

"*Camp* will star a number of people here in the colony, including . . ." Alice stopped chewing her gum and looked pointedly at me and my friend Edward Yitzkowitz. At that moment, I was busy inventing a way to hang upside down from the bench while chewing on a plastic necklace. Edward was shredding the rim of a Styrofoam cup with his teeth. "Including," Alice cleared her throat, "some of our *very own* children.

"Edward," Alice called across the barn. Like many of the colonists, Alice had a thick Brooklyn accent. She pronounced Edward not "Edward" but "Edwid." In fact, most of the colonists—including Edward's own Brooklyn-born mother, Carly, and thus Edward himself—pronounced Edward "Edwid." For years, I believed that was his real name. *Edwid. Edwid Yitzkowitz.* (Only when we were grown up, and I bumped into him in the East Village, did he inform me that his real name was "Edward." Or *had* been Edward. Sick of the wimpiness it implied, sick of its syllabic bastardization, he'd gone ahead and changed his name legally to "Steve.")

"Edwid. Little Susie Gilman," Alice called across the barn. "How would you two like to be in a *real, live* movie?"

Her voice had all the forced and suspicious cheerfulness of a proctologist—it was the voice grown-ups used whenever they wanted to coax children into doing something that they themselves would never do in a million years unless ordered to by a judge—but I was more than willing to overlook this. At that moment, I felt only the white-hot spotlight of glory and attention shining down on me: it felt like butterscotch, like whipped cream and sprinkles.

I nodded frantically. Of course I wanted to be in a movie!

The truth was, until Silver Lake, the year had not gone terribly well for me. Sure, the Vietnam War was going on, and Bobby Kennedy and Martin Luther King had recently been shot. But as far as I was concerned, there was only one national trauma worth paying any attention to: the birth of my baby brother. Not only did John's arrival demolish my status as an only child, but he was handily the cutest baby in all of recorded history. Decked out in his red pom-pom hat and his pale blue *blankee,* he was the traffic-stopper of the West 93rd Street Playground set. Other mothers abandoned their carriages by the monkey bars. "Ohmygod, he is *gorgeous!*" they'd squeal, pushing past me to poke their heads under the hood of his stroller. "Does he model?"

I, on the other hand, was cute only in the way any four-year-old is cute: big eyes, boo-boos on the knee, the requisite lisp. But my face was round as an apple, my tummy even more so. I was not too young, I quickly discovered, to have adults declare open season on my weight. If anything, my brother's adorableness seemed to compel them to point out my unattractiveness in comparison. It was as if there was only a finite amount of cuteness in the world, and my brother had used up our quota.

"Oh, your little girl, she so chubby!" bellowed the obese Ukrainian woman who ran the Kay-Bee Discount department store, where my mother bought my Health-tex clothing wholesale.

"I think she drink too much Hi-C," the teacher's aide at my nursery school suggested. "Her face, it get fat."

My teacher, Celeste, was herself a genuine sadist. This was made clear to me the very first day of nursery school, when she led our class in a game of "Simon Says" designed to inflict flesh wounds: *Simon says: Poke yourself in the eye! Simon says: Hit yourself on the head with a Lincoln Log! Stick a crayon up your nose! Whoops. I didn't say Simon Says, now did I, Juan?*"

"Well, Susie certainly does like Cookie Time," Celeste informed my mother with a naked, malicious glee. "And let's face it, she's not doing herself any favors. Have you considered taking her to a doctor?"

Halfway through the school year, I lay down in front of the door to my classroom and shrieked until my mother promised to take me home. So there I was: the Upper West Side's first bona fide nursery school dropout.

But now, Edwid and I were going to be movie stars!

"We're going to be in a movie!" we sang on the ice cream line the next afternoon. As any kid knows, it's not just that good things should happen to you, but that they should be rubbed into the faces of everyone else. "We're going to be in a movie!" we chorused again, wiggling our butts in the universal hoochie-coochie dance-taunt, successfully and immediately alienating every other kid in the colony.

In retrospect, Edwid was probably as hungry for some top billing as I was. At four years old, he was already well on his way to becoming a dead-ringer for Ethel Merman. Showy, gossipy, melodramatic, he had a great froth of curly hair which he'd brush back with a flourish, and a voice that trilled up the octaves. "Ohmygawd, you guys, listen to this!" he'd exclaim. Never mind that for some of his contemporaries, getting through *Hop on Pop* was still a major accomplishment: Edwid had not just his mother's Brooklyn accent, but her full-blown, intellectual's vocabulary. "What child talks like that?" my mother remarked. "That kid is a *yenta*."

And I adored him for this. All the girls did. Unlike other little boys, whose primary hobbies seemed to be throwing rocks and plowing into you while pretending to be Speed Racer, Edwid was opposed to any kind of activity that required you to exert yourself. A burgeoning chocoholic like myself, he was only too happy to sit in a lawn chair eating Yodels and making up elaborate stories about what would happen to everybody in the colony, if, say, aliens landed in the Barn and enslaved people based on their outfits.

Needless to say, the other little boys weren't quite sure what to make of him. They were only four years old, and yet they *knew*—just as Edwid himself *surely* must have known—*that one of these things is not like the others.*

Slurping away on Fudgsicles, Edwid and I talked excitedly about how our lives would be transformed by being stars in the movie.

The only child actress I knew of at the time was the ancient Shirley Temple. Somehow, I had the idea that appearing in *Camp* meant being the centerpiece of several vigorous song-and-dance numbers: I envisioned myself solemnly descending a staircase in a small white mink cape while a cast of adoring grown-ups fawned around me, singing songs about how wonderful I was until they left me alone in the spotlight for one of my many ballet solos. I would then proceed to perform one perfect arabesque after another, ending each one by flashing a peace sign at the camera just like the Beatles did.

Edwid saw himself more as a magician. "I'm going to be in a long purple cape and a silver top hat," he announced. "When I tap the rim of my hat with a magic wand, pet rabbits are going to come running out. Then," he added, "I'll lock my sister Cleo in a cello case and make her disappear." It went without saying, of course, that somehow Cleo would fail to rematerialize at the end of the trick. Through no fault of Edwid's, she would remain lost forever in a netherworld of incompetent magicians' assistants.

At the end of the movie, Edwid and I agreed, we'd both be in a parade, then move to a split-level house in New Jersey with shag carpets and an aquarium and a kitchen stocked only with M&M's and Bosco.

The morning that *Camp* was to begin filming, I woke up so excited, I didn't want to eat breakfast. But there wasn't any breakfast to be had—my mother was already down at the lake, watching Alice shoot the first scene.

"Come take a look, sweetie," said my dad. "It's really something."

Until that moment, it hadn't occurred to me that there might actually be other people in the movie besides Edwid and me. Following my father down to the lake, I didn't know what to expect: perhaps Alice would be seated in a director's chair while a few colonists milled around in sparkly costumes, awaiting my arrival. Maybe there'd be people practicing tap-dancing, or a collie with a red ribbon around its neck, being groomed to appear as my sidekick.

What I did not expect to see was twenty-seven hippies cramming themselves into a pink and purple VW Bug.

They were, from my point of view, practically naked. The men had only cutoff denim shorts, and the women who weren't actually topless were wearing tiny, macramé bikinis crafted by Daisy Loupes, a colonist whom even the others considered, in their words, "far out." Daisy made her living selling handcrafted bathing suits at music festivals. That people actually paid money for her creations is a testimony to the strength of the hallucinogens of the time. At Silver Lake, the older boys called Daisy's bathing suits "Bags o' Boobs" and "Saggy Titty Sacks." They weren't being uncharitable.

In place of everyone's clothes was psychedelic body art. Explosive flowers and huge Day-Glo orange peace signs were painted on their chests. Hearts framed their belly buttons, smiley faces grinned from their shoulders and knees. Butterflies alighted from their clavicles. One woman had yellow and orange rays of sunshine radiating from her crotch; my friend Annie's brother, Jerome, whom I already considered a freak because he was a white guy who insisted on wearing his hair in an Afro, was entirely covered in paint. Stripes of color swirled around him like a green and magenta barber pole. The Fleming twins, a pair of teenaged girls who'd baby-sat me once, had the words "Groovy" painted on one leg and "Sock It To Me!" on the other, and "Make Love, Not War" emblazoned across their tummies.

Each hippie had a number painted on their stomach, too, and as Alice stood behind her tripod, she called out the numbers as if she were operating a deli counter. I noticed that she was counting backward, "Fifteen . . . Fourteen. . . ." Whoever's number was called had to stuff him- or herself into the VW.

My father led me over to Alice. "You see," he pointed at her camera, "Alice is going to have of all these people jump out of that tiny car just like clowns in a circus." He seemed to think I would be entertained by this, though the truth was that clowns—along with puppets, forest fire commercials, and badly drawn coloring books— scared the shit out of me. Hippies, so far, weren't faring much better.

"This scene is called 'Ode to Joy,'" added Alice, not looking up from her viewfinder.

I had no idea what an "ode" was, but trying to stuff twenty-seven grown-ups into a VW bug didn't look like joy to me at all. It looked like wishful thinking.

I watched my friend Abigail's father, a compact man with giant purple daisies painted on his nipples, crawl under the dashboard in a fetal position, while the Fleming twins wedged in behind the stick shift. "Number Six!" Alice shouted. That was Larry Levy, my friend Lori's dad. He was six foot two and had hot pink and yellow flowers painted up the trunks of his legs and a peace sign on each cheek. Watching him bend down and try to contort himself into the trunk of the VW was beyond painful; it was practically traumatic. Yet my father was grinning. "Give it up, Levy!" he shouted. "You can't do it!" Larry turned around, smiled broadly, and gave my father the finger. Then he jumped down into the trunk and pulled the hatch closed behind him with a flourish, and everyone hooted and applauded. My dad put both fingers in his mouth and whistled. It seemed to me like every dog across New York state heard him and promptly commenced yowling.

"Okay!" shouted Alice, "start cuing the music." A portable plastic record player had been set up under a tree with the help of half a dozen extension cords, and I watched Alice's teenaged son, Clifford, slide a copy of Jefferson Airplane's *Surrealistic Pillow* out of its sleeve and place it on the turntable.

A queasiness started to come over me, similar to the one I'd felt each morning before nursery school. I stood there with my father and tried to pretend that all of this was okay—that this was how any other kid from my nursery school would be spending their summer vacation.

No one paid the least bit of attention to me.

"Okay, people," shouted Alice. "It's 84 degrees out and I don't want anybody suffocating to death. Once my camera starts rolling, haul your ass out of that car as fast as possible!" Then she shouted,

"Clifford! Music!" and the reverberating, psychedelic, maraca-laced opening of the Jefferson Airplane song "She Has Funny Cars" boomed across the lake.

"Roll 'em!" Alice shouted. The original idea, apparently, had been to have the car "drive" up into the clearing and then have all the hippies emerge, but once everyone was crammed inside, steering the car became physically impossible. "Just get out when I call your number!" yelled Alice. "One!"

Slowly, the car door opened and Adele Birnbaum, who'd smushed herself in just a minute earlier, emerged. A lightning bolt painted on her stomach hadn't fully dried; it bled into the purple "1" above her belly button, creating a Rorschachy mess, but Adele just grinned and wiggled and danced right into the camera while the crowd hooted and cheered. "Two!" Alice yelled, and Sidney Birnbaum emerged, dancing the funky chicken with an American flag wrapped around his waist.

It all went smoothly until Alice got to hippie Number Six. It seems Larry Levy had pulled his back out leaping into the trunk of the VW. Alice had to stop filming while my father and Sidney Birnbaum carefully extracted him from the back of the car and whisked him off to the emergency room in Brewster. Nobody thought to remove Larry's body paint beforehand, and I wondered what the nurses would make of it. Oddly, it comforted me to think that Larry's kids might be even more embarrassed by all this than I was.

By the time Alice got to filming her thirteenth flower child, most of the real children had lost interest. They'd wandered over to a grove of trees by the lake, where they invented a game in which one person farted into a bag, then everyone else took turns sniffing it. But I had no interest. I went off and sat on a rock by myself. The vague upset I'd felt at the beginning of the shoot had metastasized into a full-blown stomachache.

"Sweetie, it's just make-believe," my mother said gently.

"I don't like it," I said.

"Why not?" she asked. "They're just having fun. They're playing—like you do."

For some reason, hearing this only bothered me more. Grown-ups weren't supposed to play. They were supposed to be stodgy and boring. More importantly, they were supposed to be stodgy and boring while paying attention to *you* while *you* played. They weren't supposed to be dancing the funky chicken while you went off and farted into a bag. It started to dawn on me then why hippies really frightened me: they were competition. Their face paint, their bubble-blowing, their naive and garish clothing—they wanted kids' stuff for themselves. They wanted to be silly and irresponsible, twirling around in the grass. But then what did that leave for us real kids to do? And if grown-ups were busy being flower children, who'd be left to be the grown-ups?

I made a great show of turning my back to my mother, though I was flooded with gratitude that she and my father had opted not to pop out of the VW themselves. "I just don't like it," I said. "That's all."

Kneeling beside me, my mother gently brushed a piece of hair from my eyes. "Alice says she's going to film you and Edward dancing together by the lake tomorrow."

This news had its desired effect. I was a sucker for vainglory. "Really? I'll get to dance?" I said.

Suddenly, I imagined Edwid in a sequined top hat and tails—not unlike his magician's costume—twirling me around in the sand and lifting me gracefully in the air in a diaphanous gown. The hippies might "do their thing," but Edwid and I would waltz along the water's edge, looking preternaturally glamorous and beautiful.

———

The next morning, my mother woke me up in the dark. "Okay, movie star, let's get going," she sighed. "Why Alice has to do this at sunrise is beyond me."

While it clearly wasn't my mother's idea of a good time, I liked being the first people awake in the colony. It felt to me like we'd won some sort of contest.

I pulled on my tutu and skibbled out onto the patio as the first blush of sun seeped over the hills. Outside, it was chilly—colder than I'd imagined—but the sky was streaked with gold and shell pink, and the air was sweet with morning fog. I'd never seen a morning look so magical: no garbage trucks, no sirens, just wet leaves and a few ambivalent sparrows. When my mother and I arrived at the lake, Edwid's mom, Carly, was already there. Carly must have been close to 250 pounds, yet her weight seemed a necessity given the size and volume of her personality. With her booming opinions and a laugh that could shake fruit off a tree, she was a one-woman piece of agit-prop theater, a force of nature in plus-sized bell-bottoms and paisley caftans. She carried Edwid slung over her shoulder like a small bag of laundry; he was still in his Snoopy pajamas, wheezing, spittle-lipped, crusty-nosed, half-asleep.

Before I could ask about his magician's costume, a car pulled up, and Alice climbed out, followed by Clifford, who unloaded what seemed to be a great avalanche of equipment. Though it was five-thirty in the morning, I was impressed to see that Alice was already dressed in a lime green maxi-dress with a matching turban and full makeup. Her jaw was going frantically.

"Okay, people," she said, snapping her gum, "let's set up down by the beach as quickly as possible. We're racing the sun here. Saul? Where's Saul?"

Suddenly, I saw Saul Shapiro rounding the bend in his pajamas. Saul was my friend Wendy's father, and he was easily the largest man in the colony—he even made Larry Levy (now Larry Levy of back-brace-emergency-room fame) look somehow insubstantial. He was barrel-chested, with enormous hands and feet and a corona of thick white hair. His baritone made anything he said—whether it was "Get that gerbil out of the laundry hamper" or "Iris dear, hand me a pretzel"—sound like the song "Some Enchanted Evening." Occasionally mistaken for Walter Cronkite, Saul had special license plates on his car, because, my mother said, when he wasn't lying on the beach in plaid bathing trunks, he was actually a prominent New York state assemblyman—whatever that was. All I knew was that he was Goliath. He terrified me.

Now, Goliath was wearing a peppermint-striped nightshirt and a matching, tasseled cap. I thought he'd also been too sleepy to get dressed, but Alice explained that Saul was going to be in the movie with us. The scene, titled "Ode to Innocence," would consist of this: Edwid and I would dance around the beach at dawn, chasing a butterfly, while Saul stood amid us in his nightshirt and nightcap, playing a flute.

Obviously, not quite what I'd imagined. But okay.

Soon, however, we had a butterfly problem. Butterflies, it turned out, could be real divas on a movie set. Unlike the rest of the cast, they could not be ordered to show up. They had to be coaxed; they had to be courted. Barring that, they had to be caught. While Alice set up her tripod, Clifford was dispatched to the marshes with a butterfly net and an old gefilte fish jar. After ten minutes of watching him swing away blindly, Edwid fell back asleep and Alice wondered aloud if she could spray-paint a moth. But then, Clifford's luck changed. He came upon not one, but two monarch butterflies—*in flagrante,* no less—and easily nudged them into the gefilte fish jar. We were in business.

Saul took his position at the end of the lake with a tiny plastic flute that looked doubly preposterous in his oversized hands. Carly plopped Edwid down on the sand, "Edwid, enough with the sleeping," she said loudly, pinching his cheeks until Edwid yelled, "Maaa! All right already!" and stood up unassisted.

My mother knelt down and combed my hair and fluffed out the tulle of my skirt. I felt regal and prim, very nearly perfect. Then she and Carly retreated to the stone terrace overlooking the beach, where Alice had set up her camera. "Everybody ready?" Alice called from behind the viewfinder. Saul, Edwid, and I all nodded. Then she straightened up, clearly displeased. "Um, could we lose the tutu and the pj's?" she said.

I looked at my mother.

"No tutu, Alice?" she said.

"Ellie, Ellie, Ellie!" Alice cried. "This is the 'Ode to Innocence,' not the 'Ode to Las Vegas' and 'Ode to Corporate America.' I want children—*naked* children—children like cherubs, dancing around the Pied Piper at sunrise, chasing a butterfly. This is not a place for sequins. This is not a place for trademark cartoon puppies printed on a pair of synthetic pajamas. This is about nature."

Hearing this, Carly shouted over to Edwid. "Hear that, Edwid? This is about nature. Take off your pajamas!"

My mother looked at me, unsure of how to proceed. "Susie, Alice would like you to dance without your tutu," she said carefully. "Do you want to do that?"

"What's a cherub?" asked Edwid.

"Who cares what a cherub is?" boomed Carly. "It's a pagan symbol appropriated by Christians for their paintings of the afterlife."

"No it's not. It's a naked angel," said Clifford.

"I don't want to take off my pajamas," said Edwid. "It's cold out."

"Oh, Mr. Yitzkowitz, it's not that bad," Saul chuckled avuncularly.

"Easy for you to say," said Edwid. "You're wearing a nightshirt and a stupid hat."

"Edwid!" shouted Carly. "Don't talk fresh to Saul. He's a Socialist." She turned to Alice. "I don't know why he's being difficult. Once, when he was two, he took off all his clothing in the middle of Gimbel's department store."

"They're also called 'seraphim,'" said Clifford to no one in particular.

"Do I get to be an angel?" I asked my mother. I had to admit, this sounded pretty good to me, though I wasn't crazy about the "naked" part. Every day, I changed in and out of my bathing suit on the beach—all the little kids did in full view of everyone—but I wasn't a toddler, like my brother, who ran around naked all day long, and good luck getting him into a diaper and a onesy for a trip to the Dairy Queen. Being naked in a movie did seem slightly embarrassing, but maybe not if I was a *cherub* . . .

"The sun's rising, folks," said Alice. "Are we here to create art, or are we here to discuss the epistemology of cherubs and complain?"

"Edwid, stop being such a prima donna and take off your clothes," said Carly.

"Well, Suze?" said my mother.

Edwid shrugged, so I did the same. Frankly, I didn't know what else to do. The general consensus was that shrugs meant "yes," so quickly, our mothers helped us out of our clothes. The truth was, Edwid and I mooned each other regularly—our friend Freddy Connors had invented a game called "Butt In Your Face," which was a big hit on the ice cream line—but standing naked when it was officially sanctioned somehow made us very shy. We avoided eye contact with each other.

"Oh, that's beautiful!" said Alice, ducking back behind her camera. As soon as she said, "Roll 'em!" I decided I changed my mind. I wanted my clothes back on. *Now.* But Saul was playing "Greensleeves" on the flute and strolling toward us, and Alice was saying, "That's it. Great. Now, Susie and Edwid, dance around Saul."

And since it was freezing, and dancing was preferable to just standing there, Edwid and I just threw ourselves into it, breaking out our best dance moves from our own, personal repertoire.

"Stop! Cut!" Alice yelled. "Ellen," she called to my mother, "what's Susie doing down there on one leg? What's wrong with her hand?"

"Oh," said my mother. "She's performing an arabesque and flashing a peace sign. It's a little ballet thing she likes to do."

"Oh for fuck's sake," said Alice. "Little Susie Gilman!" she shouted down from the terrace. "Enough with the arabesques and the peace signs. And Edwid, what's with the shimmying?"

What Alice had forgotten is that Edwid and I hadn't been raised on Julie Andrews musicals. We'd had our diapers changed to Otis Redding. We'd learned to walk listening to Donovan's "Sunshine Superman" and Tina Turner's "River Deep—Mountain High." In the bathtub, we regularly sang along to the entire soundtrack of *Yellow Submarine*. When ordered to dance, Edwid had launched into his version of the pony mixed with go-go moves he'd seen on the Sunday morning kiddie show *Wonderama*. This, apparently, was not what Alice had had in mind.

"Forget the dancing, you two," she ordered. "Just skip. Skip joyously around Saul."

"Like this!" Carly shouted. She lifted up the hem of her caftan and mimed skipping joyously across the terrace. Even Alice looked a bit stunned at the sight. She turned back to the camera. "Skip," she said.

Saul resumed playing his flute and Edwid and I skipped around him furiously, in great, spastic movements with big, imbecilic smiles plastered on our faces that we hoped approximated joyousness. We twirled and flailed, pretending to conduct an enormous, invisible orchestra with our entire bodies. We leaped. We pranced. We waltzed. We sashayed. Neither of us had any idea what the fuck we were doing.

"Beautiful, beautiful!" said Alice. "You're children! You're innocent! You're natural! Keep skipping!" She cued Clifford to release the butterflies. One of them had clearly been asphyxiated in the gefilte fish jar—it wafted down pitifully like a dry leaf—but the other fluttered about wanly, and we chased it with exaggerated dedication, our gusto fueled, mostly, by the fact that we were freezing.

"Skip! Chase the butterfly!" Alice chanted.

We skipped and chased, skipped and chased, and then suddenly, Alice yelled, "Cut! It's a wrap!" and Saul pulled off his nightcap and wiped his forehead with it, and my mother came down and pulled me quickly into my tutu, and Edwid was buttoned back into his pajamas and flung over Carly's shoulder. Clifford was collapsing all of Alice's equipment and carrying it back up the hill to the car, and Alice was muttering "Where the hell did I put my thermos? I need coffee *now*," and then she was off, and I heard her car sputtering as it started, the tires crunching over gravel, and Saul was waving goodbye to us, and the gate was swinging closed with a *tlink!* behind him and then, that was it. It was all over.

One butterfly had vanished, the other lay dead on the sand, sacrificed to art, to the "Ode to Innocence." The sun glinted over the horizon. The lake was glassy and eerily still, as if we had never existed, as if it had been preserved in time long before humans started prancing about with their Super-8 cameras. My mother and I stood alone on the beach.

"Well," she sighed, "I guess that's one for the history books. Shall we get you back into bed?"

That afternoon, Edwid and I didn't say anything to the other kids on the ice cream line about our less-than-stellar movie debut, and they didn't mention it either, which was all just as well. The new point of interest was Terry, the substitute ice cream man filling in for Jack, the octogenarian regular, who was away on vacation in the Adirondacks. Terry was a college kid. To make a tedious job interesting, he'd made up scatological and sexual nicknames for all of the frozen novelties, which he shared with us in a conspiratorial whisper. If we asked him for a "Chip Candy Crunch," Terry would wink, "Oh, you mean a Chip Candy *Crotch*?" sending us into convulsions. Nobody cared about some movie called *Camp* when you could listen to Terry saying, "Here you go. Two Dixie *Cunts* and a *Poop*sicle."

In fact, Edwid and I never spoke about *Camp,* period, even when it was aired for the entire colony at the Barn, three weeks later, as part of the annual "End of Summer" banquet held the Saturday night before Labor Day. We sat on the wooden picnic benches beside our parents, quietly clutching our Styrofoam cups full of Very Berry Hi-C, watching the shaky camera work of the opening shot, in which a disembodied hand spray-painted the word "Camp" on a woman's bare midriff to the trippy sound of the Byrds' song, "Turn! Turn! Turn!"

We watched the jiggly, lint-ridden frames panning over the lake to the pink and purple VW bug. Applause and hoots sounded from both the audience on film and the audience in the Barn, which was essentially one and the same, as each hippie-clown emerged again from the tiny car (the biggest cheers erupted when Larry Levy emerged, strung awkwardly between the shoulders of my father and

Sidney Birnbaum). Then came scenes I hadn't seen before: My mother and a guy named Morris, dressed in evening clothes, having a fancy candlelit dinner on a wooden raft in the middle of the lake, while being waited upon by a swimmer . . . the Fleming twins singing Dylan's anti-Vietnam song, "Masters of War" accompanied by Clifford on his vibraphone in a rowboat . . . some "avant-garde" scene in which finger puppets alternated between reading aloud sections of the Warren Report and poetry by Kahlil Gibran . . . halfway through this mess came Edwid and me, dancing frantically on the beach around Saul, who was occasionally decapitated by the camera angles. I was sure everyone would burst out laughing at the sight of us, but instead of snickers, there was an almost universal "Aaaaawwwww" throughout the Barn as assorted mothers gushed: "Oh, that's little Susie and Edwid! Aren't they cute!"

Before I could drink in this wave of admiration, however, the camera cut away again to a playground in Brewster, filled not with children, but with more hippies from the colony. The heading "Ode to Innocence" filled the screen for a moment, graffitied on a piece of fluorescent poster board, and then the camera zoomed back to the playground, where it showed a montage of grown-ups running into a sprinkler one by one, then piling onto a carousel loaded down with an assortment of pinwheels, umbrellas, flowers, balloons, and peace signs. Clearly, this was more the spirit of innocence that Alice had been looking to capture: the rest of *Camp* followed the hippies playing on seesaws and pushing each other on the swings for what seemed like a good fifteen minutes.

The final shot, however, did feature two children again—Daisy Loupes's twins, Sasha and Eli, aged three, walking naked, hand-in-hand, down one of the colony's dirt roads. On Sasha's tush was painted the word "THE" and on Eli's the word "END." Upon seeing this, the entire Barn went nuts—clearly, the colonists found this supremely cuter than anything else—and I was suddenly indignant that such a plum role hadn't been awarded to me instead. *Why hadn't I been filmed with the movie's closing credits painted across my ass?*

For one frantic moment, I tried to edit the scenes in my head, refilming myself so that my dancing was more memorable, so that I didn't look nearly as silly as I had, so that I'd switched places with Sasha. I even considered telling people that it was *really* me and Edwid, *not* the Loupeses, in the final scene.

But the lights came on, and as the adults all went about congratulating each other on their performances, some kids in the balcony began chanting "Nudie Boy! Nudie Girl!" and throwing balled-up paper cups over the railing. Whether they meant to hit me and Edwid or Sasha and Eli really didn't matter. Because only then did I remember where I was: I was in a barn full of Socialists. A freak among freaks.

For years after the dubious premier of *Camp,* I practically got a migraine just thinking about it. It was an independent film that I could only hope would remain forever independent of such things as an audience and a projector. Ironically, I later became incensed not by the fact that my parents had been hippies, but that they had not been hippies *enough:* "You put me in some nudie Granola-head home movie, but didn't take me to Woodstock?" I once shouted at my mother. "It was 1969. Silver Lake was only an hour away from Yasgur's farm. What were you thinking?" It seemed galling to me that if I was going to have to be preserved for all time dancing naked on a beach while a state assemblyman played "Greensleeves" on a flute, at least I could've also gotten to say, *Well guess what, man? I saw Pete Townsend bash his foot through an amplifier.*

Sometimes, I wondered why I cooperated. Okay, I was four—generally not an age noted for its impulse control or savvy business sense. But I could have lain down on the sand and shrieked my head off like I did at my nursery school. Little kids think nothing of throwing a fit at the foot of an escalator, or ruining an entire day at the zoo over a forbidden hot dog, or whining loudly, "I'm bored. Can we go home?" during a funeral. They're experts at defiance. Why hadn't I exercised this age-given gift?

For a time, I even wondered if Alice cast me and Edward in *Camp* because I was a pudgy girlie-girl and, for all intents and purposes, so was Edwid. Could she have sensed that we wouldn't be the type of kids to object—we were already at a disadvantage—that we'd be hungrier, more vulnerable, more eager to please?

Only years later, I'd meet a girl named Dyanne, whose Tennessee mother insisted on dressing her and her two sisters up in identical sailor suits and pulling them through the town in a wagon decorated to look like a boat for the annual Fourth of July parade, during which time they were all bidden to sing interminable and quasi-patriotic "boat songs" like "Sailing, Sailing, Over the Bounding Main" and "Row, Row, Row, Your Boat" even though they'd grown up land-locked. I would date a Robert Redford look-alike when I was sixteen, whose mother used to dress up as "Mrs. Pumpkin" for Halloween and insist that he be photographed with her in a vegetable patch for her Christmas newsletter. How humiliating! There would be other boys whose mothers would be only too happy to pull out family albums to show me snapshots of their little darlings caught for eternity picking their noses and peeing in the dog's dish—one, even, dressed up like a girl by his older sister and installed at a tea party. I would meet girls who were forced as children to sing "Sheep May Safely Graze" in church while actually dressed up as sheep. Who were carted out to dance the tarantella for relatives. Who were encouraged to recite abominable rhyming poems written by their mother entitled, "Reflections on a Menopausal Picnic." Girls who were paraded about in ludicrous Easter bonnets, who were photographed sitting on the toilet wearing only Mickey Mouse sunglasses and a feather boa, who were ordered to play the ukulele for neighbors, who were preserved in both film and memory in the shipwreck of school talent shows. I would come to realize that for everyone, childhood means having limited power, at best, in the face of adults' pathetic and misguided ideas about how children should behave. It means being hamstrung between the desire to please and desire, period. Welcome to the world.

But back in New York, in the days immediately following our return from Silver Lake, I thought about none of this. Thanks to my own gnatlike attention span, I quickly became consumed by such new, all-important projects as rearranging my crayons, lobbying for a mink coat, and figuring out how to clip rhinestone earrings to my hair without ripping it out of my head. Forgetting the shame of my movie debut, I took away from it only one lasting impression: if I was truly going to be a star, it would simply not be enough to perform. Oh, no. I would have to direct as well. Thanks to Alice Furnald, I added that to my list.

Chapter 2

A Girl's Guide to Bragging and Lying

THE DAY I STARTED kindergarten I made a jarring discovery: all the other girls, it seemed, wanted to be just as fabulous as I did.

The first morning of school, after the critical business of nap blankets was settled, our teacher, Mrs. Mutnick, had our class sit in a circle on the rag rug by the piano.

"Now, we're all going to say our names and what each of us wants to be when we grow up," she said brightly. "For example, my name is Mrs. Mutnick, and when I grow up, I want to be a kindergarten teacher."

"But you *are* a kindergarten teacher," said Gregory Dupree.

Mrs. Mutnick gave a fluttery little laugh, a sort of falsetto hiccup. "Oh, dears, I'm saying it as an *example,*" she explained, "so that you'll understand how to answer, you see? Now Gregory, you try."

Gregory thought a minute. "My name is Gregory Jackson Dupree," he said. "And when I grow up, I want to be a member of the Black Panthers."

Mrs. Mutnick removed her large tortoiseshell glasses, then put them back on again. "I see," she said. Her eyes darted quickly around the circle until they landed on redheaded Brian McConnell, who was already in the process of chewing the hat off a Fisher-Price policeman. "Brian," she smiled encouragingly. "What do you want to be when you grow up?"

Brian chewed thoughtfully. "I want to be a Black Panther, too," he said.

"Me too!" shouted Timothy Wang.

"Okay, class," Mrs. Mutnick inhaled. Obviously, the discussion wasn't headed in the direction she wanted.

"What I'd like to know is what kind of *job* you'd like to have," she said. "For example, do you want to be a mailman? Do you want to be the president?"

"Richard Nixon? *Yech*. Who wants to be him?" said Christopher Kleinhaus. Christopher was taller and heftier than everyone else in the class because he'd already been left back twice. God only knew what you needed to do to flunk kindergarten.

Mrs. Mutnick shot him a look that communicated she was running out of patience. "Do you want to be an artist? Do you want to be an astronaut?" she prodded.

I understood what she was asking, and my hand shot up. Usually, I found the question highly irritating. Adults who asked what you wanted to be always assumed children had nothing better to do than think about being grown-ups. The fact was, we had far more interesting things to concern ourselves with. Such as, for example, seeing what happened when you emptied an entire bowl of M&M's into your grandmother's silk evening bag, then set it on top of a radiator while you ate them.

But earlier that morning, Mrs. Mutnick had let me select a pink circle from the "Shapes and Colors" box to decorate my cubby. I felt a rare impulse to make her life easier.

"Mrs. Mutnick, my name is Susie Gilman," I said proudly, "and when I grow up, I want to be a ballerina, and a model, and a movie star, and a director, and a stewardess." Then I leaned back with a sort of "tah-dah!" look on my face that would eventually endear me to my fellow classmates almost as much as my ass-kissing.

Predictably, Mrs. Mutnick beamed. "Well," she said, giving her little, startled laugh, "you certainly are ambitious. You want to be all sorts of things, don't you?" She turned to the girl sitting next to me. "Carmen, what about you? What do you want to be?"

Carmen pressed her finger to her chin. "Hmmmmm. I want to be . . . let's see . . . a singer . . . and a fashion designer . . . and a trapeze artist . . . and a bride."

Mrs. Mutnick smiled indulgently, and I wanted to hit Carmen. Not only was she clearly copying me, but her answers were generally better than mine.

"Sara, what about you?"

"I want to be a ballerina, too, and a bride, too, but also a princess, a nurse, a gymnast, and a drum majorette," said Sara.

This time, I couldn't contain myself. "Oh, me too! I also want to be a princess and a nurse. I forgot to say!"

Carmen nodded furiously in agreement. "And I forgot drum majorette," she said. "I'm also going to be that."

Each time one of the girls said something new, we all shouted out and added it to our lists. Predictably, when we said things like "hairdresser" and "ice skater," some of the boys made barfing sounds. When they, in turn, said they wanted to grow up to be things like helicopter commandos and dump truck operators, we responded, in kind, with a collective "Eeeeewww."

What strikes me now, of course, was how stereotypical our choices were. Born just as the women's movement was catching fire, my classmates and I were being raised by mothers who would be the first on line to buy copies of *Free to Be . . . You and Me* and multiracial, anatomically correct baby dolls. And yet not a single girl longed to be a mathematician or a pulmonary cardiologist. When I first informed my grandparents that I wanted to be "an actress, a model, and a stewardess," they chuckled delightedly. *Susie wants to be a stewardess! Isn't that adorable?*

I'm sorry, but a *stewardess?* Let a little boy pledge allegiance to the service industry and see if his relatives find it endearing. The fact was, I had no idea what a stewardess actually did. I didn't even realize they got to *travel*. I'm sure if someone had said to me, "Little girl, how'd you like to grow up to push a cart full of drinks up and down the aisle of an airplane while people bitch at you about needing more pillows?" I would have thought they were insane.

What it really boiled down to, I realize now, was the "-ess" in the word "stewardess." Somehow, my five-year-old brain had grasped the idea that "-ess" was the culmination of all things feminine and highly desirable. It was a suffix that separated the girls from the boys in the best of all possible ways. Princess, goddess, actress, countess. What was there not to love? A flight attendant, *feh*. But a stewardess? "-Ess" made any profession sound glamorous. A laundress, a sorceress, an adulteress. To this day, I'm convinced that, if someone had only been enterprising enough to call female MDs "doctresses" and female scientists "nuclear biologesses," I would have been equally enthusiastic about becoming those, too.

No matter. After my classmates and I recited our career litanies about a zillion times each, they began to lose their luster. They didn't sound like lists of possibilities anymore so much as lists of *chores*. Plus, since we *all* wanted to be everything, it was getting pretty hard to distinguish ourselves from one another, which was the whole point of our ambitions in the first place.

And so we began not only ratcheting up our visions, but transforming ourselves. "Okay," we'd say feverishly, before embarking on a routine game of "House" or "Space Ship." "Pretend I'm a princess, and my name is Melanie, and I have long red hair and green eyes and I'm wearing a silver miniskirt and a fur coat and I have a magic ring that makes people freeze whenever I yell 'Freeze.' "

The boys, I happened to notice, didn't do nearly so much elaborating. They tended to declare that they were Batman or Wilt Chamberlain and that was it. They didn't feel compelled to give themselves a total makeover in the process. They never said, "Okay, pretend I'm an astronaut, and my name is Chad, and I have brown hair and blue eyes, and I'm wearing a tuxedo shirt . . ." Well, not the straight little boys, anyway.

Early on, somehow, we girls came to think of ourselves as malleable, as rough drafts, as "before" pictures, eager for and requiring an "after."

Even our own imaginations weren't enough sometimes to satisfy our aspirations. We soon began staking out starring roles for ourselves in an even more fantastic world.

As the children of liberals, television for me and my friends was largely contraband. At my house, for example, my brother and I weren't allowed to watch the news because my parents didn't want us traumatized by footage from the Vietnam War. At Michelle's house, we weren't allowed to watch the *The Flintstones* or *I Dream of Jeannie* because her mother said they were sexist. At the Richmonds', any situation comedy in which black people were servants was strictly off-limits. At Annie's house, her teenaged brother Jerome refused to let us watch *The Brady Bunch* because he said it was "a case study in capitalist oppression." *The whole family is dependent upon one proletariat worker,* he explained, *and what does Alice get for her labor? Nothing. She only gets to date another proletariat, Sam the butcher, who can't even spend the night with her. It's the bourgeoisie controlling the means of production.*

Annie's mother, however, actively encouraged us to watch *The Partridge Family,* because, she said, it taught little girls that women didn't need men in order to raise a family. My mother, however, objected to *The Partridge Family* solely on the basis of its music.

By the time everybody finished weighing in, my friends and I were basically left to watch *Romper Room* and, a few years later, the Watergate Hearings—both of which struck us as entertainment for idiots.

Yet somehow, we managed to sneak in an impressive amount of off-limits viewing. And whenever we did, we scrambled to touch the TV screen as soon as the opening credits for a particular show came on.

"I call I'm Ginger!" we'd yell, lunging at the television, trying to be the first one to press her palm over the seductive cathode-ray smile of Tina Louise before the picture flashed to the infinitely duller

Professor and Mary Anne. The rule was: whoever touched a character first got to "be" her for the duration of the show.

"I call I'm Marcia!" we'd shriek, vying to tag the upper-left-hand corner of *The Brady Bunch* grid first, leaving the losers to fight over insipid Cindy and consolation prize Jan. We'd compete to be Marilyn on *The Munsters,* Penny on *Lost in Space,* Laurie on *The Partridge Family.* Cartoons were equally fair game: we "called" Melodie, Daphne, Betty, Valerie, Veronica, Wonder Woman, Trixie, and Judy on the *Jetsons.*

For me, however, one character was the apotheosis of all that I admired and ever hoped to be.

By day, Barbara Gordon was the brainy, Jackie Kennedy–esque daughter of Gotham's police commissioner. And yet, with one flick of a switch, her vanity table rotated around and she was transformed into Batgirl, as pornographic a crime fighter as could be seen on prime time, with stiletto heels, a peek-a-boo black mask, and sparkly latex bodysuit that made her look as if she'd been dipped in liquid rubber.

For Batgirl's big "fight move," Batman and Robin would lift her off the ground like two chorus boys and *Wham! Bap!* Batgirl would kittenishly swing her pointed, dominatrix boots right into the jaw of an oncoming henchman. Unlike the ditzy molls cowering in the corner, Batgirl leapt into the fray and held her own. And, once the battle was over, and the Riddler and his sidekicks were left drowning in their own vat of pancake batter or whatever, Batgirl whirled around and vanished, leaving Batman and Robin awestruck in her wake:

"Batman, who do you think she really is?"

"We'll never know, Robin. I believe we'll never know."

They'd never see her, but we—the audience—would, riding her electric purple Batcycle into the sunset with the wind in her hair while a groovy, Muzaky chorus sang: *Batgirrrrrl, Batgirl! Yeah, whose baby are you?*

Pretending to be her made me almost dizzy with yearning.

There were only two small problems:

She was fictional, of course.

And—she didn't wear a tutu.

Out of all the girls in kindergarten, Audrey Abromowitz became my closest friend. Audrey was a red-haired drooler who lived in a grubby red-brick apartment building across the street from our grubby gray one. She and I were obsessed with ballerinas. All the other aspirations on our lists were really just filler. When it came right down to it, both of us would happily forfeit the chance to cure cancer to save the planet from a nuclear holocaust if it meant we'd be assured an opportunity to prance around in a tutu.

Frustrated by our inability to stand out in school in any way, we longed to up the ante somehow. We wanted to establish ourselves as *the real* ballerinas of K-5—the genuine article among pretenders—even though, of course, neither one of us had ever taken a dance class in our lives, and I was pudgy, and Audrey was bowlegged. But we were at that stage in life where we truly believed that what you wore was infinitely more important than what you actually did. And so, one day, we decided to wear our tutus to school.

My new tutu, campaigned for vigorously and received on my birthday, was a frothy white satin confection that I topped off with a gold cardboard crown and three appalling rhinestone necklaces given to me by my grandmother. Audrey's tutu had a pale blue bodice covered with satin roses, and it came with a tiny satin cape that tied around her shoulders with a ribbon. When we paraded into kindergarten dressed in this finery, Christopher Kleinhaus immediately began making elaborate throw-up noises. The other girls looked on with a mixture of admiration and envy—or, it occurs to me only now, possibly disgust.

"Oh, how delightful!" Mrs. Mutnick exclaimed.

Over our heads, our bedraggled mothers looked at her apologetically.

"It was this or nothing," said Audrey's mother helplessly.

"Trust me," my mother sighed, rolling her eyes, "It's better than the alternative. Last year, she lay down in front of the door to her nursery school and screamed."

"Don't be silly," said Mrs. Mutnick. "They both look adorable, and it's not hurting anybody."

Our teacher's aide, Mrs. Flores, begged to differ, however.

Our tutus, it turned out, were a bitch to take off whenever we needed to pee—which we needed to do almost constantly. Audrey and I were probably the two most frequent pee-ers in the entire New York City Public School System. Between us, we had a bladder the size of a Froot Loop. Whenever one of us had to pee, Mrs. Flores would have to walk us down the hall to the girls' room, where she had to help us wriggle out of our crackling, sequin-crusted leotards, then roll down our pilled and staticky tights, then wait outside the door while we "made," then help us again, squirming and distracted, first back into the tights, and then back into the skin of our leotard, making sure to ease the tutu gently over the bodice so as not to rip the tulle and incite hysteria.

And no sooner had she finished doing this for one of us, when, back inside the classroom, the other would invariably tug on the hem of her skirt, and whisper softly, "Mrs. Flores, I have to go, too."

In our defense, Mrs. Flores was an unpleasant woman. Like all teacher's aides, she was overworked, underpaid, and underappreciated, yet she took out her frustrations not on the administration but on us kids. She made no attempt to disguise her loathing of us, and she tended to communicate mostly through scowls, except on the occasions when Mrs. Mutnick left the classroom for a few minutes, in which case she berated us openly. Her favorite threats seemed to involve us spending a lot of quality time with the devil.

"If you don't sit still," she hissed, "you play with the devil!" If we picked our noses, she informed us, we'd be playing with the devil, too. Ditto for getting off our nap blankets before "sleep time" was over.

For some reason, though, we took Mrs. Flores in stride. After all, she was a fabulist preoccupied with punishment—which was pretty much what we five-year-olds were. In the schoolyard, we constantly invented dire consequences for ourselves—"Step on a crack, break your mother's back"—and that sort of thing. Because of Mrs. Flores's fire-and-brimstone disciplinary tactics, we tended to regard her affectionately as one of our own.

"Look, Mrs. Flores," we'd call out cheerfully after spilling finger paint all over the piano bench. "We're playing with the devil!"

I'm sure Mrs. Flores complained to Mrs. Mutnick about our ballerina costumes. But Mrs. Mutnick loved the idea of free expression almost as much as she hated conflict. As far as I knew, she never sent any notes home demanding civilian clothes for school. And so, after two weeks of Audrey and me flouncing around in our satin and tulle, Mrs. Flores took matters into her own hands.

"Boys and girls," she announced at snack time, "today, everyone has to wait for milk and cookies because Susie and Audrey have to go to the little girl's room *again,* and as we all see, they're dressed in their tutus."

Clearly, it was her goal to shame us—if not to generate an all-out Christians-to-the-lions scenario in which our cookie-starved peers ripped us and our sequins to shreds.

But what Mrs. Flores hadn't counted on was that, once they saw the special attention Audrey and I were getting, a lot of the other little girls decided they wanted to wear tutus to school, too. The next day, Mary Berns arrived in a fire-engine-red number, while Claudia Ramirez and Iyala Lev arrived in pale pink versions of my tutu. Carmen trooped in wearing a gold-sequined leotard with a white tutu, and Jocanda Johnson came dressed in a dark-rose-colored tutu that her mother had sewn based on a photo from *Life* magazine. By mid-November, half the girls in our class had horned in on the action. We were a legion of ballerinas, and from then on, we spent virtually our entire time in kindergarten waiting to pee.

———

Of course, once tutus became practically the school uniform, I had to find yet another new way to distinguish myself. Being part of "team ballerina" was all fine and good, but it was nothing compared to getting singled out as a prima donna.

Happily, I found another spotlight soon enough, and quite by accident.

Show 'n' Tell in our classroom was your basic mundane parade of rubber bugs, paperweights, food stamps, and snow globes. Once, Christopher Kleinhaus brought in a bong, which was immediately snatched out of his hands and transported, along with Christopher, to the principal's office—none of us had any idea what had happened—*What did he say he brought in? A gong? A bog?* Another time, Jocanda Johnson stood up and sang a song she'd sung at her church. Her voice was better than the teacher's—she sounded like a record—and it was such a grown-up and powerful sound that I forgot to be jealous and just sat there, rapt, wanting her to sing it over and over again. But unless a kid came in with some kind of head wound, Show 'n' Tell was usually of little interest to any of us. The only truly attentive person was Mrs. Mutnick; the rest of us either squirmed around impatiently or boned up on our napping skills.

One day, I planned to show a pair of souvenir maracas my grandparents had bought on their honeymoon. Yet when my turn came, I discovered I'd left them at home. Determined not to give up my slot, I informed Mrs. Mutnick that I had something to "tell" instead.

I hadn't planned anything. I just stood up before my classmates. "Tomorrow, my parents are changing my name to 'Rhinestone,'" I announced.

For some reason, this caught people's attention. Mrs. Mutnick adjusted her glasses on the bridge of her nose. "Really!" she exclaimed. "You're going to be called 'Rhinestone Gilman'?"

I'd never liked "Susan" because wherever I went, there were always at least two other girls with the same name. Only one of us ever got to be just "Susan"—the other two were inevitably relegated to using our initials—we became "Susan K." and "Susan G.," auxiliary Susans, backup singer Susans, second- and third-runner-up Susans. "Rhinestone," on the other hand, was sparkly and, I was quite certain, original. But hearing it said aloud with my last name attached, it suddenly sounded a lot stupider than I'd imagined. *Rhinestone Gilman?*

"No, wait, I mean 'Sapphire,'" I said quickly. "They're changing my name to Sapphire. *Sapphire Gilman*." Yes, that was much better. Plus, I got to keep my initials.

"Isn't that interesting!" said Mrs. Mutnick. "Are you going to court to change it legally?"

I had no idea what she was talking about. "My mommy and daddy are just going to call me that from now on," I explained. "I asked them, and they said yes."

(Part of this was not exactly a lie. I had recently asked my mother if she'd call me another name I liked a lot—Beulah. "What, are you kidding? You want the name of a black maid on a racist TV show?" she said. "Not a chance.")

"Well, I think that's very good of your parents," said Mrs. Mutnick. "It's important to let children have a say in defining themselves, isn't it, class?"

Everyone nodded.

"Would you like us to call you 'Sapphire' from now on, too?" Mrs. Mutnick asked me.

I couldn't believe my good fortune. Flooded with gratitude, I nodded vigorously.

"Well then, Sapphire," Mrs. Mutnick said kindly, "thank you for sharing today. You can sit down now."

That was the moment it dawned on me that the real purpose of Show 'n' Tell was not to show off Frisbees or spoon collections, but to provide me, personally, with a forum for passing off all of my wildest fantasies as bona fide truths.

The next day, when Mrs. Mutnick asked who had anything for Show 'n' Tell, my hand went up again.

"Yes, Sapphire?" she said.

"Today I have something else to tell," I said. "My family and I are moving to Passaic."

Earlier that year, my aunt and uncle had moved to Passaic, New Jersey, and I was completely enraptured by it. All the houses on their street were identical, with tiny, scalloped awnings over the windows and pastel aluminum siding. In their bathroom, they had a toilet seat covered in pink faux fur, a pearly pink plastic shower curtain, and an enormous box of pink rosebud soaps that dissolved like chalk in your hands whenever you used them. We'd been out to visit them twice so far, and I'd spent the entire time in the bathroom, washing and rewashing my hands, then peeking out the frosted glass window to look at their next door neighbor's raised swimming pool. In Passaic, nobody's white mother wore kente cloth and big purple sunglasses she'd bought at the local head shop. Nobody's father walked around in a "Fabulous Furry Freak Brothers" cartoon T-shirt and clogs.

"Really," said Mrs. Mutnick. "When are you moving?"

"I don't know," I shrugged. "Maybe next year. For my birthday. We're going to have a pink bathroom and a swimming pool," I added. "And a pink fake fur toilet seat cover."

"Oh," said Mrs. Mutnick. "Won't that be lovely."

The next day for Show 'n' Tell, I informed my classmates that I would be dancing that weekend in the *Nutcracker Suite* ballet at Lincoln Center.

"What a coincidence!" Mrs. Mutnick exclaimed. "So are Lucille Suggs and David Gonzales in Mrs. Lowey's third grade class! Are you in the Jacques D'Amboise program, too?"

I had no idea what she was talking about. As luck would have it, the famous choreographer Jacques D'Amboise had just started a pilot program to bring ballet to inner city schools; from it, a handful of children were recruited to dance "backup" in some productions with the New York City Ballet. Although I'd planned to tell the class that I was going to be dancing the starring role of Clara, it suddenly seemed like a better idea to agree with my teacher.

"Mmm-hhmmm," I said.

"Well, that's just wonderful," said Mrs. Mutnick. She turned to the rest of the children. "Maybe on Monday Sapphire will tell us all what it was like to dance at Lincoln Center. Won't that be nice?"

But by Monday morning, I'd clear forgotten my whopping lies of the previous week and had even better things to share.

"This weekend," I announced, "my mommy had another baby."

"Oh, my! I had no idea!" said Mrs. Mutnick, clasping her hands together. Even Mrs. Flores's face took the shape of something less than an all-out grimace. "A new baby? Sapphire, that's wonderful!"

"It's a girl," I told her. "A girl like me." In real life, my parents had ignored my wishes and coughed up a boy instead, but that didn't mean I couldn't correct the situation with a little creativity of my own. "Her name is Sylvia Goldia. Sylvia Goldia Gilman."

Saying this, I could almost see my beautiful new sister for real. She was named Sylvia Goldia after my two favorite crayon colors, and she wasn't a toddler like my brother, but practically my age already, capable of playing "Super Star Girl" in which I was a super hero named "Super Star Girl" and she was a pet dog who didn't say very much unless I told her to.

"I got to pick out her name," I added proudly.

"Yes," Mrs. Mutnick smiled. "I somehow suspected that."

My life, from then on, was a dream. I danced around the playhouse with my friends, instructing them in proper ballet technique, which they now looked to me for, seeing as I had appeared at Lincoln Center. Everybody called me Sapphire and inquired thoughtfully about my new baby sister. Carmen and Sarah even decided they should make a card for her drawn entirely in silver and gold crayon. "Welcome Sylvia Goldia!!!!" it read. I promised both of them that they could come visit me in Passaic when we moved, and that we'd all play in the swimming pool together, then wash our hands with pink soap. Everything was going perfectly for me—I was even contemplating what to say next for Show 'n' Tell—that I'd be spending Christmas in Hawaii? That I was going to appear as a guest star on *Captain Kangaroo*? That my little brother had to be put up for adoption now that there were two girls in the house?—when, suddenly, my mother walked through the door. It was two o'clock. I'd completely forgotten: time to go home.

"Mommy!" I shouted, running over to give her a voluminous hug.

To my horror, Mrs. Mutnick rushed over to her at the exact same moment.

"Oh, Ellen, congratulations!" she said, clasping both my mother's hands in her own and shaking them vigorously. "I'm so surprised to see you. They let you out of the hospital so early!"

My mother looked confused.

"Your new baby," prompted Mrs. Mutnick, smiling. Then she looked down at the stroller. My brother was sitting in it in his red pom-pom hat, chewing on the end of a drool-covered pretzel.

"He's right here," said my mother, pointing to John. "Though, Greta, he's not that new anymore."

"But Sapphire said you'd given birth to a baby girl over the week-end."

"Sapphire?" said my mother. "Who's Sapphire?"

They both looked at me and I suddenly realized it would be a very good idea to develop an interest in the chalk tray right about then.

"Oh dear," sighed Mrs. Mutnick. She leaned against the door frame and massaged the bridge of her nose beneath her glasses. "I'm guessing there's no house in Passaic?"

My mother shook her head.

"And she didn't dance in the *Nutcracker Suite* ballet this weekend, either."

With this, my mother threw her head back and laughed and shook her head. Tears came to her eyes, and she wiped them on the back of her glove.

"Just out of curiosity, Greta, what did she say her new baby sister's name was?"

Then they both said in unison, *"Sylvia Goldia."*

"Mm hm," said my mother, eyeing me dryly.

"Actually," said Mrs. Mutnick, "at this age, making up stories and names for themselves is fairly common. Until recently, I'd be suspect about a name like 'Sapphire.' But this year alone, I've got a 'Sunshine' in one of my classes, and a 'Stokely,' and a 'Rainbow,' and a 'Che.' Ruth Lowey has two 'Arethas' and a 'Moonbeam.'"

"Well, my kid does have a vivid imagination," said my mother.

Mrs. Mutnick chuckled and shook her head. "No shrinking violet, your daughter."

For a moment I assumed I was off the hook; it was usually a good sign when grown-ups talked about you in the third person bemusedly. But the next thing I knew, the other kids had all gone home, and my mother had taken me out of my winter coat, and she and Mrs. Mutnick were sitting me down at the table—one on either side of me, stuffed into those Lilliputian kiddie chairs—and they were reading me a book. It was illustrated with woodcuts, and it was titled "The Boy Who Cried Wolf."

You all know the story.

When the boy was finally devoured by wolves, my mother shut the book and asked, "So, Susie, do you understand why it's bad to tell lies?"

I nodded. "Because you don't want to get eaten by wolves?"

My mother looked at Mrs. Mutnick.

"Good enough," she sighed.

———

The next day, newly chastened, I came to school as Susie again, and raised my hand for Show 'n' Tell. Mrs. Mutnick called on me proudly. "Susie has something very important to tell the class, don't you, Susie?"

"Uh-huh," I nodded. I stood up. "Last night my mother was hit by a truck."

This time, Mrs. Mutnick didn't wait for the end of the day. She telephoned my mother, and during Juice and Cookie Time, they sat down with me again.

I believe it was Freud who once said that the definition of insanity is doing the same thing over and over, hoping to get different results. But then, Freud never had to deal with raising a five-year-old. Out came "The Boy Who Cried Wolf" again, and again we had the discussion roughly entitled "Why It Is Bad to Lie."

Somewhere along the line, my mother had the insight that I was lying not to be difficult, but to be special. And since appealing to my sense of morality was obviously a lost cause, she decided to appeal to my vanity instead.

When we got home from school, she said, "Why don't we try to come up with the most interesting *true* thing for you to share? That way, you can show everybody at school how smart you are."

Then we looked at the maracas I had originally planned to bring in. They'd been crafted from coconut shells with the word "Havana" painted on them in black.

"Oh, there's a story behind these," said my mother. "Do you know where Havana is?"

I shook my head.

"It's in Cuba, in the Caribbean Sea," said my mother, pulling an atlas off the shelf. She showed me a picture of an island shaped like a newt. "This is where your grandparents had their honeymoon many years ago. And a lot of big things have happened in Cuba since then."

The next day, I trooped into kindergarten armed with my maracas. I noticed Mrs. Mutnick seemed hesitant to call on me for Show 'n' Tell, but when she did, I stood up and said, "Today, I'm going to tell about something true. Today I'm going to tell you about the Cuban Revolution." Then I held up my maracas and shook them for effect.

"Cuba is an island south of the United States. It has palm trees and beaches," I said. "When my grandma and grandpa first got married, they went there on their honeymoon. But then, things changed in Cuba. The country had a revolution. What's a revolution? Sometimes, my mommy says, it's when people in a country don't like the way the country is. Sometimes lots of people are poor, and only a few people are rich. Or sometimes—"

I looked up and noticed that Mrs. Mutnick was looking intently at Mrs. Flores, who was staring at me with a kind of disbelieving fascination. I had never seen her look that way before. She tilted her head slightly toward the door. "Susie, do you mind waiting a minute?"

Mrs. Mutnick said. "Mrs. Flores and I think Mr. Alvarado might like to hear this."

Mr. Alvarado was our principal. Of course, I had no way of knowing that both he and Mrs. Flores had been born in Havana. After a minute, Mrs. Flores returned to the room with Mr. Alvarado following behind her. They both squeezed down into the tiny kindergarten chairs with the rest of the class, looking no longer scary, but suddenly miniaturized and silly. Mr. Alvarado smiled at me expectantly. I looked at Mrs. Mutnick, who was beaming. I had everyone's attention. Everybody was focused on me. Not because of my costumes, or who I was pretending to be, but because of what I had to say. It was my moment. Finally, I was a stewardess. I was a prima ballerina. I was Batgirl.

Yet I was not destined to become any of these things.

Perhaps I was simply a typical five-year-old, compelled to do exactly what I'd repeatedly been instructed not to do. Or perhaps, I was exhibiting the first signs of what I would, in fact, one day really grow up to be. Because my mother had told me the history of Cuba as accurately as she could. She'd pulled out our *World Book Encyclopedia* and a few old, cracked copies of *Time* magazine. She'd gone over the history with me. I'd gotten the facts, I knew the truth.

And yet, I couldn't help myself. The impulse to embellish, to put my own fantastical little spin on things, was simply too strong. "The Cuban Revolution was led by a man named Fidel Astro," I announced. "He was named after the dog on the *Jetsons*."

Chapter 3

White Like Me

AS WITH MOST EVERYTHING ELSE in life, I first decided I wanted to be Puerto Rican based on the clothes.

One Sunday when I was six, I spotted two older girls from my school, Carmella and Lisa, standing on the steps of the church across the street from my building. They were wearing white party dresses that looked like spun sugar and tiny crowns made of seed pearls. Most unbelievably, they each had on a real lace veil. Seeing them dressed like that made me spastic with envy.

"Mom! Look at Carmella and Lisa!" I shouted, bouncing up and down and pointing. "Can I be that? Can I? Oh please Oh please Oh please?"

My mother laughed. "You want to be a Puerto Rican girl in a communion dress?" she said. "Honey, we're not even Catholic."

Until that moment, I'd thought being Puerto Rican simply meant you spoke Spanish and were allowed to get your ears pierced. But now, child genius that I was, I saw that it also meant you got to parade around on the steps of the Church of the Holy Name dressed like a miniature bride. A whole new vista of desire opened before me, and immediately, I set about campaigning to become Hispanic.

Fishing a doily and a tiny, beaded basket out of my closet, I stuck them on my head and promenaded around our apartment, enunciating loudly, *"Uno, dos, tres. Cuatro, cinco, seis. Leche."* Counting to six and saying the word "milk" was just about the extent of the Spanish I'd picked up around the neighborhood, but it seemed to me like a good start.

"Blanco!" I shouted, pirouetting around the kitchen. *"Mira. Dos frittatas por favor. Adios. Muchachas."*

Sitting at the table, my father glanced at my mother.

"Our child now wants to be Puerto Rican," she informed him. "God knows where she got the idea that it's optional."

My father chuckled. "Hey, Susanita," he called to me. "Is that what we should call you from now on? Susanita?"

"Please," my mother said tightly, my disgraceful kindergarten career still fresh in her memory. "Don't encourage her." Then she set down her wooden spoon on the countertop and looked at me.

"Speak all the Spanish you want!" she shouted. "But for the last time: You're not getting a communion outfit."

Years later, when I went to college, I dated a guy from Maine who told me that the first black people he'd ever seen were Gordon and Susan on *Sesame Street*. This both amazed and appalled me. Growing up in my neighborhood meant that I spent much of my time confronting racial issues, thinking about racial issues, and completely misunderstanding racial issues.

With its rubble-strewn lots and highly interactive junkie population, the Upper West Side of the early 1970s was what was optimistically known as "a transitional neighborhood." Its butchered sidewalks were spangled with broken glass, and rows of vacant lots were boarded up using doors salvaged from demolished tenements.

Broadway—the main thoroughfare—was lined with pawn shops, check-cashing services, Off-Track Betting parlors, Chicken De-Lite takeaways, and furniture discounters that sold sofas on layaway. Many of the signs were in Spanish, including the marquee of the

Edison porno theater, which led several local boys to believe that speaking Spanish was a prerequisite for getting laid.

In this neighborhood, it was simply a given that everyone came in different colors. The kids in our high-rise apartment building were black, white, Hispanic, Asian, interracial, tri-racial, you name it—though when we played together, the main thing on our minds, of course, was the same thing that was on the minds of most kids in America: namely, what we could get away with without getting caught by the grown-ups.

Behind our building was a long walled-in area euphemistically called "the backyard." Devoid of any plant life, it was a wet dream for cosmetic dentists and personal injury lawyers. Virtually every surface was concrete, except for the jungle gym, which was made from cast iron and about as safe and appealing to play on as a giant perforated skillet.

My playmates and I ran around this yard like the Rainbow Coalition on amphetamines. We zoomed about playing freeze tag, then "Hot Peas and Butter," then "Red Light Green Light," then staged kamikaze jumps off the monkey bars, then got into elaborate pile-up crashes on our assorted tricycles, bicycles, and Big Wheels, then held competitions seeing who could leap off the highest section of the concrete retaining wall without knocking out a tooth.

No one had to tell us that our skin might be different colors, but underneath we were all the same. Given the amount of blood we spilled in that backyard every day, we saw this firsthand.

Still, our parents weren't taking any chances. Flush with the activism of the 1960s, they were determined to raise us free from all prejudice—a goal which they seemed to attempt primarily through the strategic use of T-shirts, lunchboxes, and sing-alongs. Every kid's Fisher-Price phonograph had "Free to Be . . . You and Me" spinning around on its turntable. For our birthdays, we received black Raggedy Ann dolls and consciousness-raising children's books with titles like *The World Is a Rainbow* or *Che Guevara: An I Can Read Book!*

On television, we watched animated versions of the Harlem Globetrotters and the Jackson 5 every Saturday morning, as well as the cartoon *Fat Albert and the Cosby Kids,* which, just like *Josie and the Pussycats,* ended each week with the characters playing in a rock band and singing snappy songs about loving each other and getting along. The head shop on 94th Street sold "Black Is Beautiful" T-shirts, peace sign necklaces, and buttons that read "America: Let's Get It Together" that showed a map of the U.S. constructed from profiles of people of different races. Every day, we jumped rope and played freeze tag to the funky Top 10 hits that emanated from transistor radios on stoops throughout the neighborhood. The scorching anthem of "Brother Louie": *She was black as the ni-ight/Louie was whiter than white . . .* Sly and the Family Stone singing *"I-hi-hi love everyday people . . ."*

On weekends, we were trotted over to the Goddard-Riverside Community Center for special multicultural "family events," where a white woman named Minna Bromberg had us sing Swahili folk songs and drink unfiltered apple juice. Minna was a pale woman with cheekbones like paper cutters and blue-black hair pulled back so tightly it virtually improvised a face-lift. Although she dressed in tie-dye and armloads of hammered brass jewelry, she was really far too high-strung to be a hippie. "Goddamn it," she'd mutter as she scrambled amid the onslaught of hysterical, folksinging six-year-olds. "Where the hell are those peace posters? Could we please have a little more quiet in here, please?"

Other weekends, my friends and I sat squirming and poking each other as we watched multiethnic "Shadow Box" puppet shows, listened to Hopi storytellers, and clapped in time as a bearded banjo player named Satchel led us in one interminable round after another of "He's Got the Whole World in His Hands."

"Remember, children," Satchel instructed cheerily at the end of each concert, "when you look at people, don't see the color of their skin. Only the content of their character." He always said this extra slowly and loudly for emphasis, as if we were not actually children but mildly retarded beagles.

To my playmates and me, this was perplexing. That everyone was equal was obvious to us. As far as we were concerned, the only legitimate reason to ever discriminate against anyone was if they happened to be your little brother or sister. In that case, it was perfectly acceptable to relegate them to the role of "deaf-mute orphan" and "houseplant" whenever you made up games.

But how weren't we supposed to see another person's skin? As kids, we noticed *everything*.

We knew, for example, that only Tabitha Cohen could roll her eyes back and fake a truly convincing epileptic seizure. Gregory Dupree was double-jointed and could dislocate his own thumb. Ricardo had a scar like a piece of dental floss from his wrist to his elbow from the time he ran through a plate glass window. Chieko ate strange and frightening seaweed for lunch. Peter could play "The Battle Hymn of the Republic" with armpit farts. Karis had a special condition that made her eyebrows fall off.

In the backyard one day, Michelle, Adam, Juan, and I tried to figure out how, exactly, to be color-blind.

"Okay, look at me," said Adam, balancing precariously on the rim of the jungle gym. His skin was the golden brown of pancake syrup, and the rest of us squinted at him, trying to make him appear translucent. "Do you still see it?"

"Mm-hm," we nodded.

"Still black," said Juan.

"Try me!" I volunteered. Adam, Michelle, and Juan screwed up their faces and squinted at me fiercely.

"Still white!" they chorused.

William, Adam's fifteen-year-old brother, sauntered over to us, followed by his friend Georges.

"Ay, Adam. What's up? Skins," William said, slapping Adam's hand, then running his palm smoothly across it. He walked around the jungle gym and "gave skin" to Juan, Michelle, and me, too, which made all of us feel enormously grown-up and privileged and worshipful and cool. "You all okay over here?" William asked.

"Uh-huh," nodded Adam. Then he squinted up at him, practicing.

"We're trying to be color-blind!" I explained.

"Huh?" said William.

"Satchel the Banjo Player said we should all be color-blind," Adam said.

"He said we shouldn't see people's skin," I said. "So we're trying not to."

"So far, it isn't really working," Michelle said.

"Yeah," said Juan, squinting up at the sky and lolling his head back and forth like Stevie Wonder. "So far, everyone's just a little fuzzy."

William and Georges looked at each other.

"Ho, shit, man," Georges said, shaking his head. He exhaled with a whistle, then threw his basketball against the wall and caught it on the rebound.

"Color-blind? Are you kidding me?" William hooted. "You're supposed to pretend you don't see who people are? You supposed to act handicapped? Shit. That's the dumbest thing I ever heard."

He leaned down and draped his arms around me and Michelle conspiratorily.

"Look. Let me tell you something," he said gently, squeezing our forearms in a brotherly fashion. "Every day of my life, I *know* that I'm black. And Georges here, he *knows* he's Puerto Rican. And both of us, we *know* that you two are white. And *you* should, too. In this world, everyone's gotta know who they are and where they come from. Understand? Don't let anybody tell you it's not important. Because it is."

Then he stood up and grinned at us. "I don't want any of you pretending to be blind, you hear? Not color-blind, not blind-blind, just 20/20, you got that?"

Obediently, we all nodded. He smiled and made a "Right-on!" fist at us, and we all made one back. Then he and Georges headed off to play basketball.

Sure enough, as we got old enough to walk to school by ourselves, we started to see things. Not just things like Puerto Rican girls wearing communion dresses. Things like the white proprietor of the corner bakery giving my brother and me free Swedish candy when we stopped by after school, but ordering our friends Jerry and Tremaine, two black kids from our building, to leave if they weren't going to buy anything.

But mostly what we saw was that, while the adults around us might have been singing "Joy to the World" and reading aloud stories like *George Washington Carver: Father of Peanut Butter!,* a lot of kids in the neighborhood were simply interested in kicking each other's ass.

Every day during recess at PS 75, boys in my first grade class tumbled onto the asphalt and pummeled each other mercilessly. Christopher and Ricardo against Barry and Juan. The fights were like dance contests, really. When boys fought, there was a blunt, muscular grace to it, a choreography, a parsing of the air, and as they locked together, other kids encircled them, cheering, clapping, hooting.

Sometimes, Christopher Kleinhaus yelled, "I call 'Boys against girls!'" Then it was a frenzy of yelling, chasing, and running. When this occurred, my friends Audrey, Sara, and I took refuge in the bathroom until the bell rang. We had a reputation as crybabies and cowards, and saw no reason to contradict this. Some of our other friends fought back, though, especially the black and Hispanic girls. The moment the boys flew at Alissa and Shana, they proclaimed flatly, "Excuse me, but I don't think so," then slonked them expertly in the kneecaps. "That's right. You *better* run," they shouted after them gleefully.

Still other times, two older girls fought each other. Then the temperature dropped dangerously. The schoolyard became frozen, suddenly vicious and terrifying. There was no prelude, no sense of decorum, just an instant eruption of violence.

"Excuse me. What did you just say?" one girl would say, stopping dead in the middle of the asphalt.

"You heard what I just said," another would reply venomously. "What? You deaf?"

"Whoa, that's it, bitch. I'm gonna fuck you up."

Then it was if a starting gun had been fired, and they lunged at each other, tearing out each other's hair in clumps, clawing each other's faces, clamping on to each other in a mutual, squalling death-choke until some hapless teachers finally managed to pull them apart.

No matter how much liberal gloss the adults tried to put on it, our neighborhood was simply a rough place. A decade before I was born, it had been riddled with Irish and Puerto Rican gangs. Now the gangs had gone, but the sense of foreboding and antagonism remained, crackling in the streets like static electricity.

When Michelle and I walked to Carvel for ice cream, boys and girls we didn't know hung on the chain link fence of the basketball court and taunted, "Hey. You. Ugly white girl. In the ugly pink coat. Yeah, you."

Standing on a movie line at the Olympia, Audrey and I heard snickering behind us, then whispering in Spanish, followed by a sharp poke. Turning around, we saw two girls sticking us in the butt with the pointy tips of their umbrellas.

"What?" they glared. "You got a problem?"

Audrey and I consulted each other nervously. We'd been instructed to love everyone and that "violence is not the answer," but now what were we supposed to do?

"If we yell at them, will they think we're prejudiced because they're Puerto Rican and we're white?" Audrey whispered.

"I don't know," I said. But meanwhile, why were the girls picking on us? Since they didn't know anything about us, except what they could see, were they ganging up on us *because* we were white?

Some of the older kids in the neighborhood seemed to have no use for us. Their contempt was palpable for the white so-called liberal culture, with its smiley face stickers, its patronizing "famous Negro" storybooks, and its TV jingles that professed to want to teach the world to sing in perfect harmony while really selling you a Coke. They knew what I couldn't possibly have known at that age: that all of us might be low-income at the moment, but that not all of us would be in ten or twenty years' time, and odds were that *they* would not be among the ones "movin' on up." To them, we white kids weren't "brothers and sisters" or "amigos" at all.

Being little kids, however, my white friends and I didn't understand this. All we saw was that some kids seemed to loathe us on sight. We struggled to understand why. What had we done wrong?

With no working knowledge of history, and without the usual host of prejudices to fall back on, we were left to develop our own. And the prejudice we developed was this: we white kids were disliked because we were so hideously un-cool.

When it came right down to it, declared my white friend Andrew, we had to face facts: white people came in dead last in the Hip Pageant. We were the lowest branch of the Cool Tree. We were losers in the Lottery of Soul and All-Around General Funkiness.

As he said this, our friends Juan, Steven, and Adam looked down sheepishly. "Aw, c'mon," said Steven halfheartedly. Steven was black. But why should he apologize? We white kids could see it for ourselves. Every morning, when we all walked down the hill to PS 75 together, we stopped to look in the window of the Ottowa Record Store. There were two albums always on display, set at right angles to each other: *The Partridge Family's Greatest Hits* and *ABC* by the Jackson 5. "Like, doy, who's better?" said Andrew disgustedly, rolling his eyes.

White dorkiness was glaring and embarrassing. Augh, how we wanted to wriggle away from it! Our black and Hispanic friends seemed all-knowing, almost invincible to us. They were like the superheroes of the neighborhood. They were clearly the best at anything that truly mattered to us kids: Loyalty. Cracking Jokes. Thinking Quickly. Musical Taste. Opening Up a Big Fresh Mouth. Playing Stickball and Basketball. Bravery. Resisting Pompous Authority Figures. Jumping Rope. Beating People Up. Telling It Like It Is. Hairdos.

Compared to them, we white kids were hothouse flowers—pampered, hesitant, gutless children who followed instructions and clung to our mothers. We were callow. We thought nothing of selling each other out for a baseball card or a Zagnut bar (I personally could be persuaded to change seats in the lunch room for a can of 7-Up).

By contrast, if I just *looked* at one of the older Puerto Rican girls on the cafeteria line, her *friend* would say to me: "Ay, who you lookin' at, girl? You lookin' at my friend Diana, here? You better not be."

With black and Puerto Rican kids, it wasn't enough just to have the right dolls or an extra package of Devil Dogs. You had to be initiated into their friendships and prove your allegiance. "If you're really my friend," Alissa told me in the corridor at school, "then whatever you have to say, you say it to my face or not at all. You're either straight with me, or you're not with me. You got that?"

Of course, the great irony was that the black and Hispanic kids in our neighborhood were among the most vulnerable populations in America. Their toughness wasn't a luxury or a fashion statement. It was a survival kit, plain and simple. But we little white kids were too young and naive to see that. All we saw when we looked at them was their strength and indifference, coupled with style—the fundamental essence of Cool. Black and Hispanic kids gave the impression of having thrown off all the humiliating albatrosses of childhood that the rest of us suffered with: the obedience, the dependence, the frustrating helplessness. Strangely, if they threatened us, it only fueled our desire to become more like them.

Remember, this was pre-MTV. This was long before white suburban kids started going around in baggy jeans with their underwear hanging out, rapping about being gangstas and givin' a shout-out to their peeps. But already, we felt the irresistible tug: any white kid with kinky hair coaxed it into a "Jewfro," then walked around with a pick stuck in it like a trophy. White teenaged girls started wearing T-shirts reading "Black Is Beautiful." My friend Amy's older brother hung out only with "the brothers," dated only black and Hispanic girls, and spoke Spanish on the basketball court. All of us imitated the clothes, the speech, the walk of our black and Puerto Rican peers. *Yo, gimme some skin. Cool man, that's cool, baby. Hey, blood, qué pasa?*

All of us, essentially, were now campaigning for that communion dress.

"You know," my white friend Michelle told me one day while we were sitting on the monkey bars. "Nobody knows this," she whispered, "but, my mom's mom *was really Puerto Rican.*"

"Nuh-uh," I said, seized with equal amounts of jealousy and skepticism.

"Uh-huh," she nodded.

Michelle herself had hair as light as sunflower oil and eyes the color of a chlorinated pool. If she could be one-quarter Puerto Rican, well then, I decided, I could do even better.

"Well, do you want to hear a secret that you can't tell anybody?" I said. Glancing around to make sure no one was watching, I cupped my hands tightly around Michelle's tiny pink ear, and whispered, *"My great-grandfather was black."*

———————

A girl in our building named Miriam was the first white girl to actually join one of the neighborhood's Puerto Rican girl gangs. One day, Miriam was attending St. Hilda's and St. Hughes in a pleated pinafore and writing book reports on *The Red Pony.* The next day, she was cutting school, donning platform shoes and a pink lamé halter top, calling herself Mira, and beating up white girls on Amsterdam Avenue with her "amigas." The adults in our building were all horrified—hadn't Miriam sung "What's Going On" once at folk mass? Weren't both her parents Freudian psychoanalysts? We kids, however, were all very impressed.

We also found it sort of funny—not *funny ha-ha* but *funny strange:* Miriam's mother had always encouraged her to play with children of different colors. So now that she was, what was the problem?

The next week, my friend Audrey's older sister, Rochelle, joined a gang of Puerto Rican girls, too. Instead of going to Hebrew school one afternoon, she plucked out all her eyebrows, painted them back on with liquid eyeliner, then went to smoke cigarettes in full makeup with three girls in the park, who later that day beat up Tara Eisner, one of Rochelle's Hebrew school classmates, because, Rochelle said, "Like, I didn't like her face, okay?"

Hoping to catch a glimpse of the new, improved, Hispanic Rochelle, I went out of my way to play at Audrey's house. My efforts paid off when Rochelle stormed through the door while we were sitting at the kitchen table cutting out Sonny and Cher paper dolls. "Ay. Audrey. Jew see my Marlboros?" Rochelle said.

Since Rochelle couldn't speak Spanish like a Puerto Rican, she tried to speak English like one, parroting the accent and English-as-a-second-language speech patterns, then punctuating them with ghettoish, serpentine head bobs and finger snaps. This kind of speech was known as "Spanglish," and lots of white kids in the neighborhood were starting to adopt it. In reality, of course, it was as contrived and offensive as a Frito Bandito cartoon, but we were too dumb to know that.

Flinging her keys down on the kitchen counter, Rochelle dumped the contents of her crotchet shoulder bag out onto the table. She was wearing enormous hoop earrings made from silver wire, and her skintight Danskin blouse looked more like a bathing suit top. Silver bangles jangled along her forearms as she sifted frantically through the contents of her bag. I noticed a tall, cool Puerto Rican boy waiting for her by the entrance to the kitchen. He leaned languidly against the door frame, working a piece of gum slowly around in his mouth, his eyes following Rochelle as she stormed about, pulling open the utility drawers by the sink. He seemed to have all the time in the world.

"So, li-eeke, I told my muth-thuh, like, riiight?" Rochelle said, clearly for her new boyfriend's benefit and not ours. "Like, I ain't goin' to no bat mitzvah class an' shit no more, riiiight? Li-eeke, fuck Hebrew school, man."

That evening, when I reported this to my mother, she laughed. "Serves Sheila right," she said.

Sheila Abromowitz was Rochelle's mother. She and my mother had had a huge argument the year before, when both of them spent the day volunteering at my kindergarten. That day, all of us kids were supposed to make our own books, which meant, essentially, that we scribble-scrabbled wildly over a bunch of folded-up papers, then tried to invent some story for the mothers to write down.

When my mother got to Gregory Dupree, he pointed to his picture and said, "Okay, please write, 'This boy ain't got no shoes.'"

"All right," smiled my mother. "But Gregory, let's phrase it correctly. Let's write 'This boy doesn't have any shoes.'"

No sooner did my mother begin to transcribe Gregory's story in her decorative serif print than Sheila asked if she could have a word with my mother in the hallway.

The door had barely clinked shut behind them when Sheila said, "How dare you alter that boy's original words?"

"Sheila," said my mother. "The whole purpose of this is to teach the children grammar."

"Gregory is expressing himself using his own culturally indigenous, Afro-American speech patterns," Sheila said acidly. "What you call 'grammar' is just a white, cultural conceit."

"Oh you think so?" said my mother. She set her hands on her hips, then took aim. "Well let me tell you what I think is a white, cultural conceit: a white woman holding a black child to a standard of English that she'd never allow her own children to use."

My mother turned around and twisted open the door. "The day that Harvard University accepts students who express themselves exclusively in 'indigenous Afro-American speech patterns,' you let me know, Sheila. Until then, I'm teaching Gregory the kind of 'cultural conceits' that'll actually give him some power in this world."

"Sheila Abromowitz ought to be slow-roasted on an open spit," my mother fumed to me on the way home from school. "*Indigenous Afro-American speech patterns.* What a load of racist, liberal bullshit. It's just an excuse, you know, to keep black children disenfranchised."

I nodded in agreement. I had no idea what "disenfranchised" was, but my mother sounded exactly right to me. Just a few weeks before, my brother and I had come up with our own language. We called it "Farty Fartese," and it essentially mimicked Pig Latin, except that it inserted the word "fart" between the word and the "ay" sound. *I-fart-hay. Ow-fart-hay are-fart-ay ou-fart-yay?* As soon as my mother heard it, she said, "Okay, that's enough. I don't want to hear that annoying and stupid talk in this house, again. Understood?"

It seemed to me that if John and I couldn't use our own special language, Gregory Dupree shouldn't get to use his either. Besides, Gregory and I had a huge crush on each other. I wanted him to go to Harvard—whatever that was—and do the best and win at everything because we'd agreed to get married as soon as we both turned seven.

Now, Sheila Abromowitz's eldest daughter appeared to have adopted the indigenous cultural speech patterns of a bunch of delinquent Puerto Rican girls.

"Ah, yes," smiled my mother. "Payback is sweet."

However, she didn't seem to think it was nearly so sweet later that night at dinner, when I was dawdling over my carrots, and she pointed to my plate. Getting John and me to eat anything resembling a vegetable was a major source of contention in our household, and the level of difficulty had only increased over time.

At first, my parents had tried employing the artificial, suspicious enthusiasm of gum surgeons, game show hosts, and incompetent clowns: *"Hey, kids, let's all eat three forkfuls of yummy broccoli on the count of three. Mmmm. Isn't this FUN?"*

When this eventually proved useless, they tried out-and-out bribery: "Eat three pieces of celery and I'll pay you a quarter," my father said wearily.

Now they'd simply resorted to bullying. "Finish your carrots," my mother ordered. "Now."

Looking down at the congealing, lurid carrot wheels I'd succeeded in pushing around my dinner plate for the past half-hour, I suddenly thought of Miriam, Rochelle, and their *amigas*.

"Li-eeke, I don't dink so, all riiiight," I said in my best possible Spanglish.

"Excuse me?" said my mother, setting down her fork.

"What? Jew deaf?" I said. "Like, I ain't gonna be eatin' no carrots an' shit, riiiight?" I repeated, this time making a little turkey bob with my head.

My brother slid off his seat down under the table, and my father removed his glasses and began massaging the bridge of his nose.

"Oh. Are we back to being Puerto Rican again?" said my mother.

"Das riiiight," I said proudly.

"Well then." She dropped her napkin crisply down onto her plate. "In that case, let me put it to you this way. Open up a big, fresh mouth to me like that ever again, and I'll slap you so hard you'll be prying your teeth out of the floorboards. This that clear, *amiga?*"

My eyes filled up wetly and I nodded.

"Bueno," said my mother.

I had to give her credit. None of the kids in the neighborhood had anything on my mother.

———————

Jerome, my friend Annie's older brother, soon put the kibosh on another one of my ideas.

"Black and Puerto Rican kids don't beat us up because we're uncool, Susie," he told me. "They beat us up as historical payback."

Even though Jerome was probably all of fifteen, I considered him a grown-up because he had a beard. Whenever I went to Annie's house, Jerome was skulking around the kitchen in his suede vest, eating organic yogurt and complaining about the Nixon administration. As Annie and I played checkers or Candyland in her bedroom, we'd hear Jerome yelling at the television, "Henry, you goddamn fascist!"

Jerome had the habit of talking to me and Annie as if we were grown-ups and not in elementary school. Usually when people did this, it was flattering. But with Jerome it was just scary, because he tended to view all grown-ups as either dimwits and criminals. Once, when he overheard me mention to Annie that I liked the song "The Candy Man," he came storming into the living room yelling, "How can you possibly like that song? Don't you know Sammy Davis Jr. campaigned for Nixon? Don't you realize that royalties from that song are supporting an administration that's engaged in the covert bombing of Cambodia?"

I was six years old. I had no idea what Cambodia was. I liked the song simply because of its lyrics, *Who can take a rainbow, wrap it in a sigh? Soak it in the sun and make a groovy lemon pie?*

But after Jerome explained it to me, it was fairly impossible to listen to "The Candy Man" ever again without thinking of Henry Kissinger napalming babies.

Now Jerome leaned back in his chair. "You don't know a thing about imperialism or slavery, do you?" he said incredulously.

I did so. "Imperial," I informed him, was the name of a yo-yo as well as a brand of margarine. As for slavery, I knew all about it from a picture book my parents had given me on Harriet Tubman. Unfortunately, from reading it I'd somehow gotten the impression that the African slaves had been a small, finite group of people—rather like the crew of a shipwreck—whom the heroic and fabulous Harriet Tubman had rescued single-handedly while driving a railroad train and wearing many interesting but not terribly glamorous disguises.

Jerome looked at me disgustedly. "The slaves were not like the crew on *Gilligan's Island,* Susie," he nearly spat. "They were millions of people." He then cleared away our half-finished game of Chutes and Ladders and spent the next hour educating Annie and me about the full, epic atrocities of slavery and colonialism.

When he finally finished, he crossed his arms triumphantly. "See," he said smugly, "that's the *real* reason why black and Spanish kids beat us up. They're pissed off. We white people are the biggest assholes in history."

I suppose he thought he was enlightening us, but all he really managed to do was to give me a massive stomachache. If I'd wanted to be black or Hispanic before, by now I was pretty much ready to tear off my skin, then run away from it as quickly as possible yelling, "I call 'Not it'!"

"Dad, did we own slaves?" I asked my father that evening.

"Did we own what?" he said.

"Jerome said that over a hundred years ago, white people owned black people as slaves. Did we?"

My father shook his head. "A hundred years ago, our ancestors were living in Russia, eating rancid potatoes, and getting chased by Cossacks."

"Oh, that's good," I said. "What a relief."

"Why? What did Jerome tell you?"

"He said that the black and Puerto Rican kids on the street beat up white kids as historical payback."

My father sighed and shook his head. "Sweetie. The reason that black and Puerto Rican kids on the street beat up white kids is because you're all kids on the street. And that's what kids on streets do."

He folded his newspaper and tossed it aside. "Listen, when I was growing up, the Italians would beat the shit out of the Poles, then the Poles would beat the shit out of the Irish, and then the Irish would beat the shit out of the Jews." He said this almost nostalgically. "In fact, if there weren't any Jews around, the Irish just beat the shit out of each other. That's street life. Come to think of it, that's history. Someone's always beating the shit out of someone else. It's not right, but it happens."

"But what about slavery?" I said. Personally, it seemed to me that if someone had made me be a slave, I'd want to beat the shit out of them, too.

"What about it?" said my dad. "Black people have absolutely no reason to like or trust white people. That's a fact. *That's* historical payback. But the world is full of horror and cruelty and distrust. The Irish were starved and treated like dogs by the British for eight hundred years. The Armenians were slaughtered by the Turks. The Jews . . . Loads of people can make the case. If you start thinking that the kids in this neighborhood are beating the shit out of you *only* because they're black or Puerto Rican, *that's* when you have a problem," said my dad. "Because then you're not seeing them as human beings. You think that they behave the way they do because of their group, not because of their humanity."

"So the girls who poked me at the movies and the older boys who threaten John do so because we're all human?"

"Of course," said my father. "Only humans do crazy stupid shit like that. The day a cow or a Chihuahua hits you in the ass with an umbrella or threatens you with an ice pick, you let me know."

That spring, a brand-new playground opened near 100th Street in Central Park. Soft wooden jungle gyms were linked by rope ladders and jute bridges that led to malleable plastic slides. Fat, cushy tire swings hung from redwood frames, and every single structure was set in an enormous sandbox, so that you could swing, dangle, slide, jump, and fall wherever you wanted to and still keep your teeth in your head. It seemed to have been designed precisely as an antidote to the cement proving grounds of our own backyard.

The day it opened, a whole group of kids from our building went there with our parents. We'd never seen anything like it before—it was a paradise for little maniacs like us—and every other kid living in a two-mile radius of West 100th Street seemed to be there, too. It was the newest, best thing in the neighborhood, and a sign that maybe we mattered.

One Saturday afternoon, when the playground was filled to bursting, all the tire swings were occupied. There was no time limit, of course, to how long you could be on the swings, and since they didn't require anyone to push you, kids could conceivably hang out on them for hours, converting them into make-believe spaceships or private camper vans—which is exactly what I planned to do, actually, as soon as I got hold of one myself. I waited for what seemed like hours, but no one got off. It was almost summer, and as the heat prickled and burned at the back of my neck, I began roasting with impatience.

Finally, a group of three big girls abandoned the tire to my left. They were older than me by at least three years, and they had that tough, hard-baked look of the kids who lived even farther north than I did—it was the look of the hard-core projects, the look of danger, hunger, suspicion. For a moment, my instincts told me not to get on the swing just yet, but I climbed on greedily anyway.

I'd barely begun to spin around, when the three girls returned. "Hey girl," the biggest one said. "You're on our swing."

I clutched the chains that suspended the rubber tire from the redwood frame and looked at her. My instincts also told me to get up quickly and relinquish the tire, but the rest of me was hot and cranky, and told me to ignore my instincts. Hadn't these same instincts instructed me to do nothing in the past when Christopher Kleinhaus yelled "Boys against girls" in the schoolyard? Hadn't they told me to do nothing when the two girls at the Olympia poked me with their umbrellas? I decided then and there that I was sick of doing nothing. I was sick of trying to love everybody instead of just slugging it out with the rest of humanity.

Looking the biggest girl fiercely in the eye, I said, "It's not your swing. The park is for everyone."

Only a child of hippies, I realize now, could ever imagine these might actually qualify as "fightin' words."

Hearing this, the girls looked at me incredulously. "Ho, snap," one of them laughed—though whether this was at my audacity or stupidity was unclear.

"Look, I'll tell you again," the biggest girl said. "Get off of our swing."

I inhaled as deeply as I could. I was suddenly aware only of my own pulse, pounding in my ears. "It's my turn now." I tried not to betray the tremor in my voice. "This park is for sharing. You can have it back when I'm done."

The girl cocked her head. As if cued, her two friends moved into position alongside her, polishing their fists. "Girl. I'm telling you. One last time. GET. OFF. OUR. SWING."

"NO. I WON'T!" I shouted, emboldened by my own, righteous bravado. "MAKE ME." Remembering the protocol from the schoolyard, I then added, "BITCH!"

Throughout our childhoods, my mother had always taught me and John to be grateful for even the very smallest things in life. In one swift moment, I was grateful for perhaps the very smallest of them all: sand. Millions of grains of it. Because that was what quickly came between me and the concrete as the oldest, biggest girl batted me off the tire swing with a single motion, then straddled me and began pounding me methodically into the ground. I assumed her friends were kicking and punching me from both sides, but I couldn't be sure. It was such a blatantly unbalanced fight—I was so clearly a nonopponent—that they could've decided it wasn't worth the effort and simply whipped out a nail file and a compact mirror and sat on the edge of the tire swing primping while they waited for their friend to finish me off.

Oh, I *did* fight back. I flailed my hands spastically and shrieked "Stooo-ooop it!" in a shrill and girlish whine. I swatted blindly, windmilling at the air. Pinned beneath her legs, my own kicked at nothing but sand. I did get in a couple of slaps before I felt a blow or two on the side of my torso, a kick on the side of my thigh, then a wallop to my face, followed by a meaty, metallic taste in my mouth and a hot wetness around my nose. Then the girl climbed off me with the same easy swagger you'd use to climb off a mechanical rocking horse outside Woolworth's. She brushed off her hands with expert efficiency, then calmly resumed her place on the swing. The other two girls took their original places beside her, and in a moment, they were spinning around and laughing as if nothing had happened.

I just lay stretched out in the sand, listening to the rasp of my own breath and waiting for the internal pounding of my pulse to subside. Then, slowly, I sat up, clutching my bloody nose. I scanned around the benches for my parents and saw my father talking to Michelle's mother, not fifteen yards away. He glanced in my direction, but I couldn't tell whether he'd seen me or not.

Once I discovered that no major damage had, in fact, been done, I struggled to my feet. I was perfectly fine, but sand-covered and dazed. I made a beeline for my father.

"Daddy!" I sobbed. "I got into a fight."

"I know," he said, handing me his handkerchief. "I saw you."

"You saw me?" I cried. "Why didn't you come?"

"Sweetie," my father said. "You took on three girls. They were older than you. They were bigger than you. And they were clearly looking for a fight. You had no backup. And you had never thrown a punch in your life. About the only thing you *did* do right was not have your daddy come running to your rescue." He smiled and mussed my hair. "Besides, I didn't want to hurt your pride, now did I?"

"My pride?" I thought. "What about my nose?"

"Hey. If you want to play tough," he said, "those are the rules."

My nostrils felt jewel-encrusted. My head throbbed, but not so much from being hammered repeatedly against the sand as from the shock and adrenaline.

"How are you?" my father said after a moment.

I sniffled tearfully and shrugged. Right before the other girl had thrown her first punch, I'd felt a momentous bolt of confidence. But now I just felt foolish and embarrassed and despicable. I had misjudged everything. There was so much about the world that I did not understand. Rivulets of my own blood were starting to congeal on the back of my hand. They turned my skin from maroon to deep brown, and in the mid-afternoon sun, they glistened darkly.

Chapter 4

Christmas Trees, Jews, and Virgins

KARL MARX ONCE SAID that religion was the opiate of the people. What he hadn't counted on was that this observation actually made religion more attractive to my grandmother, who had no use for God, but thought the world of opiates. Thanks to Communism, my grandmother discovered religion could be worthwhile, provided you regarded it as one giant bartending opportunity.

By the time my brother and I were born, heresy had become a family tradition. Our mother—who also loved a good party almost as much as she hated dogma—raised us as pagans, really: we had chocolate bunnies, Christmas trees, and menorahs without ever once having to attend Sunday school or nod off during a sermon. It was an "all gain, no pain" approach to religion, and as you might imagine, it was just fine by us.

Certainly, it had never been in the plans to send me to Presbyterian school. But one summer, our local school board must have smoked a kilo of Peruvian hash because it was suddenly decided that my public elementary school—renowned for its academic traditions—would really do much better as an experimental "open corridor program."

"Like, why should a school have *walls,* man?" a board member explained, raking his hands through his hair. Ray described himself an "education activist," but really, he looked more like a guy you'd find at a Rainbow Gathering inhaling nitrous oxide from a canister of Reddi-wip. "Schools are like prisons, man. They kill children's natural instincts. I mean, leave kids alone, let them do their own thing, and they'll learn from each other."

Even *I* knew Ray was an idiot. Having experienced my classmates' natural instincts, killing them off as quickly as possible was just fine by me. And sure, I was an enthusiastic learner, but who were we kidding? If left to my own devices, all I would do all day was color.

Which is exactly what I did. Thanks to the educational free-for-all known as the "open corridor program," I spent all of first grade drawing pictures of fashion models and anthropomorphized bunnies. Around me, my thirty-one other classmates "did their own thing," too. They hit each other over the head with plastic buckets. They built huge towers of blocks, then shrieked "Geronimo" and plowed into them with a Big Wheel. They ate library paste. They played "How Loud Can I Yell in Your Ear Until You Go Deaf?" Luis Morales and Barry Brenig discovered that if you held a G.I. Joe under the lamp in the reading alcove long enough, you could melt his head and accidentally set off the fire alarm.

"This isn't education. It's anarchy," my mother said. "I'm taking you out of there."

The next September, I was enrolled in a tiny private school run by the Second Presbyterian Church of New York. I was one of its few scholarship children, its charity cases. As my mother explained, it wasn't like we had a lot of options. "It's either the Presbyterians or the lunatics," was how I believe she put it.

Located in a small warren of rooms adjoining the church, the school felt like an antique jewelry box. My teacher, Mrs. Tumbridge, spoke with a British accent. "Everybody, this is Susan," she informed the class in a high, chipper soprano, sounding as if she might have just come in from a fox hunt in the Yorkshire dales. "Let's give her a warm welcome, shall we?"

The boys sort of grunted. The girls chewed on their pencils and stared. Most of them were wearing the school uniform—a stiff navy blue blazer with the gold school emblem stitched over the heart like a shield.

The solemnity of the school made me feel studious and anointed. As I sat down and arranged my new school supplies symmetrically on my desk, I imagined a documentary being filmed of my life for some fascinated and adoring future audience: *"Susie Gilman is arranging her school supplies symmetrically on her desk,"* the narrator intoned. *"It is here, in this tiny Presbyterian school, that she will first exhibit the signs of genius that will catapult her, one day, to greatness."*

What I hadn't counted on in this documentary were three girls, Courtney, Samantha, and Jennifer, sidling over to my desk at lunch.

"Hi, Susan!" grinned Samantha. Samantha, I'd noticed, loved horses. She kept a picture of one in the corner of her desk and wore little gold horse barrettes in her hair. She also wore patent leather Mary Janes to school—the kind I was allowed to wear for special occasions only.

"Hi, Samantha!" I smiled back.

For some reason, this made them giggle.

"Susan, we were just wondering," said Jennifer thoughtfully. Casually, she picked up the end of the fringed suede belt I was wearing and stroked it with exaggerated affection. "Where did you *ever* get this *amazing* pink belt?"

I beamed. Recently, I'd begun developing my own personal style, predicated largely on the belief that if one floral pattern was good, three were even better. For my first day at school, I'd worn hot pink bell-bottoms, an eye-blindingly flowered shirt, and my long, fringed, rose-colored belt. The idea was to play up any resemblance I had to Laurie Partridge.

The pink belt had been given to me by my baby-sitter, Gina Gold. Gina wore hand-crocheted vests and bangle bracelets like the black girls, and her room was covered with pictures of David Cassidy, Bobby Sherman, and Tony DeFranco. I wanted to be just like her, and whenever she gave me the clothes she'd outgrown, they automatically became my favorite things to wear. It was like getting cast-offs from Cher.

"This belt was a hand-me-down from my baby-sitter," I said to the girls.

As soon as I said this, their faces illuminated like flashbulbs, exploding with bright malice and gleeful disbelief.

"A hand-me-down!" Courtney cried. "Eeeeeeeeewwwwww!"

"You wear other people's old, rejected clothing?" exclaimed Samantha.

"Ohmygod," laughed Jennifer. "That is sooooooo gross! It's like you're wearing *garbage!*"

———————

Never mind our classroom's proximity to a church. Never mind the lessons on dinosaurs, Pueblo Indians, and phonics that Mrs. Turnbridge imparted to us each day. One of the first things I learned at my new school was that boys might be fighters, but girls could be terrorists.

Girls could pinpoint a weakness in another girl, then torture her for it, stealthily and psychologically. *Everybody give Gabriella the silent treatment today . . . Now, let's all pretend to like Charlotte and make her think she's really popular, but then, once she thinks we're her friends, we'll tell her she can't come to Serena's birthday party.* Girls plotted. Girls made a group project out of inflicting misery.

Arriving at school the following week, I found anonymous notes folded up into puffy rectangles and left on my chair.

Ten reasons why we hate Susan.

Nicknames for Susan: Fatso. Super-Fatso. Fat-head. Fatgirl. Add yours here _____.

Is your name Susan? If so, you could be a retard.

The girls in my class, I discovered, fell into essentially two categories: the Spanish Inquisition and everyone else.

The Spanish Inquisition was a tightly clenched fist of five girls.

Calculating, self-possessed, and precociously snide, Courtney was the queen of the group, trailed by four ladies in waiting: Samantha (the freckle-faced horse lover), Jennifer (the clothes horse), Molly (a nearly mute, ethereal beauty), and Serena (a skinny, self-possessed gymnast). The prettiest girls in the class, they spanned the hair color spectrum from blond to auburn to brunette, looking like a set of paper dolls, each one with a lithe ballerina body and prim knee socks pulled up to match her corduroy skirt. There was not a homemade haircut among them. By neighborhood standards, all five of them were hopelessly white and un-cool, and yet strangely, this didn't seem to bother them in the least. The girls in the Spanish Inquisition all lived across the park on the impossibly aristocratic Upper East Side—in town houses and apartment buildings with uniformed doormen. They took the cross-town bus to school together each morning and made a big show of decorating their notebooks with the same smiley face decals and sharing the same bottle of pink nail polish. Dressing alike and talking alike, they seemed almost incapable of delivering a book report on *Amelia Bedelia* without a support group. Ironically, the one area in which they demonstrated extraordinary imagination and initiative was in coming up with ways to make the rest of us miserable.

Weighing in for the victims' team was me, of course, the chubby hippie kid. I was joined by Georgette, a gangly Albanian immigrant with two different-colored eyes; Gabriella, a tomboy; Alice, the one black girl in the class. And Charlotte, a shy diabetic with learning disabilities and frizzy red hair who had the unfortunate habit of absentmindedly scratching her crotch whenever she stood at the blackboard. We were also all indigenous peoples, members of the great proletarian unwashed, the natives who lived within walking distance of the school.

Yet while the Spanish Inquisition was generous in its disdain for us, they singled out Charlotte and me as particular targets.

Within weeks, going to school for me became the social equivalent of Cambodia. I lived in constant fear of stepping on a landmine. I never knew when something I said would set off a burst of taunting, when something innocuous I'd do would blow up in my face.

"Augh, Courtney, what smells so fishy and disgusting?"

"Eeeew. I don't know, Samantha, but it's coming from Susan's desk."

"Look, she's eating tuna fish for lunch!"

"Oh gross. Okay, everyone who thinks Fat Pig Susan stinks more than her sandwich, raise their hands!"

Soon, every time I set out for school, my stomach started to feel like someone had put it through a paper-shredder. Of course, all across America, kids were going to school feeling like this. The perfectionists. The gay kids. The unathletic kids. The kids with strange last names. The artistic kids. The poor kids. The legions of kids who were never sure if they were "in" or "out" on any given day.

When you're little, it's nearly impossible to understand that being a scapegoat is a fairly typical experience. Even more strangely, it's really nothing personal. Oh, it *feels* personal when kids call you Douche Bag or Faggot or Fuckface—when they mimic the way you talk, or chase you home after school, or play "Keep-Away" with the hat your grandmother knitted. But oddly, their teasing has little to do with *who you really are*. Some kids have an instinct for cruelty. Before they ever met you, they were itching, they were hungry, they were jonesing for a victim. You just happened to amble along as they were casting about. If it wasn't you, it would be somebody else. Anyone, really.

But of course I didn't know this. And since my new school had only one class per grade, there was no hope of a reprieve after the summer, no chance of a fresh social mix come September. My classmates were mine until middle school. Once I was branded an "Eeeewww" girl, there was no escaping it.

To be fair, I did not exactly do myself any favors either. Socially, I had about as much savvy as a wood ant.

When Courtney and Samantha chanted, "Susan eats snot!" I yelled back, "Stop it! I do not!" then burst into tears right in front of them.

It was inconceivable to me that some girls could actually *enjoy* being vicious—or that picking on me might be their idea of a self-esteem program. Naively, I assumed that if people didn't like me, it was simply because I had yet to win them over. And of course this could be done! If I just showed them how good I was at drawing, how quick I was at reciting the multiplication tables, and how I could build a medieval castle out of nothing but Styrofoam cups, they would admire me and want to be my friend. "Wow, isn't Susan intelligent and entertaining?" I imagined them concluding after I'd won the class spelling bee for the second week in a row. "We were wrong about her, girls. Let's invite her to our next sleepover."

Of course, if people are already refusing to partner with you for a group project on "Flags of Many Nations," announcing that you got fourteen A's on your latest report card isn't going to win you any fans.

If your nom de guerre is already "Blimpo," raising your hand and saying, "Mrs. Tumbridge, can I write a book report for extra credit?" virtually guarantees that no one will ever notice any of your lurking inner beauty.

And feigning surprise when the teacher hands you back a pop quiz—slapping your palm dramatically against your forehead and saying aloud, "Another 100! And I thought I failed!"—well, you might as well make a sign reading "Kick Me" and tape it to your ass yourself.

Amazingly, I never figured this out. The more I got teased, the more I became a world-class show-off. My talents, my opinions, my imagination, even my kindness—in my innocence and desperation, I held nothing back. If I could only just prove I was the Best at Everything, I figured, than surely someone, *someone,* would believe I was worthy enough and want to be my friend.

(Pathetically, I would employ this same losing formula to attract guys in college, but that's another story. Later, in college, too, I would read Plato's dialogues. In them, Socrates argues that it is only logical that people will always choose that which is good and virtuous and eschew the wicked and unpleasant. Reading this, it struck me that Socrates obviously never spent any time with eight-year-old girls.)

That November, our class began rehearsals for the school's annual Christmas pageant. Held inside the church, it was considered a pretty big deal. For six weeks, we spent every music period singing "I Saw Three Ships" and "O Christmas Tree" over and over until we no longer needed mimeographed sheets to remember the words.

The Friday before the pageant, we had a dress rehearsal. It was my first time inside the actual church, and frankly, I was disappointed. The interiors of other churches in our neighborhood looked like giant dashboards, like enormous, glittering control panels full of ornaments, statues, and stained glass. But the Second Presbyterian Church was adorned only with two rows of wrought iron chandeliers that looked like medieval weaponry. These were suspended from the skeletal, vaulted ceilings by thick black chains. Except for a burgundy carpet running the length of the aisles, there was no other decoration to speak of. I found it cavernous, bleak, intimidating.

But the day of the pageant, everything was magically transformed. The aisles were lit with long white tapered candles. A huge Christmas tree shimmered by the altar. Filled to overflow with beaming, festooned parents, the pews were ablaze with color. As we proceeded solemnly into the church as instructed ("No waving at your parents! Eyes straight ahead, please!") our music teacher pounded away at the church's monstrous organ and a collective "Ooh" and "Aah" rose from the congregants. Flashbulbs went off and perfume came over us in waves as fanatical mothers leaned into the aisles with their Instamatics.

It was only then that I realized the kids from the upper grades were in the pageant, too. The older girls were costumed as angels in white robes, the boys as shepherds. After our headmaster, the Reverend Alcott, welcomed the parents, the organ sounded portentously, and these students rose and launched into a rigorous series of carols I'd never heard before. The singing was punctuated by readings from the

New Testament, which the students tended to recite with about as much enthusiasm and comprehension as the Pledge of Allegiance.

But still. By the time Mrs. Tumbridge cued us for our song, I was almost paralyzed with awe. Somehow, I made it up the steps with my classmates, and as soon as we started singing, the audience began grinning like maniacs. Because, since the majority of us were missing our baby teeth, our songs came out as, "I Thaw Thwee Thipth" and "O Cwisthmath Twee."

Afterward, the story of Christmas commenced. A girl in a gold tinsel halo came forward and sang a song called "The Angel Gabriel," which I instantly decided was the most extraordinary piece of music I'd ever heard. Following that, a girl dressed as Mary in soft blue robes sang a lullaby that made me feel like weeping. Then, all the other students launched into an anthem called "Torches" that echoed majestically off the vaulted ceilings, and down the aisle came the three biggest boys in the sixth grade class, dressed resplendently as kings. With a great, dramatic flourish, they knelt before Mary and presented her with three coffee cans spray-painted gold.

Watching this spectacle, I was overcome with a sense of wonder and longing. Oh, I wanted to *be* that beautiful, to sing with such heartbreaking lyricism, to make the church swell with music and glory.

It was then that I seized upon a plan to win over my classmates.

———————

In America, there is an enduring myth of redemption that is, not insignificantly, a favorite staple of after-school TV specials and rated-PG movies.

The story line is always the same: A kindhearted, ugly duckling dork is ostracized at school. After class lets out, she returns home to the equivalent of a trailer park. One of her parents is missing, dead, or drunk. The other is unemployed or almost mentally ill.

One day, the dork's principal announces the school's annual homecoming contest or talent show. For all the importance accorded it, you would think this event was a summit on nuclear disarmament or the treaty at Yalta.

"Oh, I wish I could enter, but I'd never win," the dork sighs ruefully to her sidekick. (It is important to note here that the sidekick is certifiably eccentric and hideous-looking, whereas the dork is unattractive simply because she wears glasses.)

"But you *can* win!" the sidekick says. "I've seen you—and I *know* you're the best!"

"Oh, I couldn't possibly," says the dork.

But then, we see montage shots of the dork in training—jogging, sweating, getting a makeover, holding up outfits in front of a department store mirror while a bevy of salesclerks frown and shake their heads, then nod approvingly—until the Big Night. Inevitably, some school bully or bitch tries to sabotage her plans. And inevitably, last-minute obstacles pop up, threatening to jettison the whole evening. Maybe her limousine breaks down. Maybe her father has a pulmonary embolism.

But inevitably, our heroine finally arrives in the school gymnasium transformed into a jaw-dropping beauty. The other kids gasp, part around her like the Red Sea, and she then wows them with her hidden talent—which, more often than not, consists of dance moves. She wins the talent show, the homecoming crown, and, not coincidently, the heart of the school's supreme love interest. Her nemesis, meanwhile, ends up tearing her hair out with jealousy in the parking lot while a car veers past and splatters mud all over her taffeta bubble dress. In the final scene, the dork is hoisted up on her classmates' shoulders and paraded around the school gym—or is shown in profile, kissing her new boyfriend—while her sidekick gives her the thumbs-up from the punchbowl.

The moral of these stories was never lost on me: namely that, with the right makeover, it was possible to reverse years of social ostracism in a single evening.

And so I became convinced that if I could only land the role of the Virgin Mary in the school Christmas pageant, I could win over my fiercest critics. I pictured myself sitting beatifically in the center of the altar, draped in pale blue silk, singing Mary's lullaby with such extraordinary, chilling grace that my classmates would sink to their knees. "Oh, Susan," the girls would sigh reverently. "That was so gorgeous. We're so sorry for teasing you the way we have. Please, come to our birthday parties. Join us for after-school gymnastics. Allow us to decorate your dollhouse."

From then on, whenever I was forced to take my bath, I practiced singing. I had to say that, ricocheting off the putty-colored tiles in our bathroom, my voice sounded surprisingly good to me. I sang every carol I could remember from the pageant, from "The Angel Gabriel" to "O Come All Ye Faithful."

"What the hell is she doing in there?" I'd hear my father say. "It's the middle of August."

I practiced this way for the next three years, crooning in the bathtub and in the back of our VW bus on the drive to see our grandparents in the Bronx. I sang in my bedroom and lying on the couch. Soon, in addition to Christmas carols, I found myself singing television jingles for Country Kitchen Noodles, Coca-Cola, and Levi's blue jeans. I began covering songs from my parents' record collection, too. I sang along to Carole King's "I Feel the Earth Move" and Roberta Flack's "Killing Me Softly." Listening to WABC radio in the mornings before school, I belted along to such great 1970s hits as "The Night Chicago Died," "Love Will Keep Us Together," "Rock the Boat," and "Tell Me Something Good" by Chaka Khan and Rufus. Granted, this wasn't exactly church music, but I figured a song was a song.

In sixth grade, it was finally my class's turn to audition for the pageant's main roles, and I was ready. When the big lunchtime topic of discussion turned to "Who do you want to be in the pageant?" I felt like I finally had a right answer, the secret password to help me fit in belatedly.

"I want to be Mary," said Samantha.

"Me too," said Courtney and Serena.

"Me too," said Molly. "Definitely Mary."

"I want to be Mary, too," I said.

All the girls stopped and looked at me.

"Augh," Courtney rolled her eyes. "You're so stupid! You can't be Mary."

"You shouldn't even be in the Christmas pageant," said Samantha. "I don't know why they let you in."

"Why can't I?" I said. I'd heard everybody sing in music class, and as far as I could tell, my voice was as good as anybody's by now.

"Because, moron, you're Jewish. Jews don't get to celebrate Christmas," said Samantha.

Really? I was Jewish? And Jews didn't celebrate Christmas? This was all news to me. In between Passover seders—and attending an occasional "folk mass" to sing Peter, Paul, and Mary songs with a hippie priest with a banjo—and listening to my mother quote the guru Ram Dass—why, we'd always celebrated Christmas!

As far as I could tell, the only difference between our family's Yuletide festivities and those shown on television was that my parents had a Christmas rule that I believed qualified as child abuse. On the morning of December 25, John and I were not allowed to wake up our parents until 9:00 A.M. Which would've been okay except that on Christmas morning—and only Christmas morning—we always woke up at exactly a quarter to four.

Jittery with glee, we'd dash into the living room, where a glittering avalanche of presents spilled beneath our tree, and rip open the one gift we were allowed to touch immediately—our stockings. They'd always contain a chocolate bar—we'd devour it—we'd squeal "It's Christmas!"—we'd jump up and down—we'd hold up our candy wrappers—and only then would we start to realize that it was 3:47 in the morning, and we had exactly five hours and thirteen minutes to wait.

We'd take every single book we owned off our shelves, and I'd read them to my brother, one at a time.

"What time is it now?" John would ask after I'd finished *Clifford the Big Red Dog*.

"Four twenty-seven," I'd say. "Augh! Four hours and thirty-three minutes to go!"

By the time 9:00 A.M. arrived, we were certifiably insane. We'd spent over five hours fondling the presents, gazing hungrily at the tree, and reading and re-reading *Curious George* in what can only be described as a delirium of Kiddie Christmas Foreplay. As soon as that big hand finally hit that twelve on the clock and the small one slid onto the nine, John and I barreled into our parents' room and pounced on top of their bed shrieking "PRES-SENTS! PRES-SENTS! OPEN THE PRES-SENTS!"

Then we'd race to the tree and tear ecstatically through one gift after another—holding things up, dancing around the room, crying, "Oh yes! Oh thank you! It's exactly what I wanted!"—before tossing the wrapping into the air and moving on enthusiastically to the next gift. We stood up proudly as our parents opened our gifts to them— a Play-Doh paperweight! A macaroni necklace!—announcing what every gift was before they'd finished ripping off the paper. And then suddenly, inexplicably, it was over. We sat there amid a wreckage of tinsel and foil paper, feeling that same sort of shivery despair we felt sitting in the bathtub, watching the last of the water swirl languidly down the drain.

Five hours and fifteen minutes of buildup, over in exactly twenty-two minutes. That was our holiday.

"Well, my family celebrates Christmas," I shrugged. "So what?"

"Well, you're not supposed to!" said Jennifer. "My family's Jewish, and we don't. It's going against God!"

"Why?" I said.

"Because," said Samantha, exasperated. "Christ is not your Lord and King like he is ours."

"You have a king?" I said. "But I thought we were a democracy."

"Augh! You are SUCH an IDIOT!" shouted Courtney.

That night at dinner, I asked my parents. "Are we Jewish?" My mother stood up and went into the kitchen and spooned noodles into a serving bowl.

My dad just continued cutting up a piece of chicken. "Sure. We're Jewish," he said, as if he'd only just decided.

"Well, what makes us Jewish?" I said.

He thought for a minute as he chewed. "I dunno," he shrugged. "We eat bagels and lox. We read the *New York Times* and argue about it."

Up until that moment, I'd been under the impression that "Judaism" and "Christianity" were like zodiac signs, blood types, eye colors—vague variations of some even vaguer commonality that people had. Religion, as I understood it, was a collection of fabulous stories that resulted in even more fabulous theme parties. Rudolph the Red-Nosed Reindeer. The Miracle of Chanukah. The Birth of Baby Jesus. Santa Claus. Frosty the Snowman. Moses. Peter Cottontail. Lazarus . . . All of these ran together in my mind, merging into one enormous "Fantasia" that fueled all the holidays.

"Well, Samantha says that Jews can't celebrate Christmas and Jennifer says that if you're Jewish and you do, you're going against God."

My mother came back into the dining room, frowning. She set down the bowl of noodles with a clatter. "You tell Samantha and Jennifer that as Americans, we have freedom of religion and you can celebrate any damn thing you want."

"Don't say 'damn' though," chuckled my father. "You'll piss off your teacher."

"In fact," said my mother, pointing at me with the serving spoon, "you can tell them that if they're so concerned with religion, they should start practicing it for a change and do unto others."

"What does that mean?" I said.

"That they should stop being so nasty to you," said my father.

My mother began dishing out the noodles. She wasn't really paying attention to what she was doing and gave my brother more than he could possibly eat. "And while you're at it, you can tell those little snot-noses in your class that organized religion has created more problems than it's solved," she said. "The only way this world will come to any good is if people remain open-minded."

"So can we still celebrate Christmas?" said my brother, clearly focused on his priorities.

"Well, what's the difference between Judaism and Christianity anyway?" I said.

My mother set down her spoon. "There's something called a messiah," she said wearily. "It's a savior, a messenger who's an embodiment of God. Christians believe that Jesus was the messiah. Jews don't. Jews believe the messiah has yet to arrive. That's why Christians celebrate Christmas. It's the birthday of their Lord."

"Why do we celebrate it, then?" asked John.

"Because your grandmother thinks she's a Communist and your mother loves parties," said my father. "Now eat your supper."

"So is that why Uncle Arthur hides his Christmas tree in the bathroom?"

Uncle Arthur was our father's best friend. His family celebrated Christmas, too. But recently, his son, Todd, had started Hebrew school, and whenever the rabbi dropped by their apartment, Arthur and Todd made a mad dash to put the Christmas tree in the bathtub. "Whatever you do, don't serve the guy anything liquid!" Arthur would shout. "No water, no soup. Nothing. Don't let him pee!"

"So hold on. Jews have to wait for a messiah *and* we don't get to celebrate Christmas?" I said. Suddenly, Judaism was sounding like a really bad deal to me. Why did *we* have to wait? I hated waiting. I hated waiting for anything. I could barely wait for the ice cream man—hell, I could barely wait for the *bus*. Now I had to wait for some messiah?

And all we really got was *Chanukah*? That *sucked*. "Eight nights of presents"—as if a candleholder and one irritating dreidel song could possibly measure up to Santa Claus, Christmas trees, Christmas carols, Christmas morning, and all the apartments around us lit up like brothels?

"Forget it," I announced. "Christmas kicks Chanukah's ass. I'm being a Christian."

My mother gave a little, mirthless laugh. "It's not that simple," she said. "But God doesn't really care if you decorate a pine tree in your living room or if you light candles. God cares how you treat other people, and how you treat yourself, and how you treat the world. That's all that matters. The rest, as they say, is just commentary."

She passed me the platter of chicken. "More than anything else, your relationship with God is your own business," she said. "Don't let anybody tell you otherwise."

———————

Still, after that, I couldn't help but feel that celebrating Christmas was a little like wearing Gina Gold's belt: sure, it was beautiful, but it belonged to somebody else first. I worried that I was no longer entitled to it, that it diminished me somehow. Some sort of concession seemed to be in order on my part. But what? The plain truth was, I was far too greedy and lazy and smitten with Christmas to actually give it up.

"I decided I don't want to be Mary anymore," I announced to the girls at lunch.

I thought they'd be impressed but Courtney just rolled her eyes. "Ugh. What do you want?" she said. "A medal?"

"No," I said, glancing at Jennifer. "I decided I'm not right for the part."

"Why?" Samantha grinned wickedly. "You're not a virgin?"

"Well, of course not," I said.

As soon as I said this, the girls acted as if they'd just stuck a fork in a light socket. They began jumping up and down spastically and flailing their arms. "OHMYGOD! I CAN'T BELIEVE SHE JUST SAID THAT! DID YOU HEAR WHAT SUSAN JUST SAID?" They ran from desk to desk, shrieking with glee, "SUSAN SAYS SHE'S NOT A VIRGIN!"

For the first time ever, they actually ran outside to tattle to the teacher, who always took a ten-minute lunch break on the bench just outside the classroom. "MRS. GOLDSMITH!" they called, flinging open the door. Only Jennifer stayed behind. She glared at me. "You know, it's hard enough, and then you have to go and say something like that."

"What? What did I say?"

Mrs. Goldsmith appeared in the doorway. "Susan, would you please step out here a moment?" she said. The whole room went silent. Everyone looked at me.

"Ooooowwwwwhhh," the whispers chorused, like the opening bars of a hymn. "Susan's in trouble!"

"Class," said Mrs. Goldsmith sternly. She led me by the elbow into the hallway and shut the door sharply behind her.

"Susan, dear, I need to ask you a question," Mrs. Goldsmith said gently. "Courtney and Samantha said you told them you're not a virgin. Is this true?"

I had never been in trouble before. Choked up, I nodded.

Mrs. Goldsmith looked shaken. "I see," she said slowly. "And can you tell me why you said you're not a virgin?"

"Because, Mrs. Goldsmith," I burst out sobbing, "I've never given birth to a savior!"

Mrs. Goldsmith clamped her hands over her mouth.

"I see," she said after a moment, the corners of her eyes crinkling.

"Samantha said I couldn't be Mary in the Christmas pageant because I'm Jewish," I sniffled, "and so I told her that I wouldn't audition. And then she asked if it was because I wasn't a virgin, and I said yes because . . . because . . ." I started to cry again. Mrs. Goldsmith sat down beside me and put her hand softly around my shoulders.

"You know, Susan," she said. "The Virgin Mary was Jewish."

I sniffled. My nose was running, and I tried to be discreet about wiping it on the back of my sleeve. "She was?" I said.

Mrs. Goldsmith pulled a tissue out of her pocket and handed it to me. "And so was Jesus."

"Really?" *Nobody tells me anything around here,* I thought suddenly. *What else was I missing?*

"I've heard you sing. You have a lovely voice," my teacher said softly. "I see no reason why you shouldn't audition for the Christmas pageant—provided your parents agree. If they say no, you have to respect that. They have good reasons."

I blew my nose with a honk. "My mom says that as Americans, we're free to believe as we choose," I volunteered. At that particular moment, my mother's latest spiritual interest happened to be a swami. I thought of mentioning this, then decided against it.

"That's true enough," Mrs. Goldsmith said. She stood up and motioned that we should go back inside.

"One last thing." She paused before clicking open the door. "You might want to ask your mother to explain in greater detail what a virgin is," she winked. "Somehow I think you're going to want to know that at some point."

The next week, I stood nervously before our music teacher and the Reverend Alcott and sang "The Angel Gabriel" as melodiously as I could. In the end, though, Samantha wound up being cast as Mary and the role of the Angel Gabriel went to our classmate Robert, one of the few boys in the school's history whose voice wasn't changing on the day of the audition. But, our music teacher announced, two other girls had shown such promise that special solo roles had been created for them as well. Alice and I would be "archangels" dressed in silver tinsel.

My solo was probably the most ecumenical hymn the Reverend could dig up. The first verse went:

My master has a garden
Fulfilled with diverse flowers
Where thou mayst gather posies gay
All times and hours.

Not exactly "Earth, Wind, and Fire"—or *Aida,* for that matter—but it might as well have been, given how seriously I took it. And yet, I had never sung outside the bathroom before. Once I was faced with an audience that wasn't composed of porcelain wall tiles, I got nervous. My voice broke at the highest note, which fell on the word "All." It was painful to sing and even more painful to listen to. I became convinced that I was tone deaf, that I had gotten the part by a fluke, and that I would go down in history as the Jewish Girl Who Ruined Christmas—they would write cautionary fairy tales about me—I would join Scrooge and the Grinch in the pantheon of Christmas meanies and fuck-ups—on the day of the pageant, I'd crack that high note, and my voice would be so shrill and awful that the cast iron chandeliers suspended from the church ceiling would come crashing down, crushing everyone in the pews to death. The headlines in the New York *Daily News* would trumpet: ANGEL OF DEATH CRUSHES XMAS AUDIENCE—and I'd wind up in a reformatory.

For their part, my classmates seemed pretty much convinced that this would happen, too.

"Oh God, Susan's going to ruin the whole pageant," said Samantha, flinging her auburn hair over her shoulder. "Nobody's going to be able to concentrate on my lullaby because they'll all have headaches from her so-called singing."

The week before the pageant was a wash of anxiety. I'd tiptoe out of bed at night, press my forehead against the cold glass of my window, and look out at the city. The dark sky would be a fumy purple-orange. The windows of other apartments would be illuminated—bright yellow boxes of light—and sometimes I could see an elderly man in his undershirt eating cereal in a small kitchen, or a couple seated on a couch, the blue light from a television flickering across their profiles. Counting the windows decorated with colored Christmas lights, I wondered what religion everyone was.

There was a store that sold religious icons in our neighborhood, right next to Carvel. Sometimes after John and I got ice cream cones, we milled about outside looking at the Jesus calendars and wall clocks. All the pictures of Christ always showed him writhing, bloody, and nearly naked, hanging limply from a cross, clad in nothing but a diaper. Maybe, I thought, Jews didn't celebrate Christmas simply to spare Jesus any further embarrassment.

But Christian or Jewish, the concept of a messiah made me anxious. Were humans really such screw-ups that we needed a superhero from God to come to our rescue? The idea that we were all such losers and incompetents frightened me. Even with the nasty girls in my class, I somehow gave people more credit. Shouldn't we be responsible for saving ourselves—and each other?

For the first time in my life, I thought about what I believed.

When I was even younger, I'd secretly suspected that everything on earth was alive and had feelings. This "everything" included not just philodendrons and our pet gerbils, but also things like the dishwasher and the ceramic lamp in my grandparents' living room.

When my brother said the lamp was ugly, I said, "*Sssshh,* John. Don't say that in front of the lamp. You may hurt its feelings."

"Um, Suze?" he said carefully, looking at me as if he were doing a mental health assessment. "The lamp is an object, okay? It doesn't have feelings."

Then I'd laugh and quickly agree and act like I was just joking— *Of course a lamp doesn't have feelings! Sheesh, couldn't he tell when I was kidding around?* But secretly, I'd still worry.

I realized now that I tended to believe what my mother had told me: that we were all put here on earth to be good to each other . . . that we were all obligated to help improve the world somehow . . . and that every one of us had to figure out our own relationship to God.

When it came right down to it, I guessed that was the essence of my religion: wanting to do right, and feeling protective of everything, even the lamp.

———

The morning of the Christmas pageant, I wandered around our apartment singing "All, All, All" over and over again, practicing this high note until my throat was raw, the strain making my voice crack even more.

My classmates, consistent to the end, made sure to let me know how little faith they had in me.

"I'd say break a leg, but you're probably just going to break a note instead," said Courtney. Then she wrapped her forefinger and thumb loosely around her wrist to show off how skinny she was before walking off with a snort.

I stood alone in the antechamber of the church, letting my music teacher adjust my silver tinsel halo and tie garlands around my waist. "You'll do fine," she reassured me. "You look lovely."

I should have felt beautiful, but instead I felt clumsy and fraudulent. The organ music began thrumming, and Alice and I proceeded solemnly into the packed church the way we'd practiced. I couldn't look at my parents—I couldn't look at anybody. My solo was toward the end of the pageant. I tried to sing the other carols, but I felt nauseated so I just mouthed the words and tried not to cry.

Then, halfway through the pageant came the scene between the Angel Gabriel and Mary. I'd seen it played out countless times before, but I was always too busy admiring my own angel costume to pay much attention.

Robert stood up. Instead of gold tinsel, he'd been given a much more masculine outfit to wear, a burgundy vest over a white robe. He walked over to Samantha, who was draped solemnly in pale blue.

"And the Angel said unto her, 'Fear not, Mary, for thou art chosen among women,'" recited Robert.

Fear not, for thou art chosen among women. The words landed heavily. *Mary,* I thought suddenly. Why, Mary was poor, frightened, outcast, and Jewish—just like me. Nobody wanted much to do with Mary, it seemed; she was in pain and in labor, but there was no room at the inn for her. Maybe the kids teased her, too. And yet, the Angel Gabriel came down and said: *Fear not.*

Sitting there beneath the Gothic arches and the chandeliers of the church, I imagined that the Angel Gabriel was swooping down to visit me. Fear not, he was saying, for God has chosen you among women, too. And fireworks seemed to go off in my chest, as it occurred to me that if there had been hope for poor, forsaken Mary, then perhaps there was hope for me, too.

Messiahs, saviors, they were beyond me, but Mary I could understand. Maybe that was what her story was meant to be about—that in the darkness of winter, in the face of poverty and prejudice—I should fear not—I would be taken in—I would be chosen yet—fear not! There were children to be born—and stars to appear—and kings to arrive—Fear not! God had not overlooked anyone! God had not overlooked me, as unattractive and unlikable and pathetic as I was.

I suppose you could say that as I stood there, quivering in silver and white, I had my first spiritual moment, in all its hokey innocence. I felt suddenly lightened; my stomach unclenched slightly. And then, the organ was pounding the introduction to my song. It was time for my solo. I stood up carefully in my long white robe—my heart punching my rib cage—and walked to the edge of the steps leading down from the altar. I opened my mouth as wide as I could, and I began to sing.

If I were being my smart-assed, cynical, literary self, I would alter the facts and recast this next moment: After a spiritual awakening, I'd tell you, I stood boldly before my teachers, classmates, and a churchful of parents, and sang as badly and as painfully as ever, anyway. In this version, the audience would wince and cover its ears, pigeons would alight squawking from the rooftops, even the kindly Reverend Alcott would grimace. Surely, this scenario would make for a darker, more unexpected, but somehow more human story.

Yet that isn't what happened. Instead, I opened my mouth to sing. And when I got to that high note, I nailed it. I mean, I really drove it right through that church ceiling. I hit it with strength, vibrato, and a self-assurance that I hadn't felt since my first day at school. The note seemed to fill the transept, the clerestory, the coatroom in the back. It was so high, powerful, and clear, I couldn't believe it had come out of me; there seemed to be an audible gasp from the audience. I hit that note, then continued, finishing my solo about my master's garden, filled with diverse flowers, with my voice so astonished and joyful, all you could hear were the lyrics and the thunderous power of the organ. My classmates' collective sigh of relief was completely drowned out by the music.

Afterward, my music teacher put her arm around me radiantly. "See? I had faith in you," she said. My parents, too, were ecstatic— not only because I'd hit the high note, but because now they'd no longer have to listen to me stomping around the house singing "All All All" with the frequency of a busy signal.

"That was beautiful," my mother cried. "You were simply wonderful."

Gleefully, I hurried upstairs to the library, which had been converted into the girls' dressing room for the day. The rest of the procession had already arrived there, and I didn't want to miss my grand entrance. When I walked in, no doubt, the girls would finally cheer, "She did it! She did it after all!" and Courtney would apologize for being so nasty to me.

When I reached the library, Alice was already standing outside the door dressed in her street clothes, flanked by her family.

"Great job, Susan," she said, while behind her, her parents nodded vigorously. Alice's father was a preacher. When he gave my shoulder a little squeeze, my heart felt like an enormous flower.

Opening the door, I stepped into the library. All the girls were in various stages of undress. I walked amid the desks slowly, triumphantly, my footsteps ringing against the varnished floorboards. I walked directly over to where Courtney, Serena, and Samantha were changing their clothes and planted myself before them. Then I just stood there, my hands on my hips. The room grew hushed, pregnant with expectation.

Yet none of them lifted me up on their shoulders and shouted "Three cheers for Susan!" None of them had a change of heart and suddenly felt compelled to invite me to their Christmas party after the pageant. In fact, none of them said anything. They simply looked at me viciously for a moment, then turned away and quickly resumed packing their white angel robes into their dry cleaning bags. The library was strangely quiet. Grabbing their winter coats off the pegs by the doorway, they hurried off. Only Jennifer acknowledged me. As she was halfway out the door with her mother, she glanced back and sniffed, "Well, thank God you didn't screw *that* up."

Alone in the library, I slowly packed up my angel costume. The silence seemed to reverberate. Carefully, I put on my coat, then went downstairs to where my parents and John were waiting. By then, the church was almost empty. The pageant was over, and the custodian, Mr. Hernandez, was making his way up the aisle with a stepladder, carefully snuffing out each of the dying candles. My family and I stood at the front of the church for a moment, staring up at the Christmas tree sparkling beside the altar. Beneath the cavernous, vaulted ceilings, we formed a tableau, a unique crèche of sorts: father, mother, brother, sister.

I didn't feel as euphoric or as exonerated as I'd expected. Strangely, though, I didn't feel defeated, either. I was simply too drained. The dorks in the movies: they all made it look so easy. Trying to prove yourself to your classmates was exhausting, and I realized I was tired of doing it. It was time to put my faith elsewhere. I reached up and began unfastening my halo, one bobby pin at a time. "Okay," I sighed. "I'm ready. Let's all go home."

Chapter 5

Love and the Maharishi

EVERY SO OFTEN, when our living situation fell into chaos, my mother would decide that we were in desperate need of a motto. "Remember, children," she liked to remind us. "Reality is for people with no imagination."

John and I tended to dismiss this the same way we dismissed her requests to clean up our rooms and take our feet off the coffee table. But really, we should have paid more attention. Because as our mother became decreasingly enamored with reality, she became increasingly imaginative in her quest for alternatives.

The week before my tenth birthday, John and I returned home from school to discover she'd signed our entire family up to learn Transcendental Meditation.

We had no idea what Transcendental Meditation was, but it sounded like something that would only confirm our status as Freaks of the Neighborhood.

"No! Please!" my brother gasped. He staggered around the kitchen as if he were being mortally wounded. "Don't make me learn Transcendental Meditation . . . Anything but that! No! Aaaaahhhhh!" Then he fell to the floor writhing in a fit of mock epilepsy, and we both started to giggle.

"Oh, stop it," said our mother. "TM is a relaxation technique, not electroshock therapy."

She took a brochure out of her canvas shoulder bag and smoothed it out on the table. "Everyone gets a word called a mantra. You say it over and over again, and it creates a sense of calm. Your father and I are going to learn it this weekend, then you kids will get initiated next Thursday after school."

John and I leaned over and studied the brochure. It showed pictures of an Indian man with long, gray hair and a tumbleweed for a beard. He was sitting cross-legged on a rug, fondling a daisy. His face, I noticed, had a peculiar, dopey smile on it, as if he had just finished eating an enormous piece of cake, then gotten clubbed over the head.

"That's the Maharishi," our mother said. "He teaches people to achieve inner peace."

Dress him in a Hefty bag, I thought, and he could easily pass for any of the local lunatics who staggered around Amsterdam Avenue singing "Flashlight" and pushing a stolen shopping cart into traffic. In several of the photos, the Maharishi was sitting in a circle with his followers. They were all slightly cadaverous, pale to the brink of translucency: blissed-out albinos in bedsheets. "Transcendental Meditation changed their lives—let it change yours, too!" the caption read.

"Do we have to do this, Mom?" I said. "It looks creepy."

"It's not creepy," said our mother. "Lots of respectable people do TM. Merv Griffin does TM. So does Burt Bacharach. Maybe you don't realize it, but I'm giving you a tool that can help you for the rest of your lives."

That past week at school, Mr. Grimaldi, the professional bloodletter known as my gym teacher, had organized a massive game of boys-against-girls dodge ball. Somehow, my classmate Charlotte and I found ourselves the last two girls left in the game. We cowered in the corner while our teammates screamed, "Catch the ball, you morons!" and the boys counted to three, then slammed a barrage of rubber into us with all the force they could summon, breaking Charlotte's glasses and leaving our thighs imprinted with hot pink grapefruits. My brother, meanwhile, had gotten chased home from school by a gang of older kids with an ice pick who told him, essentially, that his sorry white ass was theirs. As far as I was concerned, the only tools either of us really needed at that moment were blunt instruments.

The next weekend, however, our parents went to the TM Center to receive $200 worth of enlightenment. Despite our secret fear they'd be brainwashed, they returned home a few hours later laughing breezily and carrying a bagful of bagels. Nothing seemed to have changed until that evening, when, just before dinnertime, our mother lit a stick of cinnamon incense and took the phone off the hook. "Okay, kids, Dad and I are going to meditate!" she sang out. "Please cool it for the next twenty minutes."

Then she and my father sat down rigidly on the sofa, side by side, with their eyes closed, while the apartment slowly started to smell like an overcooked muffin. John and I were instructed to stay out of the living room, but since their eyes were shut, we figured, how would they know?

"Did you see anything strange?" I whispered to my brother, as he tiptoed back into the hallway.

"Nuh-uh. They're just sitting there."

"Are they breathing?"

"Dad's wheezing through his mouth like he always does. Mom looks okay. No blood or drool or anything." He sounded slightly disappointed.

Me, I worried—not about my parents' vital signs, but that somebody might actually discover this latest tableau of Gilman family weirdness. What if our neighbor, Mr. Garcia, came by to borrow our blender while our parents were sitting there like zombies? What if the apartment caught on fire, and the cops wanted to know what our parents had been doing when the blaze broke out, and I'd have to say, "They were *meditating*, Officer"? Then the newspaper headline would read: BIZARRE PARENTS IN TM TRANCE WHILE

BUILDING BURNS. Worse still, what if the girls at school somehow found out? Bad enough that I was chubby, Jewish, and your basic social retard: now I had to have a mantra, too? I might as well just give my class free run of an arsenal.

But most distressingly, I learned that the TM Center was located on the southeast corner of 72nd Street and West End Avenue—at 277 West End Avenue, to be exact.

Whenever gays and lesbians say that sexual orientation is something you're born with—that you "just know" whom you're attracted to early on—I've never doubted it. Because the very first day I walked into second grade, I saw a boy standing alone by the terrarium. He was carefully patting down some soil at the base of a rock with his fingertips. A lock of his wavy, reddish gold hair fell into his eyes. I was seven years old, but romantic longing and vaguely sexual yearning shot through me like mercury. I fell instantly, torturously in love with him.

Lincoln Anderson was the tallest boy in our class, and the smartest, and one of the best athletes, and probably the shyest, too, though I mistook his aloofness for flinty, masculine cool. *Lincoln Anderson.* Augh! Just his name alone—a name of great emancipators and Vikings—left me practically asthmatic with desire! *Lincoln Anderson.* Every time he got up to write on the blackboard. Every time he crumpled up a Ding Dong wrapper and aimed it in the wastepaper basket. Every time he scored a goal in hockey, or presented to the class one of his many masterful social studies reports entitled "Vasco da Gama: Finder of Oceans" or "Autumn Comes Early to the Adirondacks," I watched him with secret, shining adoration.

The other girls in my class actively loathed boys. A cherished pastime, in fact, was to shriek "Eeew! I'm contaminated!" anytime they bumped into Ian by the pencil sharpener. Terrified that my crush made me some sort of mutant, I played along with them, doling out "cootie shots" to any poor girl who accidentally brushed against

Patrick or Jimmy in the milk line. But once I was alone, sitting in the library during "reading period," I concocted elaborate fantasies about me and Lincoln that I'd replay lovingly in my head, lingering over the details, altering and embroidering them, stoking my ardor. These daydreams were drawn shamelessly from television, comic books, movies. In them, Lincoln was always Lincoln, but I was somehow a teenaged version of myself—breathtaking and curvaceous, with soft winds blowing perpetually through my hair—as if I'd just stepped blithely off the cover of a Harlequin Romance. My personality was utterly transformed, too, from the one on display in gym class, where I routinely faked a limp in order to get out of kickball.

One of my favorite daydreams, inspired by *The Poseidon Adventure,* began with our whole class taking a field trip to Staten Island. It would be a lazy spring morning—everybody would just be milling around the deck feeding peanuts to the gulls. But then, suddenly, a freak tidal wave would wallop the New York harbor, and the Staten Island ferry would capsize. Our teacher and the captain would be knocked unconscious. Amid the flames and roiling waters, it would fall to Lincoln and me alone to save the entire ship.

Lincoln would say something like: "Susie, take my hand, let me pull you up this escape hatch to safety!" and then I'd respond, "But Lincoln, we must make a human chain, and save the others!"

Our classmates would all be blubbering or semicomatose—a mass of jelly and grapes, really—but Lincoln and I would remain cool, commanding, laserlike in our intelligence, witty beyond compare, and encyclopedic in our knowledge of maritime engineering.

Muscular, sensuous, streaked erotically with soot and our clothes ripped dramatically to expose our best body parts, we'd jury-rig a Morse Code transmitter, send out an SOS, then courageously lead our classmates through a perilous labyrinth of ventilation ducts. Alas, while crawling across a steam pipe dangling above a burning tank of gasoline, Courtney would lose her grip and plunge, horribly, to her death. And I, being a delicate creature of enormous sensitivity, would pause, my lower lip trembling, looking gamine with grief. But Lincoln would grab my hand.

"Susie, you mustn't!" he'd shout. "We've got to get out of here before the whole ship blows!"

Just in the nick of time, we'd deliver the rest of our classmates to safety at the exact same moment that our teacher regained consciousness. Aboard the deck of the Coast Guard rescue ship, Lincoln and I would be wrapped in satin bathrobes, hailed as heroes, and surrounded by fawning reporters. Only then would the enormity of our ordeal catch up with me and, going into shock, I'd faint gorgeously in Lincoln's arms, collapsing like an exquisite, injured swan.

"Gosh, she's so beautiful, and she doesn't even know it," Lincoln would marvel, gazing adoringly at my unconscious body. "And I couldn't have done it without her."

Okay, now: do I even have to say that in real life, Lincoln completely ignored me?

Whenever it was my turn to be "milk monitor," I went out of my way to hand him a little red and white carton of homogenized milk personally.

"Here, Lincoln," I'd say breathlessly, holding the milk as if it were a quivering bird, the Hope Diamond of dairy products. "Here's your milk."

"Mffhmph," Lincoln would mumble. Then he'd toss his head slightly to get his hair out of his eyes and saunter back to his desk. Besides these occasional grunts—which I optimistically translated as "thank you"—Lincoln had only ever said exactly one thing to me: "If you're such a feminist, why don't you clean out the gerbil cage?"

And now, suddenly, miserably, I found myself about to enter his sacred sphere of existence under the most mortifying circumstances imaginable. Because the borough of Manhattan, as I figured it, had approximately two million miles of sidewalks, 300,000 city blocks, and 17 zillion buildings. And yet, out of all the possible spaces for the Transcendental Meditation Center, the Maharishi and his dingbat followers had chosen to set up shop at 277 West End

Avenue—the very apartment building where, according to the mimeographed class list on our refrigerator, Lincoln Anderson lived.

On Thursday of our TM initiation, John and I were both excused from school early for what we begged our mother to describe in her note as simply "medical reasons." As we rode downtown on the bus, I bit my nails into bloody crescents while my mother chatted cheerfully about how meditation would make us all so much more relaxed. All I could think was that it was 1:30 P.M. If it took thirty minutes to get to the TM Center, I calculated, then another hour and a half to get "initiated," we'd be leaving the TM Center at exactly the time when Lincoln would be returning home from school.

If we bumped into him on the street, maybe that would be salvageable. With all the stores and discount supermarkets, there were thousands of reasons we could be in his neighborhood. But what if we collided with him just as we were emerging from the TM Center? The only possible thing I could think of was to pull my coat over my head and stumble out the door like a headless person, hoping he somehow wouldn't notice.

The TM Center was in a corner of Lincoln's lobby by the service elevator, and we slipped in inconspicuously enough. Inside, the reception area was funereal. A gaunt woman in aviator glasses and a stretchy green turtleneck came out from behind a musty curtain. Her long hair was parted severely down the center of her scalp and when she smiled, she looked pained, as if she had a horse's bridle in her mouth and some unseen hand was yanking at the reins behind her.

"Ellen, how very good to see you again," she said. Then she turned to me and John. "I'm Agatha," she said. "On behalf of the Maharishi, I welcome you."

That week, John and I had been told that, in order to "show our dedication to the Maharishi," the TM Center required us to donate a week's allowance to him, which only confirmed our suspicions that his holiness wasn't a guru but a panhandler.

"Hi," I said glumly.

My brother got more to the point. "Does the Maharishi still want my allowance?" he asked.

Agatha gave a brittle laugh. "Oh. Yes. But it's not for him. It's for *you*," she said. "It's a sacrifice you're making for yourself. For self-improvement. And for this reason only, the Maharishi thanks you."

John and I looked around, expecting to see the Maharishi emerge from the curtains behind the desk.

"Oh!" she said, sensing our confusion. "His holiness isn't here. He's in India. Now, Ellen," she said to our mother, with a speed clearly designed to head off any questions John or I might have about where, exactly, our allowances were going if his holiness was in another hemisphere, "do you mind waiting here? We prefer to initiate children alone."

Agatha whisked us behind the curtain into a dimly lit room with high ceilings. Thick velvet curtains had been drawn over all the windows, and the room was empty except for a Persian carpet and two threadbare armchairs. On one end was a fireplace with a giant poster of the Maharishi taped above it. The mantel was cluttered with flower arrangements in various stages of decay, bowls of fermenting oranges, and an assortment of steaming incense burners that made the entire room smell like the underside of a throw pillow.

"Now, sit down and we'll watch a little movie first," Agatha said. She used the tone adults use when they haven't the faintest idea how to relate to children—the vocal equivalent of aspartame. A filmstrip was projected onto the bare wall in front of us: *Transcendental Meditation: Pathway to Inner Peace*. It consisted of jiggly shots of the Maharishi, sitting cross-legged on the grass somewhere in India, talking about TM. He spoke softly with a mincing accent—it was hard to make out what he was saying—and I found it only slightly more interesting than a filmstrip called *Silt* I'd been forced to sit through at a recent school assembly. Pieces of lint flickered around the peripheries of each frame, and I wound up paying more attention to these than anything else.

Afterward, another woman entered the room. She had long, oily hair parted in the middle just like Agatha's, and a turtleneck that almost looked like a neck brace. Acne was splattered across her chin and her forehead. She reminded me, vaguely, of a baby-sitter we once had who spent the entire evening seeding a nickel bag in the sleeve of our parents' *Magical Mystery Tour* album.

"I'm Pamela?" she said anemically. "An instructor? And, I just want to say that doing TM is, like, really, really good for you? It's like, eating vegetables for your soul?" She spoke so hesitantly, it seemed as if she was afraid to commit to the actual vowels and consonants required to construct a language.

"John, you're going to go with Pamela. Susie, you're coming with me," Agatha explained. "We're going to give each of you your very own, private mantra. This is a special word that the Maharishi has formulated just for you, personally. It's been designed to give you a sense of peace when you say it. If you tell this word to anyone, it will lose its power, so you've got to keep it secret. Do you understand?"

John and I nodded.

Agatha looked at us, unconvinced. "Not even to each other, not even to your best friend, not even to your mom."

"But what if someone overhears you while you're meditating?" said John.

"You say it to yourself in your head," said Agatha. "You think it. You don't say it out loud."

"But what if we forget it?" asked John.

"Tell your mommy that you forgot your mantra, and have her call the TM Center for an appointment to renew it."

This seemed like an enormous waste of time to me. "Couldn't we just write it down?" I asked. "Or have you remind us over the phone?"

Agatha shook her head vehemently. "A mantra is not a casual word. It's something holy that can only be transmitted by teacher to student in person. Is that clear?"

John and I nodded again. Pamela held out her long, limp, bony hand and led my brother silently through a door on the left. Agatha motioned for me to follow her through a second door on the right. I thought fleetingly of Hansel and Gretel, then wondered how the Maharishi knew how to formulate a special mantra just for me when he'd never met me before in his life. Did he have ESP? Somehow, I doubted it. Perhaps my mother had sent the TM Center information about me that Agatha had forwarded on to India. I tried to guess what my special word would be. For obvious reasons, "S" was my favorite letter in the alphabet, and I hoped my mantra would begin with it. When I was seven, I'd had an "S" birthday party, "Saluting Susie's Seventh" the invitations had read, and everyone who was invited had to wear something that began with "S." We'd served spaghetti, sundaes, and soda—just about my three favorite foods—along with "sweets," which was a convenient catch-all for an obscene amount of gummy bears, M&M's, and Blow Pops. Maybe my mantra would be "Sugar," I thought hopefully. Or, better yet, "Superstar." Couldn't that be a mantra? That sounded like a good one to me.

Agatha led me into a room that was even darker than the first. It also had two armchairs in it, another huge picture of the Maharishi, and a level of incense that could have very well been what motivated Congress to pass the Clean Air Act of 1970. It suddenly occurred to me that the word "suffocate" began with "S" also.

"Okay now, Susan, I'm going to whisper your mantra to you, and then I want you to repeat it back to me three times, so I'm sure you've got it," said Agatha. Then she pulled me so close to her, I could smell the orange rind on her breath, and she whispered my special, secret, personal mantra.

At first I thought I hadn't heard right. It wasn't even a word. Why, it was barely a diphthong. It was a vowelly, gibberishy syllable, devoid of any possible meaning. I didn't know how the Maharishi had come up with such a mantra for me. Frankly, I was insulted. How could he think that this tiny, unappetizing little sound reflected *my* innermost being? For starters, it didn't even have an "S" in it.

"Now, repeat it to me three times," Agatha commanded.

I wanted to say that I didn't like this mantra and could I please have another—something with a little more *oomph* in it, something that, when I was finished meditating, might double as a great name for a magazine or a female superhero I was going to invent. But Agatha flashed me a squinty look I'd seen on dentists and traffic cops. I did as I was told.

"Excellent," she whispered. "Now close your eyes. Keep repeating your mantra to yourself. Let your thoughts flow organically. That's it. Now, breathe."

Then I heard a rustle, and a click.

"I'll be back when your time's up," she said curtly.

Suddenly, alone in the dark, I felt ridiculous, but I soon realized that keeping my eyes shut was preferable to staring at the poster of the Maharishi, who looked more and more to me like a lawn troll in drag. Slowly, I began to meditate. Agatha had explained that my thoughts would eventually drift—this was part of the "inner peace process"—but, somehow, all I could think about while saying my mantra was how much I hated it and wanted another one.

Still, I kept repeating it. For all the anguish TM had caused me, I wanted it to work. At Silver Lake that past summer, my friends and I had played a game called "hyperventilation." It wasn't so much a game as a pleasurable massacring of our brain cells. With hyperventilation, you breathed in and out frantically while counting to 30. Then you held your breath while your friend gave you the Heimlich maneuver. If they squeezed enough air out of your lungs hard enough, you blacked out for a second or two. When you came to, you felt gobsmacked by bliss. You got a massive head rush that made your whole body tingle deliriously. You felt completely disoriented, giddy, and weightless. "Ohmygod, how long was I out?" we'd always squeal, stumbling around dreamily. When our friends informed us that barely three seconds had passed, we cried, "Wow! It felt like forever!" Then we'd have to wipe drool from our chin and the beginnings of a horrendous migraine headache would begin to take hold, but who cared? We wanted to do it again immediately. Hyperventilation was drugs without the drugs, brain-kill without the middleman.

With TM, I assumed I'd feel the same sort of rush I got making myself pass out at day camp. But nothing happened. Instead of inner peace, I began feeling irritable. I thought of my mother, sitting outside in the waiting room. She'd paid $200 for this little syllable of mine. This money was the last of the tiny sum she'd inherited when her grandmother died. It was the rest of her life savings, and she'd spent it on TM, hoping it could improve our lives in some way.

Yet what was so wrong with our lives, I wondered? We weren't starving to death or getting slaughtered in Cambodia. Sure, it was true that my dad kept getting laid off. As a civil rights lawyer, he worked for nonprofit agencies where he earned only slightly more than his clients. Whenever there were budget cuts, he lost his job. He hopped from one short-term position to another, and these increasingly took him away to ho-hum places like Cincinnati and Houston. And okay, when he came home, he and my mom tended to fight—a lot. And most of the time, even when he was working, we were pretty much broke; when my mom and I went to the corner grocery store where we could "sign" for bologna and bread, Murray, the butcher, politely asked if my dad had plans to pay our bill anytime soon. Whenever people said to me, "You're dad's a lawyer, so you guys are rich, right?" I assumed they were being sarcastic.

And then, of course, there were the dangers in our neighborhood: a bomb had gone off at Rust Brown's, the new nightclub next door, spraying glass all over the sidewalk, and across the street on Amsterdam Avenue, someone had been shot to death in front of Hanratty's Restaurant, leaving bloodstains soaked into the asphalt that immediately became a major tourist attraction for all the kids in the neighborhood. And oh, yeah: there was my brother's thyroid condition that had mysteriously caused him to stop growing for a year. And then, I suppose, there were our relatives, a number of whom seemed mentally ill; that past Christmas, in fact, my mother's father had given John and me an advanced calculus test at the dinner table, then called my dad a pedophile. Since then, my mother had barely spoken to her side of the family.

Clearly, our lives *did* have some problems, and thinking about all of them, I suddenly became unbearably sad. My mother had invested so much money and so much faith in trying to solve them. Yet even though I was barely ten, I knew: the problems we had were far beyond the reach of Transcendental Meditation or anything else she could hope or imagine. And this made my heart ache even more.

Afterward, back in the waiting room, Agatha and Pamela informed our mother that our TM initiation had gone smoothly. All we needed to do now, they said, was to meditate twice a day. They also said some other stuff about our need for self-discipline and attentiveness, but I wasn't listening. All I wanted to do was get the hell out of there. It was only 2:53 P.M.—Lincoln hadn't even been dismissed from school yet—but I wasn't thinking so much about him anymore as about escaping the nose-piercing stench of patchouli and the horrible, shivery feeling of despair that had developed in the pit of my stomach. By the time we finally left the center, I was so relieved, I skipped to the bus stop.

"See, it seems like you kids got something out of that after all," our mother said on the ride back home. "It really made an impression on you, didn't it?"

John and I nodded. "Sure," he said. Then he turned to me. "Hey, Suze," he said loudly, so that everyone on the bus could hear. "I'll tell you my mantra if you tell me yours."

For the next few weeks, our mother announced before dinner, "Okay, now is everybody ready to meditate?"

"Mmhm," John and I parroted. Then he'd go and play for ten minutes while I sat on my bed and fended off a full-blown, mantra-induced anxiety attack.

One of the benefits of TM, Agatha had said, was that it enabled you to be "alone with your thoughts." But as I quickly discovered, a lot of my thoughts were not anything I wanted to be alone with.

No sooner did I start saying my mantra than I started worrying. I tried not to, but I found I couldn't keep my lurking fears at bay. At first, I worried about pretty run-of-the-mill stuff: getting picked on at school. My dad losing his job again. My parents getting divorced. But from there, the level of difficulty and sophistication quickly escalated. I worried what would happen if both my parents died suddenly in a car accident. Would I be able to get a job baby-sitting or decorating T-shirts so that John and I wouldn't have to go into foster care? But where would we live? Earning 50 cents an hour wouldn't cover the rent on our apartment. Maybe we could sneak into the Metropolitan Museum like the kids in the book *From the Mixed-Up Files of Mrs. Basil E. Frankweiler.* But there was a meat shortage going on, and cars were lined up for blocks because of the oil shortage. Tuna fish that used to be 39 cents a can was now 53 cents. President Ford had told everybody to wear "WIN" buttons, but what if inflation continued and I couldn't make ends meet, and John and I had to go live in an orphanage? And eat gruel? And get hit with a paddle? Then I thought about a bunch of paperbacks I'd recently read including *Love Story* and a book called *Sunshine,* in which beautiful young protagonists died untimely deaths from cancer. What if I got leukemia? Would I have to die from chemotherapy, or could they maybe just amputate a leg? But then, how would I ever survive gym class? It was a nightmare *now,* and I still had my limbs.

And then there were the killer bees! We'd been studying them during "Current Events." These bees were enormous mutants, flying up from Mexico. They were apparently the most pissed-off bees in history, and they were due to get to New York City sometime around 1982, at which point they would hunt us all down and kill us! What if I got cancer, and they had to amputate my leg: how would I run away from the hordes of killer bees? And on the radio, newscasters had been talking about Swine Flu. Three businessmen had died from it already in Albuquerque, and they were saying it was an epidemic. What if I got Swine Flu? What if my whole family did? And then, there was something called the "Harmonic Convergence" that Annie's brother Jerome kept going on about. He said that in 1979, all of the planets from Mars through Pluto were going to line up exactly in the universe and the gravitational pull they'd exert would be so strong that the earth would spontaneously combust . . .

Just about then, when I was doubled over and mere seconds away from an aneurysm, my mother knocked on my door. "Hey, sweetie. Your meditation time's up," she sang brightly. "Get washed for dinner." Then she cocked her head and looked at me strangely. "Are you okay? You look a bit flushed."

"Oh, Mom," I gasped, clutching my stomach. "I think I have Swine Flu."

Soon, my brother no longer made any pretext about the fact that he was playing during meditation time. We could all hear *"Vvrrrrmmm Vrrrrrmm Vvvrrrmm"* emanating from his bedroom, followed by the metallic clatter of Matchbox cars crash-landing off the side of his dresser. As for myself, I figured that if inner peace was what we were really after here, then my TM time was far better spent daydreaming about Lincoln and brushing up on my valuable comic book reading and nail polishing skills. I found I could enjoy an entire issue of *Everything's Archie* and paint smiley faces on all of my toenails in less time than it took my parents to achieve a day's worth of enlightenment.

But in December, an invitation arrived in our mailbox. The TM Center, it seemed, was hosting a "Children's Transcendental Christmas Party." *Come!* it read. *Meet other children with mantras! Eat healthy candy! Celebrate the season of peace!*

"Yech," said my brother.

"No way," I said.

"I think it'll be fun," said our mother. "How many other children get to attend a Christmas party hosted by the Maharishi?"

"None," I grumbled.

"Exactly!" said my mother, as if this was a good thing.

After she returned the RSVP, I set about worrying all over again about running into Lincoln. The morning of the Christmas party, I attempted another of my famous fake stomachaches, but it proved as ineffective with my mother as it was in gym class.

Agatha greeted us at the doorway wearing the same green turtleneck, though now she also sported a Santa hat made of cherry red felt that drooped limply against her cheek. An artificial Christmas tree had been assembled in the center of the main room and decorated with strings of cranberries, origami whooping cranes, and little silk elephants studded with tiny mirrors and "Made in India" tags attached to their sides. The Maharishi's picture had been trimmed festively with blinking lights, giving him a psychedelic, whorish look. Again, John and I had been informed that, in the Christmas spirit of giving, we'd be required to donate another week's allowance to the Maharishi. This time, our mother gave the money directly over to Agatha, knowing full well that we'd sooner swallow our weekly 35 cents than fork it over again.

Looking around the party, I was surprised to see that there were, in fact, other guests. For some reason, I'd really believed that John and I were the only two children ever to do TM, and it both comforted and embarrassed me to discover we weren't alone. To be sure, the room was hardly packed. There was a beefy boy about my age in a burgundy and white striped rugby shirt, who was picking up the oranges on the mantelpiece one by one and sniffing them. A couple of younger, fragile-looking girls were dressed in stiff taffeta party dresses and miniature platform shoes. They were each clutching Barbies, and judging from the dolls' mutilated haircuts, either the girls had anger management problems or a real dearth of hand-eye coordination. A blond, spindly boy with bangs in his eyes and a crust of mucus beneath his nose crouched in a corner, where he appeared to be trying to hypnotize himself with a Duncan yo-yo. Another boy, about John's age, was dressed, inexplicably, in a cowboy outfit and a Stetson.

One quick assessment and it was pretty clear to me that this gathering was essentially Special Education Woodstock. The other parents had enrolled their kids in TM not to enlighten them, but to supplement their Ritalin. The party was a convention of losers and misfits, and John and I seemed to be the only losers and misfits not taking prescription medication.

"See that Bruno gets two of these by 3:00 P.M.," one of the mothers instructed Pamela, handing her a vial of pills. "Otherwise he'll go through the roof."

"They're only trace amounts of lithium," another explained apologetically, motioning to an envelope she'd left on the mantelpiece. "Still, we can't be too careful now, can we?"

I looked for our mother, but she was already standing at the door in her coat, beaming at us with what looked like pride and relief. "Santa's off to do some Christmas shopping," she sang brightly. "I'll be back to pick you up at 4:00 P.M. Be good."

Pamela slipped into the room just then. She, too, was wearing a Santa hat. A jingle bell pin—the kind they displayed beside the cash register at the drugstore—was attached crookedly to her turtleneck. She was carrying a tray laden with snacks, and immediately, everyone descended upon her like a gaggle of pigeons.

"No-ho-ho. Please?" she begged, hoisting the tray aloft so no one could get at it. "These are for later? First, we're going to play some games?"

There was a collective groan from the group.

"Okay everybody," Agatha clapped her hands together. "Let's all sit on the floor." Seeing as there were still only two armchairs in the room, this was not hard to get people to do. Once we were all settled, Agatha crossed her legs and looked around at us radiantly. "Now," she said, "I want everyone to say their name and then"—she made a gesture like she was plucking inspiration from thin air—"I want everyone to share their feelings about the Maharishi."

"Oh, let me begin," Pamela said excitedly. In her breathy voice, she said, "My name is Pamela? And when I look at the Maharishi?"

she smiled gooily, "I see a man of peace and tranquillity and truth?" Then she turned to the twin girls seated on her right. "Isabella, Francesca, what do you two see?"

Twisting shyly away, Isabella just shrugged. Francesca ignored the question and concentrated on walking her butchered Barbie along the patterns in the rug.

"I see," Pamela frowned. "Rufus, what about you?" She looked to the blond boy holding the yo-yo.

"I thought we were supposed to say our own names," he said petulantly.

Pamela laughed nervously. "Oh, of course!" she whispered. "How foolish. Sorry."

"My name is Rufus," Rufus said dourly. "And when I look at the Maharishi, I think he needs a haircut."

This elicited a couple of hoots from the circle. "I look at the Maharishi, and I think he's a fag!" the boy in the rugby shirt shouted.

"Bruno, we'll have none of that," said Agatha.

"What's a fag?" said the littlest boy in the group, who couldn't have been more than four.

Francesca set down her Barbie and looked at him with exasperation. "I told you, Percy!" she yelled. "It's the name of an evil king."

"What? No, it's not!" said Bruno.

Agatha stood up. "Okay, people," she exclaimed, "Why don't we move on to something else."

The little boy in the cowboy outfit suddenly raised his hand and started waving it frantically. "Agatha! Agatha! Can I just say one thing? One thing quickly?"

"Yes, Harold?"

"Did you know," the boy said earnestly, twisting the fringe on his cowboy vest around one of his knuckles, "that if you're Scandinavian, and you marry a woman who's Nigerian, and you have sexual intercourse with her and make children, you're increasing the gene pool?"

Nobody knew what the hell to do with this. For a moment, all the air seemed to go out of the room.

"I see," exhaled Agatha. "Well. That's interesting. Thank you for sharing that with us, Harold."

"You know, Agatha," Pamela said softly, "I think it's time for the group Christmas meditation now, don't you?"

"Yes! Everybody stand up and gather around the Christmas tree," Agatha said. "For the next ten minutes, we're going to march around the tree with our eyes closed, meditating together."

John looked at me, panicked. There'd been nothing on the invitation about this. It was like being told to participate in a collective nose-picking. To the other kids' credit, they seemed as repulsed by the idea as we were.

"That's moronic!" Bruno announced loudly. "I'm not doing it, and you can't make me."

"You said we'd get candy," whined Francesca.

"If we walk around with our eyes closed, we'll all bang into the Christmas tree," Rufus said.

"Nobody's going to bang into a Christmas tree," said Agatha. "We're all going to hold hands."

"Yeeccch. No way am I holding hands with girls!"

"Then hold hands with two boys," Agatha suggested.

"Yeah, then you'll be a homo like the Maharishi!" sang Bruno.

"Bruno!" Pamela shouted. Suddenly, the room went still. Nobody had heard Pamela raise her voice before, and the shrillness of it seemed to bounce off the bare walls and hang in the air. Pamela looked horrified and clamped both her palms over her mouth. But the rest of us were sort of impressed, actually.

"Bruno," Agatha said sharply, "we don't speak that way about his holiness. Nor about anyone else. There will be no name-calling, do you hear me? Now," she glared, "if you don't meditate, you don't get any candy."

Transcendence we couldn't understand, but bribery we certainly could. Grudgingly, we all joined hands and began trudging slowly around the artificial tree with our eyes closed. There was no way I could concentrate on my mantra even if I'd wanted to. I kept worrying that I'd trip over the rug or that someone would photograph me in this humiliating situation. I opened my eyes a moment to see if everybody else had their eyes closed.

"Hey! No peeking!" Bruno shouted at me.

Floorboards squeaked beneath the carpet, and I could hear Rufus wheezing. Outside, somebody passed by with a transistor radio. A snippet of KC and the Sunshine Band came through the window— *Do a little dance, make a little love, get down to*—then a police siren tore by.

I don't know who belched first, but I guessed it was Bruno. It was a long, guttural, repulsive belch that growled up two octaves, then climaxed gaseously. A few kids started giggling.

"Bruno," I heard Agatha say sternly.

"What? I didn't do anything. Sheesh."

A moment later, there was another burp. A few more kids giggled, and a higher-pitched farting noise followed that sounded like helium being slowly let out of a balloon.

"Children—" Agatha started, but she was interrupted by two more laborious farts and a belch. "Children," she said again, but by this time, a veritable orchestra of farts and belches had started from different locations around the room, punctuated by giggling. The more people giggled, the more brazen the farters and belchers became, and the harder everyone laughed. The circle quickly fell apart, and when I opened my eyes, I saw everyone else had opened theirs, too, including Agatha and Pamela, who looked a little deflated.

"Can we eat now?" said Francesca. "You said we could have candy."

"CAN-DEE, CAN-DEE!" shouted my brother. It was his first public act of misbehavior and, for some reason, it made me enormously proud of him. "CAN-DEE!"

"CAN-DEE!" seconded Bruno delightedly, and then, in a moment, he and my brother were leading the entire room in a chant, "CAN-DEE! CAN-DEE! WE WANT CAN-DEE!"

"Now hold on—" said Agatha.

"CAN-DEE! CAN-DEE! WE WANT CAN-DEE!"

Agatha pulled off her Santa hat, sighed, and threw it on the chair. She motioned to Pamela to bring in the trays. "Fine. Whatever," she said. "I didn't sign up for this." She turned and walked out of the room.

Pamela took the trays down from the shelves and we fell upon them greedily, grabbing at anything. But in a moment, we discovered that the snacks weren't candy at all, but some kind of freakish, pre-fabricated health food. There were fig bars that looked like clumps of tar. Congealed-looking dates hairy with coconut shreds. Sesame seed bricks that some miscreant had wrapped in cellophane with the word "treat" stamped on them, as if that was enough to compensate for the fact that the product had, essentially, the consistency and appeal of sawdust.

"Oh. Gross!" yelled the twins. All around me, kids were making gagging noises and spitting the snacks out into their hands. "Yuck!" "Ewww." "Dis-gust-o-mundo."

"What the fuck is this?" shouted Bruno. "DOG SHIT?"

"All right. That's it," said Agatha, stalking back into the room furiously. Tucked under her arm was a Kleenex box that had been outfitted in gold foil paper. "You're all out of here," she said to us. "Now."

"Agatha," said Pamela. "Think of the Maharishi."

"I called a car service. The drivers should be here in five minutes. Here are their allowances." Agatha thrust the Kleenex box into Pamela's chest. "*Bugs Bunny Superstar* starts at Loew's Cinema at 2:15. You drop them off, you get them seated, I call their parents."

"Yeee Haaa! We're going to the movies!" shouted Bruno.

"MOO-VEE! MOO-VEE!" shouted my brother, who had clearly found his calling as an instigator. "LET'S SEE DA MOO-VEE!"

All of us started squealing and cheering. We helped ourselves into our coats and mittens in record time, and fifteen minutes later, we were all squirming around excitedly in the front two rows of Loew's Cinema. With our allowances, we each bought an industrial-sized box of Milk Duds, a trough of Dr Pepper, and enough popcorn to fill up a snare drum. It was a rainy afternoon—the theater was packed to the point of violating city fire ordinances—and we hooted and elbowed each other and threw popcorn in the air like confetti and hyper-reacted to the Looney Toon characters along with the six zillion other shrieking Upper West Side kids crammed into the theater. Midway through the movie, I became aware of the heat seeping through my shoes, and the smell of artificial butter wafting in from the lobby in waves. Finally, I realized, happily, I was participating in something normal and all-American. As the sugar and cartoon stimulation began to caramelize my brain, I slid back in my seat, feeling sated and stupefied.

The next day, Lincoln Anderson stopped in front of my desk on his way to the pencil sharpener. "Uh, hey, um. I think I saw you yesterday," he said sheepishly.

You might as well have punctured my stomach repeatedly with a staple gun. Lincoln had seen me in the Transcendental Meditation Center. With all those psychotic kids and those sickly Maharishi yahoos and the plastic Christmas tree. It was the most terrible of all possible scenarios.

"Were you at the movies on 83rd Street?" he said.

"Bugs Bunny Superstar?"

"Yeah," he said. "I saw you. I was in the back. It was a good movie, I thought."

"Yeah," I nodded. "It was a really good movie," was all I could think to add.

"Bugs Bunny. He's okay," Lincoln said.

Then he headed off to the pencil sharpener.

That was it—the only one-on-one conversation we would have during our entire elementary school career. But I would remember it. I wasn't under any illusions that Lincoln suddenly liked me. I didn't replay the conversation over and over in my head, according it meaning and significance that never existed. Oh no. That stupidity would come later in life, with other boys. But at that moment in fifth grade, it simply thrilled me to think of Lincoln Anderson sitting in Loew's

83rd Street Cinema and spotting me across the mayhem of the crowded theater. I was not, after all, invisible. And sometimes, when I found myself feeling particularly wretched, or chubby, or unlikable, I thought about him stopping to talk to me about *Bugs Bunny Superstar*, his notebook held purposefully at his side, his red-gold hair winking in the fluorescent lights of the classroom, and the small, simple memory of it would bring me something like peace.

It was almost, you could say, like a mantra.

PART II

Not Just Horny,
But Obnoxious, Too

Chapter 6

Mick Jagger Wants Me

PUBERTY IS A LITTLE LIKE Chinese Water Torture. One day, a hair grows, and you have to call an Emergency Session in the bathroom with your best friend. After you've been assured you're normal, nothing happens for a while. But then another hair grows. Then you get a pimple. Then another. Then you look in the mirror, and you notice the contours of your body are changing subtly, like a shoreline. Eventually, you're smoking pot and hating your parents and writing things in your diary like, "I am SOOOO depressed. NOBODY likes me," and measuring your sex life in terms of *bases,* but by this time, at least, you've mastered the fine art of shaving your armpits.

That is, unless you were like me. Absolutely nothing occurred for years, and then—*Wham!* My hormones hit like a long-overdue locomotive.

The only clue I might've had that they were coming was that, the summer before my sophomore year in high school, I'd decided nothing would be more mortifying than to spend it with my parents.

That June, I landed my first job ever as a live-in mother's helper on Long Island. A "mother's helper," I quickly learned, earns about as much as a migrant worker for doing stuff like changing diapers, vacuuming sand off the living room sofa, and fishing plastic Star

Wars action figurines out of the toilet. But no matter: paid a whopping $40 a week for twelve-hours days with no day off, I considered myself a lucky and independent woman.

And so there I was in the summer of 1979: with thumb-tack-sized breasts and a night brace, longing to be kissed. I could barely operate an electric can opener, and yet I pretended to be capable of caring for both a three-year-old and a newborn. The misguided family who'd employed me were the Maysleses. The father, David, was a well-known documentary producer who'd made, among other things, *Gimme Shelter*, a film about the Rolling Stones that famously captured on tape the murder at Altamont.

Toward the end of the summer, *Gimme Shelter* was having its television premiere, and the Maysleses gave me the evening off so that I could go watch the movie with Vanessa, a friend I'd made who lived next door.

That evening, Vanessa and I sat around her house in damp Speedo bathing suits, eating the official snack foods of puberty: Nacho Cheese Doritos and Tab. Vanessa had an old, portable black and white RCA television that had a wire hanger for an antenna. It took a while to manipulate the reception. "If this fucking thing takes one more minute," she hollered, "I'm throwing it in the goddamn swimming pool." Having been schooled privately in both New York and Europe, Vanessa had developed an impressive mastery of profanity, which I'd made up my mind to emulate almost immediately.

Eventually, we got the picture clear and settled in. The opening credits rolled.

Strangely, about ten minutes into the film, my skin started to tingle. Vanessa, who usually talked through anything, stared at the screen in silence. Mick Jagger was singing. Neither of us had ever seen him before. He was swaggering, almost tongue-kissing the microphone, and his eyes were half closed. He was serpentine, sensual, yet just girlish enough not to be scary. He looked like he could put you in his mouth and melt you.

"Ohmygod," I whispered.

Vanessa looked at me.

I looked at her.

We didn't say anything and stared back at Mick, whirling about the stage.

Then we both moaned.

From that day on, no one could hold a rational conversation with us. All we talked about was the Rolling Stones, and we didn't so much *talk* as *shriek*. We prefaced just about everything we said with a hyperventilating, "Ohmygod" and ended everything as if it was followed!!! by!!! triple!!! exclamation points!!! The adults around us felt compelled to roll their eyes and inform us that our behavior was "really adolescent"—which only further encouraged us. After all: *Who the fuck cared what adults thought? If adults were so smart and hip, we reasoned, they would have found some way to avoid growing up and turning into adults.*

Then Labor Day rolled around, and Vanessa got sent back to boarding school, while I had to return home to Manhattan and those two genetic albatrosses known as my parents.

Back in New York, I decided that the only way to survive such humiliation was to pretend that my parents simply didn't exist— well, at least as soon as they forked over my allowance each week. I also proceeded to build a shrine in my bedroom.

I bought Rolling Stones records, Rolling Stones posters, Rolling Stones buttons, Rolling Stones books. When I trooped home carrying a Rolling Stones mural—a blow-up of the cover from their album *Black and Blue,* six feet long and three feet high—and secured it to the wall with industrial-sized two-sided tape because I swore *I would never, ever want to stop looking at it for as long as I lived,* my parents stopped coming into my bedroom.

Had there been an Internet in those days, I probably would've rotted to death in front of the monitor, clicking obsessively from one Rolling Stones chat room to another. But instead, poor, pre–digital age *moi,* I had to scavenge whatever "Stones fixes" I could find from magazines. This wasn't easy. Insipid fanzines like *16* and *TeenBeat,* were ga-ga over teddy bears like Shaun Cassidy and Parker Stevenson. *Where,* I wanted to know, *were magazines for fifteen-year-old girls in love with British bisexual cokeheads, thank you?* It was an outrage. I was an invisible, oppressed demographic. I had to make do with *Rolling Stone* and *People* magazine, scouring them for so much as a paragraph about Mick, or even his bitchy ex-wife, Bianca.

Alcoholics hate to drink alone. When my infatuation became so all-consuming that I almost couldn't take it, I called up Michelle, my oldest and best friend, who lived in the same apartment building as I did.

After calling an "emergency sleepover," I stayed up all night playing Rolling Stones music for her, showing her photographs of the band from their album covers, desperately trying to get her to see the world through my eyes, to hear it as I did: Listen to "Ruby Tuesday" I begged, playing it not once, not twice, but three times in a row. "Tell me he isn't singing about us. I mean, 'Don't question why she needs to be so free.' Michelle, is that not us? And Ohmygod, okay, you have GOT to hear '19th Nervous Breakdown' . . ."

The next day, I took Michelle downtown to PosterMat on Eighth Street in Greenwich Village, a rock 'n' roll novelty store that sold stash boxes, rainbow-colored hash pipes, incense, T-shirt iron-ons, and little calling cards with phrases like "Methinks thou art a shit-head" engraved on them in elegant script, which we thought were really outrageous and funny.

There, in the back of PosterMat, past the lava lamps and concert jerseys, I'd discovered a treasure trove of drool-a-bilia. Hung on clacking, metal display sheaves were six different Rolling Stones posters! You could stand there, just stand there, and turn back and forth between them, staring for hours: Mick in black and white, wearing a "Palace Laundry" shirt. The Stones all together in a field with "Rolling Stones" written in lolling, psychedelic script. Keith with his guitar. Mick in heavy eyeliner. Glorious image upon glorious image—they were beautiful—it was almost too much to take. Looking at them left me flushed and breathless, desire boiling off my skin like a vapor.

The posters were what finally did it for Michelle. By the time we left the store, she, too, was a fanatic.

After that, the two of us went about constructing our own little meta-reality, in which the Rolling Stones replaced the sun at the center of the solar system. We talked about the Stones as if they were our intimate friends, fantasizing and worrying about them endlessly.

"Oh, Michelle, do you think Mick is lonely?" I said one night, as we were listening to *Some Girls* for the fourteenth time in a row on her Panasonic portable record player.

"Lonely?" she looked at me and snorted. "Girl, this dude has more women than any other guy on the planet. No, I don't think Mick is lonely."

"But c'mon," I said, picking up the album cover and pointing. "Think about it: His last hit was 'Miss You.' What if underneath all his fame, he's really pining away for intimacy, and that song is, like, his plea for help? Wouldn't that be terrible? Could you imagine him, lonely?"

Michelle set down her cigarette. She'd started smoking—for effect, of course. "Shit. Maybe you're right. Maybe he's really, really depressed. That's a horrible thought . . ."

"Oh God," I said, beseeching the ceiling. "Please make sure that Mick Jagger isn't lonely. Please don't make Mick lonely . . ."

Until this point, I'd spent a criminal amount of time at home, trying to copy makeovers out of *Seventeen* magazine and whipping up chalky Alba '77 "Fit 'n' Frosty" chocolate milkshakes in the blender. If I went out at all, it was to the movies or to some marginal high school party where kids stood around awkwardly, making lame jokes and grinding Fritos into the rug.

Once Michelle and I became groupies, however, we avoided having anything to do with our parents, and stopped hanging around with any of our "square" friends at school. Musical taste became the sole criterion for our social life. You could be a pothead who came to class in his pajama top . . . you could be a kleptomaniac who'd been court-ordered to attend an "alternative high school" and dressed in a kilt and a dog collar . . . you could be one of those creepy twenty-two-year-old guys with a handlebar mustache and secondhand army jacket who still hung around his old high school, buying malt liquor for the sophomores and partying with them on the street . . . but if you believed passionately that *Exile on Main Street* was indeed *the greatest fucking rock album in the history of the world,* well then, we believed you were a genius and cool enough to hang out with us.

Jimmy Carter was still clinging to the presidency. AIDS had not yet emerged. In New York City, drugs were still considered glamorous; cocaine, in particular, was pricey, chic, and, astonishingly, considered nonaddictive. Discotheques were in full swing: It was customary to see people starting an evening at midnight and staying out until dawn. At Studio 54, people thought nothing about getting high and having sex with strangers in the bathroom, then posing for the paparazzi with a whippet stuck up their nose.

Both Michelle and I felt terribly left out.

We were convinced there was always a wonderful party going on somewhere right near us in a fancy club full of photographers, artists, musicians, and movie stars dressed in gold lamé. They did cocaine, had sex, and were admired and beloved by the world.

And the kicker was: we were *right.* The terrible tease of New York City is that there always really *is* some fabulous event taking place nearby that you're not invited to. Celebrity culture—which most Americans only read about as an abstract, faraway, glittering thing—was literally right at our doorsteps. The actor Richard Dreyfuss lived on the Upper West Side—we knew exactly where and sometimes we'd stop by his building and try to talk the doorman into letting us meet him. We knew where Faye Dunaway, Diane Keaton, and, of course, John Lennon lived. We'd seen Al Pacino once buying groceries. We read constantly about celebrity events and parties. When Woody Allen had a grand New Year's party, written up in all the papers, we felt genuinely wretched and miserable that we hadn't been invited to it.

We spent every day in Michelle's room or mine, listening obsessively to the albums *Hot Rocks* and *Sticky Fingers* and embroidering the

Stones' "lapping tongue" logo on her overalls. Saturated with estrogen and progesterone, we were so frustrated and restless, we didn't know what the hell to do with ourselves. We started smoking clove cigarettes and pot, and took No-Doz to simulate amphetamines if we couldn't nab some real ones. Augh, how we longed to do coke!

We decided that if we could emulate the Rolling Stones—the ministers of decadence—and then meet them, we would somehow be rescued from our marginalized, pathetic little lives. Only meeting the Rolling Stones, we decided, would finally transform us into the ultra-cool, sophisticated *artistes* that we really, *truly* were.

Not surprisingly, losing our virginity counted heavily in this transformation. We wanted lovers, not boyfriends. After all, Warhol girls and courtesans always had *lovers;* high school *virgins* had makeout sessions with their *boyfriends.* We regarded virginity as the sexual equivalent of training wheels and braces: the quicker disposed of, the better.

And through some twisted, fifteen-year-old logic, we equated losing our virginity with losing our virginity to Mick Jagger.

We spent inordinate amounts of time speculating who in our schools had "lost it" thus far. Had Angelina? Most certainly. What about Judy? Michelle wasn't sure. Yet for her, this guessing game was just an amusement. Lithe and smoldery, Michelle bore more than a passing resemblance to Brooke Shields. Her beauty, it seemed to me, endowed her with unassailable cool. She moved unhurriedly through the world, as if she didn't have anything to prove.

But for me, the sex lives of my classmates were a source of mounting anxiety. Only that summer had I finally begun to grow breasts, yet I still did not consider myself sexy or pretty. Throughout most of ninth grade, some of the cutest alpha boys had come up to me in the hallways and thrown their arms chummily around my shoulder. Just as my stupid heart went off like a Roman candle—*Ohmygod, does he like me? Does Ira Abrams really like me?*—they'd whisper suavely in my ear, "So, hey. When are you fixing me up with one of your gorgeous friends?"

My virginity seemed like the hallmark of failure, the ultimate testimony to the fact that I wasn't desirable. Anytime I found out that somebody else I knew had "lost it," I got a sick, twisty feeling in my stomach, convinced that the number of nonvirgins was directly proportional to the extent of my inadequacy.

––––––––––

Don't ask me why, but for some reason, Michelle and I also had the idea that in order to *meet* the Rolling Stones and *sleep* with them, it was necessary to *dress* like them. Of course, we had no idea what this really meant—so we dressed the way we imagined Keith Richards and Mick Jagger would dress *if they were women*. We assumed, of course, that they'd rather look like groupies than like the fashion models they actually dated, and so we assembled outfits that looked, really, like they'd been designed by a legion of *Soul Train* dancers let loose in the Salvation Army. At a street fair, I'd managed to buy a secondhand pair of Lucite cocktail pumps (you could see the nails in the heels) with rhinestone ankle straps, which I wore with gold socks, pink harem pants, an oversized fake-fur coat, and a gray fedora studded with antique tie-tacks. Michelle, going more for what we decided was a "Keith Richards" look, wore black jeans topped with layers upon layers of secondhand bed jackets.

We bought most of our outfits on East 10th Street at a place called Bogie's, run by two old Romanian immigrants. It wasn't so much of a clothing store as a dump. The merchandise consisted of one enormous mountain of clothing: trench coats, old negligees, baseball jerseys, sheets. The women handed us a bag and we'd climb to the top of the pile—it was the size of a haystack—and sort through it until we found things we liked. Almost everything was faded, stained, or frayed, but who cared? Only bourgeoisie goody-goodies and people who listened to disco and Barry Manilow, we told ourselves, wore clothing from actual department stores.

The women at Bogie's would weigh the bags and charge us a dollar for every ten pounds of clothing. We ended up with all these fancy old garments for two or three bucks. We wore silk teddies as shirts, petticoats as skirts—and traipsed through the city in other people's underwear. We also bought loads of earrings. Michelle wore one, I the other: lavender feathers, beaded chandelier earrings from India, rhinestones-on-steroids. We also covered ourselves with bracelets and Rolling Stones buttons. Even by New York standards, we were a freak show: we once walked into Tavern on the Green to use the bathroom, and the head waiter asked us to leave.

We took immense pleasure in lying and sneaking around.

"I'm going out for ice cream with Michelle!" I'd shout, halfway out the front door.

"I'm going out with Susie for ice cream!" Michelle would shout to her parents. Then we'd both take the bus up to Columbia University and smoke pot by the statues with some fraternity guys. Or we'd go down to Lincoln Center and hang out by the fountain, hoping to spot celebrities. One night, a thirty-five-year-old man picked us up and took us across the street to a French restaurant called La Crêpe, where the three of us ate *pommes frites* and got bombed on hard cider. Michelle and I excused ourselves to go to the bathroom, then ran out and left him with the check. Our mothers thought we were baby-sitting.

"Ohmygod, can you bee-lieve we just did that?" I giggled as we lurched across Broadway, me in my clacking Lucite and rhinestone heels, my armload of bracelets jangling.

"I am so fucked up," said Michelle.

"We are sooo bad."

"That French shit is nasty."

"Think he'll come after us?"

"If he does, we'll just tell 'em that Keith'll kick his ass."

"Ohmygod! Of course!"

We'd told so many people that we were the Rolling Stones' girl-friends, we'd actually started to believe it ourselves. We'd also made it policy to speak, whenever possible, with British accents (never mind that sometimes we sounded like Eliza Doolittle, other times like Princess Margaret—we were pretty convinced we were authentic).

One night, we told boys from Yorktown Prep that we were groupies who'd hitchhiked from San Francisco. Another night, a group of tourists from Georgia stopped to ask us for directions. High on pot, beer, and cooking sherry, we happily loaded them down with all sorts of useful information about the city.

"Wow, for British people, y'all sure know a lot about New York," one of them drawled.

"Well," I whispered, leaning in close for effect, "when you're the illegitimate daughters of Mick Jagger and Keith Richards, you tend to get around."

Is it even necessary to say, at this point, that our home lives were a misery? Michelle's parents fought so terribly that through the walls of my apartment, I could hear them screaming and slamming doors. While my family was eating dinner, I'd hear several thuds; a few minutes later, our doorbell would ring. Michelle would be standing there, crying in the hallway.

"Oh, Susie, oh, God . . ."

Similarly, I'd come home from school every day to find my mother moody and seething. She was often enraged at my father (they, too, were headed for a divorce), but I usually presented the easiest target. The smallest transgression—a fork left in the sink, a wet towel on the bathroom floor—was enough to trigger a volcanic fight. My efforts to appease her often backfired as well:

"I won a prize today at school for a poem I wrote."

She read it, looked at me icily, and threw it on the floor.

"So?" she said. "What do you want from me?"

"Well, my English teacher liked it."

"So go live with your English teacher."

Then she told me to make my own dinner and slammed her bedroom door.

When my father finally arrived home he asked, "What happened? What did you do?"

"Nothing. Honest. I just showed her a poem I wrote. Do you want to see it?"

He shook his head. "I think you owe your mother an apology," he said wearily, setting down his briefcase. "You shouldn't upset her."

He walked into their bedroom and closed the door sharply behind him. I stood there for a minute. Through the door I could hear my mother yelling, then my father stammering, "Jesus Christ, Ellen—" Then I walked slowly over to Michelle's. She answered the door and I could hear her mother shouting in the background, "Ted! Listen to me for a minute, goddamn it!"

Michelle looked at me. We didn't say anything. She just got her cigarettes and we went and sat out in the concrete stairwell. I unfolded my poem and handed it to her, and she read it as she smoked. When she was done, she hugged me.

"That's wonderful! That's really, really wonderful."

I eyed her. "You really think so?"

"Of course! Susie, you're a poet!"

"Oh. Michelle."

We hugged, and then we both started to cry.

After a little while, when we felt better, Michelle would say, "So. I had another fantasy about Mick."

"You did? Tell me." Although we'd repeatedly told each other our fantasies, we never tired of hearing them and embellishing the details. Michelle's main fantasy was that she would meet Mick Jagger at a nightclub and he'd take her around to the apartments of all the other band members so she could meet them. Then she'd hit it off with Keith Richards and travel with him in the band for a while.

My favorite fantasy was that one evening I would meet Mick Jagger at a dinner party. We would talk about music and literature; he would find me intelligent and attractive. Then we would get romantically involved and he would pick me up from school in his limousine. But the limousine wouldn't simply pull up to the curb. Oh no. Mick would actually get out and walk directly into my high school. Of course, everyone would immediately stop whatever they were doing and stare. A wave of whispers would sweep through the school—a few kids would try to approach him for autographs—as

Mick walked purposefully, straight to Room 217, where I had Third Period Geometry. He'd knock on the door, and my teacher, Mrs. Yearwood, would look on stunned, as Mick strode into the room.

"'Ello Suz-zay," he'd say jauntily. Everyone in the class would look at me and gasp. The boys who'd once ignored me would be practically apoplectic with newfound reverence and awe.

"Ohmygod," Henry Platt would exclaim. "That's Mick Jagger!"

"It's really him." Ira Abrams would say with astonishment. "For Susie?"

Some of the girls would squeal and faint, and Mick would have to step over their bodies to get to my desk. There, beside me, he'd drop to his knees and grab my hand and clasp it desperately to his heart while the whole class looked on. "I'm sorry, luv, but I just 'ad to see you. I can't stop thinking about you."

And I would just sit there, looking unbelievably glamorous.

"Oh, Mick," I'd sigh coolly, "I'm in the middle of Geometry. Can't we talk about this later?"

In November, Michelle came running upstairs with a newspaper article.

"They're here," she shrieked.

According to the *Daily News,* the Stones were back in New York, putting the finishing touches on their album *Emotional Rescue* at the Electric Lady Studios. From the Yellow Pages, we learned that Electric Lady was on Eighth Street in Greenwich Village. It was 10:00 P.M. on a Thursday night, but clearly, this was not something that could wait until morning.

I told my mother I was going to Michelle's house to bake cookies; she told her mother she was going to mine. Then we both took the C train downtown to West Fourth Street. The studio was one of the most nondescript doorways in all of Greenwich Village. Located next to a movie theater, it was a small, windowless storefront with a small door set in far from the street. Only a small brass plaque saying "electric lady" in lower-case letters distinguished it. You could walk by it a thousand times and never notice.

For the next two hours, Michelle and I stood in front of this doorway, stopping people on the street who looked like they might know something, asking them if they'd seen the Rolling Stones.

After that, we spent every weekend camped out in front of Electric Lady. We'd get downtown at about 10:00 A.M., position ourselves against a car parked right near the entrance, and wait. Michelle would smoke cigarettes while I, ever the groupie geek, would bring along books and do my homework. We flirted with strangers a bit, if we thought they were "somebody," and took beer from guys on the street. Sometimes Michelle would ring the bell at the entrance and say she was sent over from the *Village Voice* with a package for Keith Richards, but they never let her in.

———

We fell in with some other hippie-groupie types from Michelle's school who were obsessed with Hendrix, the Doors, Janis Joplin, and Zeppelin as well as the Stones. On the weekends, they often threw "the parents are away" parties out in Flushing, Queens. Since the parties lasted all night, we rarely slept at them; at 3:00 A.M. a bunch of us might try to set up beds on the floor using sofa cushions and towels, but when the sun rose, we'd all be up listening to "Free Bird" and cooking frozen pizza in the kitchen.

Most of the time, none of us knew where we were, or who we were with. People were taking speed, smoking grass, dropping acid, making out with whoever was around: it was a druggie, psychedelic mess. There would be beer and cigarette butts all over the basement floor, cans and paper, little pools of wax where candles had melted down on the coffee tables. Each party, I made out with a different guy. Making out, I'd quickly discovered, was the greatest activity ever invented in the history of the planet. As soon I started making out with boys on a regular basis, I couldn't believe that vast segments of the human population ever did anything else. How, I wondered, could people possibly pick up their dry cleaning, perform open heart surgery, or teach high school mathematics when *they could be making out instead? What was wrong with this world? Where were people's priorities?*

Yet after eight straight hours of mashing, grinding, and drinking, my lips were always swollen, and by morning, I always felt battered from alcohol. All I ever wanted to do was take a hot shower and slide between the cool, fresh sheets of my own bed. Instead, Michelle and I would take the subway to Greenwich Village and spend a few hours replacing whatever it was we had lost at the party: lipstick, change purses, socks.

We were walking across Eighth Street one of these afternoons when a limousine pulled up in front of Electric Lady.

"Michelle!" I grabbed her hand and we raced across the street. Then we leaned against an Oldsmobile parked right in front of the studio and waited to see who was coming out. We were determined to appear very cool and nonchalant about it.

Two minutes later, the door to Electric Lady swung open and Keith Richards sauntered out with his little blond son in tow. He looked, if this was possible, scraggly and regal. His black hair was tousled and he was wearing a pair of gold-mirrored sunglasses. I sized him up as fast as possible: tight black velvet pants pulled over boots, black jacket, a red-green-yellow scarf slashed around his neck. When he walked into the sunlight, he recoiled a little. Then he spotted me and Michelle, and for a second, he acknowledged us with a nod before staggering toward his limousine.

"Let's go with him. Let's do it, Susie," Michelle whispered. "Let's jump in his limo . . ."

I'd completely jelled. He was walking down the street, and all I could look at was his ass. I was watching his proud legs and his ass, packed into tight black velvet, pull and move, pull and move, with a bit of a jiggle, as he moved toward his car. *That is Keith Richards' ass,* I thought ecstatically. *I am watching Keith Richards' ass.*

Michelle grabbed my wrist and pulled me to the curb. "Let's do it, Susie," she said. "We're really going to do it."

The chauffeur opened the door and Keith's son scuttled in, followed by Keith, who paused for a moment before dipping down into the back seat. He seemed to take one last look at the studio, the street, and the people, and as he did, the sunlight glared off his glasses in flashes of gold. Michelle and I froze. The door slammed, the motor growled, and the limousine veered away from the curb, leaving us standing at the edge of the gutter, shivering, tears running down our faces.

"Keith," we shrieked as the car drove away, "Keith, we love you!"

When it was absolutely out of sight, we started laughing, crying, jumping up and down, and shouting all at once: "We saw Keith! We saw Keith Richards!"

Then Michelle said to me, "I'll bet you anything Mick is still in the studio. We're going to meet him. We'll wait out all night if we have to. But he's ours, Susie. He's finally–fucking–ours."

I should have been thrilled. I should have felt that sweet, heart-pulsing surge of expectation nearing fulfillment. But instead, strangely, I didn't. Instead, I started to feel something that felt an awful lot like dread.

And then it became instantly clear to me: in my fantasy life with Mick, I was always beautiful, sexual, confident. I was at dinner parties, I was in Geometry class. I wasn't waiting outside all night on some urine-drenched sidewalk, some scraggly kid, some *beggar* ambushing him with a carnation and an autograph book.

The idea of actually meeting Mick Jagger this way sickened me. How could I possibly cast myself that way in his eyes? For that matter, how could I cast myself that way in mine? To be so pathetic and prostrate before him—Christ, what would I be left with?

I looked at Michelle.

"I can't," I said quietly.

"What? Susie, what are you talking about?" she cried. "This is our dream come true! Mick Jagger is in there! I know it! I'm telling you! We are meeting Mick Jagger!"

I shook my head. I felt like a jerk, but somehow, I couldn't stop.

"What the hell is wrong with you?" Michelle said.

I looked down and played with the rhinestone buttons on my coat. For some reason, my eyes started watering. Maybe there *was* something wrong with me. *I mean, really,* I thought. *Look at me.* Finally, I swallowed. "Oh, Michelle," I said, "in my dreams, I always meet him at a dinner party. And somebody introduces us—I don't just come up to him. And he wants me. Mick Jagger wants *me*—"

Michelle said nothing. She just reached into the pocket of her jeans jacket and fished out a cigarette. Then, very slowly, she took out her lighter, flicked it open, and expertly lit her cigarette. When she finally looked at me, I saw on her face something I hadn't expected: pity. Pity mixed with just an inkling of fear.

"Um, Susie?" she said carefully, in a tone usually reserved for the senile—or, perhaps, the criminally insane—"Honey? That's a *fantasy* you're telling me. This?" she waved her hand across Eighth Street. "*This,* right here? This is real. Mick Jagger is in this recording studio, right here, right now, and you and I have an opportunity of a lifetime to meet him."

"I'm sorry," I whispered hoarsely. Then I started to cry.

In standard Teenage Girl Culture, this should've been considered a massive betrayal, a pivotal moment that ended our friendship. The fact that it wasn't was a testimony to how close we were. Michelle simply reached over and pushed my hair away from my eyes. "Go home, girl," she said gently. "Go home and take care of yourself."

The next morning, she called me in hysterics: at five o'clock that morning, Mick Jagger had in fact emerged from Electric Lady Studios.

"Oh, Susie," she sobbed, as I shrieked with delight. She was calling me from a pay phone on the corner of Sixth Avenue, just about fifty yards from where she'd met him. "He was so beautiful. I waited outside with three other groupies until the sun was starting to rise. When he walked out of the studio, we almost missed him because he's grown a beard and none of us recognized him. But then we realized who he was, and we started following him down the street. Susie, I must have been only three feet away from him. Then, all of a sudden, he turned right around and starting yelling at me, 'Fucking ridiculous.'

"Susie, I couldn't believe it. I thought I was going to die. I thought he was angry at me for following him. But then, he smiled right at me and said, 'This is so fucking ridiculous. I can't get a fucking cab in fucking New York City at fucking five o'clock in the morning!' It was so unbelievable. Just like that, Mick Jagger starts talking to us! I just froze. I couldn't even speak. Mick Jagger, standing right next to me, talking to me about taxi cabs and New York City! Oh, Susie. Oh, girl. I wish you had been there."

At that moment, I'd wished so, too.

At the end of January, I got a telephone call from Vanessa, my cohort from the summer. She was home from boarding school, staying at her mother's house five blocks away. She wanted to know if I would come over. Her mother, she informed me, was having a "totally fucking pretentious dinner party" for some people from France.

"I figure if she can have, like, a zillion people over, I can have *one* friend," said Vanessa. Besides, as soon as her mother started drinking, she explained, it was open season on the liquor cabinet for us, too.

Vanessa's mother lived in a sprawling, high-ceilinged apartment on Central Park West crammed with artwork by Vanessa's father and godmother. No sooner did I arrive than Vanessa got a phone call from her boarding school boyfriend, and I was left alone in the middle of a crowded living room, wondering what to do with myself. Everyone else was French and at least twice my age; all I could see were the backs of people huddled in groups for conversation. Since just about the only French I spoke consisted of such captivating and useful observations as *Le tracteur est grand* (the tractor is big) and *Voici la bicyclette* (here is the bicycle), I sat by myself and tried to look riveting as I studied the bottom of my drink.

Then the doorbell rang, and Vanessa appeared from her bedroom to answer it. I started to follow her, but stopped at the entrance to the living room. Although the party was still in full throttle, everything suddenly got very quiet around me.

There, five feet in front of me in the vestibule, stood Mick Jagger. He said hello to Vanessa's mother and unknotted his scarf.

The surge of adrenaline I felt was so powerful that, for a moment, it knocked the wind out of me. It was like having a private earthquake. My knees started to buckle and the floor seemed to tilt beneath my feet. My breathing became staccato, nearly asthmatic. Feeling dizzy, I gripped the upholstery and tried not to faint. *Cool it, girl,* I told myself, my heart thumping wildly. *Do not be an idiot. You've just been given the gift of divine fate. Blow it, and you'll hate yourself for the rest of eternity.*

Be cool, now. Be cool.

Taking the cue from my daydreams, I decided that I would look far more blasé if I was not standing there directly in front of Mick, gaping idiotically as he unsnapped his parka. Yet I suddenly found I was incapable of moving—my legs were shaking—they seemed prepared to collapse beneath me. So I just stood there and tried to avert my eyes by feigning great interest in the light fixture. Eventually, Mick looked up and saw me. Most likely, he saw a small fifteen-year-old girl with eyes as big as chestnuts and a mouth as round as a small cantaloupe, making a deliberate effort not to look at him.

"'Ello," he said plainly.

It took me a moment to realize he was actually addressing me.

"Oh, hello," I said, trying to sound as casual as possible. I shrugged and made a gesture that I hoped would communicate something like: *Yes, I always stand like this, completely immobilized, clutching the sofa. And, my, is that not the most fascinating light fixture you've ever seen?*

Just then, Vanessa appeared in the doorway and asked me if I wouldn't like to talk to her for a minute. I noticed that she, too, was trying to sound as casual as possible. Both of us were talking in singsong, our voices chirpy with restraint. We sounded like two female impersonators.

As slowly as possible, we brushed past Mick Jagger and walked ever so nonchalantly down the long hallway. We stepped into her bedroom very calmly, then shut the door and proceeded to shriek and jump on the bed.

"Ohmygod! Can you fucking believe it? Mick Jagger! Right here, in this house!"

Frantically, we brushed our hair, put on gobs of lip gloss, doused ourselves in her mother's Halston cologne, and tried to look as grown-up as possible. Then we zoomed out of her room and, acting as if we had all the cool in the world, arrived breathlessly at her mother's elbow just as she was making introductions. She introduced Mick to Vanessa, then turned to me. Her words sounded in my ears were like the opening bars of Beethoven's Fifth Symphony: "Mick, this is Susie. Susie, this is Mick."

He reached out and took my hand.

From then on, the evening was all candles and glitter, clouds of white wine, and a room the color of amethyst. I was so delirious with adrenaline, for a while I thought I was having one of those outer-body experiences that precede a heart attack.

Mick, it turned out, spent most of the evening talking to me and Vanessa. I wasn't sure whether he was simply bored by the Parisians, or if he felt most comfortable playing to a teenage audience. Perhaps, tickled by our adoration, he enjoyed giving us the thrill of our lives. In any event, soon after we were introduced, he beckoned me to come sit beside him on the couch. Snaking an arm around me, he took my hand with a great, gallant gesture.

"So," he said, "what do *you* do all day?"

"Well," I said carefully. I tried to respond just as I'd imagined I would, very coolly and sophisticated, as if having rock stars ask me about my private life was a daily occurrence. "Naturally, I *do* attend high school. But really, that's just so I can complete my education and become a novelist."

For some reason, this seemed to amuse him. "A novelist," he grinned. "Really? You don't say?"

Suddenly, I wasn't quite sure how to proceed; I found myself completely straying from my script, telling him about high school and poetry and working for the Maysleses and how I'd had to fish Star Wars figurines out of the toilet all summer and how I could never figure out how to operate the electric can opener. Then, inexplicably, I began prattling on about theater, religion, and movies I'd seen. Mick kept holding my hand and grinning and nodding and interjecting, "Really? You don't say," over and over, and I supposed that he was rapt, but try as I might, I couldn't really focus on a single thing he was actually saying to me—or that I was saying to him. All I could concentrate on was that *I* was in a conversation with Mick Jagger, and that he was holding my hand, and that I was an idiot for not having a camera.

What I eventually did become aware of, however, was that Mick couldn't sit still. He was constantly moving: drumming his fingers, winking, making funny faces, rolling his eyes. He had a small diamond set in one of his front teeth; when he spoke, first his eyes (blue) would sparkle, then his diamond, then his whole smile. He seemed to glitter blue-silver-white, blue-silver-white, like Christmas lights. Also, he was dressed very casually—a green sweater and rust-colored slacks—nothing spectacular, certainly nothing at all that looked like it had been purchased at Bogie's. But what surprised me most of all was his head. It was enormous. Proportionally, it was one of the most enormous heads I'd ever seen. It seemed much too big for his body; it gave him the silhouette of a lollipop, a helium balloon. Why, he was almost a homunculus—an attractive homunculus with a seductive British accent—but a homunculus nonetheless.

As the evening wore on, my pulse slowed and oxygen slowly began returning to my brain. After dinner, Vanessa and I sat with Mick and Vanessa's godfather, Nigel (who, it turns out, was the one who knew Mick and had invited him to the dinner), drinking champagne out of Dixie Riddle Cups. By that point, Mick seemed sort of like a family friend. I began to notice that, in addition to a big head, he also had big pores. Pores like perforations. Looking at his face, I could see them sprinkled across his nose and cheeks without even squinting. And after dinner, Mick liked to hang out in the kitchen and pick at the leftovers—eating ham with his fingers and dipping it directly in the mustard jar—just like I did. He got some ham stuck in his teeth and fumbled around, looking for a napkin. And as the party splintered off into small clusters of conversation, he wandered around a bit lost in the apartment, too, just like any other normal person. At one point, he even had to ask where the bathroom was. It never once occurred to me to flirt with him. After all, he was thirty-six years old. That was *way* too adult.

Yet he remained, in my eyes, heroic. At one point after dinner, Mick, Vanessa, Nigel, and I were all in the kitchen, telling jokes. Nigel began one, "There's this Jew, you see . . ."

Having talked to me about religion, Mick knew that I was, at least in ancestry, Jewish. As Nigel launched into the joke, Mick looked at me, rolled his eyes, and said, "Hey Nige, I don't want to hear that one right now. Save it for later, huh?" Then he looked back at me and winked.

A few minutes later, as he was leaving the kitchen with Vanessa's mother, he asked her pointedly, "The girl in the kitchen, the one who's not your daughter?"

"Oh yes," she said. "That's Susie."

"Oh," he cooed loudly, drawing out his syllables. "She's *charming*."

Did he deliberately say this within earshot of me? Today, I'd put money on it. But at the time, overhearing his praise simply made me reel. My fantasy had come true—almost right down to the finest detail. *No one will ever believe me,* I thought. All my years of hyperbole and theatrics, and finally something big had actually, truly happened to me.

Yet toward the end of the evening, I wandered into one of the rooms looking for Vanessa, and found her, Mick, Nigel, and a handful of other guests watching *Saturday Night Live* on television. Mick invited me to join them; I noticed that both he and Nigel were sniffing a lot, wiping their noses from time to time, and laughing slyly at some shared inside joke.

After a moment, Mick looked over at me.

"You know you've got the biggest titties out of all the girls here," he said plainly.

"Excuse me?" I said. Some of the other guests giggled.

"Do you know you've got the biggest titties out of all the girls here?" he repeated again, much louder this time. Then he grinned a little, and motioned to my chest.

Today if I were to write this as a short story, this comment would provide the obvious moment of epiphany: A young girl, whose sexuality is just being awakened, fantasizes about a rock 'n' roll star. She dreams that one day they will meet, and that he will find her desirable. Then, miraculously, she has dinner with him. But instead of being the charming man she dreamed he would be, he humiliates her, making lewd comments about her body in front of the other guests. When he says these things, she suddenly realizes that the man she has idolized for so long is in fact vulgar and arrogant. The event marks the beginning of her disillusionment, the end of her innocence, the start of her true coming of age.

Yet while this chain of events is the most narratively and morally logical, it is not at all what actually happened. When Mick Jagger said to me, "you've got the biggest titties," I simply stood there, astonished. For one moment, my insecurity and self-loathing, my bickering parents, my loneliness and fear, all melted away. I looked at Mick, and I beamed. I said simply, "Thank you."

Chapter 7

Puberty, Sex, and Other Extreme Sports

MY FRIEND KENNY lost his virginity to his mother's mah-jongg instructor on a felt-covered mahogany table in the middle of his living room.

"My mother and her friends were in the kitchen having coffee. I'd just come home from bar mitzvah class. The instructor took one look at me, ripped off my yarmulke, and jumped me on top of the mah-jongg tiles," Kenny said, taking a swig from a bottle of Dr Pepper, then setting it down on the hood of a Buick. At Stuyvesant High School, it was Standard Operating Procedure to sit around on the cars parked outside the school and brag about our exploits before class. We snacked, made out, flirted, and gossiped endlessly on car hoods and fenders; if you parked anywhere on East 15th Street, your vehicle inevitably wound up serving as a rec room for some three thousand teenagers.

"What could I do?" Kenny shrugged. "She'd been with a bunch of Hadassah ladies all morning. She needed me. *Bad.*"

"I know how it is," a guy we called "T.J." sighed, setting his backpack down on a fender. "The woman who seduced me in the glass elevator of the Marriott was exactly the same way."

"You lost your virginity in a hotel elevator?" said my friend Dani.

T.J. pulled out a Frisbee and practiced spinning it around on his index finger. "Doesn't everybody?" he shrugged.

"Not me," said Jessica, a round, pimply redhead, removing a pack of cigarettes from the pocket of her overalls. "The first time I did it was on top of an amplifier with this record producer named Sergio. Afterward, he composed a song for me with Jimmy Iovine but it was, like, a really boring song."

"Well, gee, don't I feel old-fashioned," Dani said with some annoyance. "I thought losing it to my boyfriend at summer camp was special. What about you, Suze?" She and the other kids looked at me.

I took a deep breath and twirled a strand of my hair around my finger.

"Well, I *would* like to tell you all the details," I said coyly. "But really. The senator swore me to secrecy."

So okay: I was still a virgin. Probably some of the other kids were, too, sitting on the parked cars outside Stuyvesant High School, fabricating tales of fornication on top of dishwashers and motorcycles with Sergios and mah-jongg instructors and middle-aged women at the Stanford, Connecticut, Marriott. But by eleventh grade, I was convinced that every semi-attractive sixteen-year-old in the Free World was having sex except me. And while virginity might have been fine for the Virgin Mary, it didn't seem to make any other female I knew particularly noteworthy.

Maybe it was different elsewhere. No doubt, I imagined, there were plenty of God-fearing farm communities somewhere in the South or Midwest where girls still walked around in lace-trimmed ankle socks with matching headbands, and boys said "gosh darn" and "ma'am" and held their car doors open for you in the church parking lot. No doubt, these were places where chastity was still considered a virtue, where every year at the county fair, some flannel-shirted guy named Billy Dwayne Jr. went around pinning blue ribbons on all of the virgins along with the prize heifers and award-winning wheels of cheese.

But as far as I and my equally smug, pretentious friends were concerned, virginity was what separated the girls from the women, and we knew which camp we wanted to be in. We scoffed at the idea that "saving yourself" was a matter of morality or willpower. Who was anyone kidding? If you were a virgin, it was simply because no one wanted to fuck you. "She is chaste who is not asked," my friend William liked to say.

"Really? Getting laid meant all that to you?" said a friend of mine later—a friend who had, in fact, come from one of those very God-fearing farm communities I'd imagined beyond the Hudson. "Jeez. For us, sex was just something to do once we ran out of beer."

Just about the only person I knew who seemed to think the word "virgin" carried positive connotations was my biology teacher, a tiny, gray-haired spitfire who practically ricocheted off the walls with energy. She was named, aptly and improbably enough, Electra Demas. With her starched white blouses pinned neatly at her neck and her severe gray bun, Mrs. Demas appeared to have been teaching biology for at least two hundred years, yet this had done nothing to diminish her passion for it.

When she spoke, her eyes glittered feverishly and her words tumbled over themselves as if her voice was on fast-forward. "Okay. Today. Class," she'd say breathlessly. "The inner respiratory and reproductive systems of gladioli. Xylem and phloem. Photosynthesis. Stamen and seeds. Augh, it is all so compactly beautiful, you won't believe it." She clasped her hands together rapturously, then flung them wide open.

"Don't look at your textbooks. Don't look at your watch either, Louis Tedesco. Don't think I don't see you in the back row there. Look at me. Look at what I'm drawing on the board. The xylem. The phloem. Like this. They're long. They're striated. And they're precisely designed to transport nutrients, to perform a simple yet complicated exchange. Repeat after me, 'Xylem and phloem. Xylem and phloem.'"

You could come to class whacked out of your mind on crystal meth and fourteen cups of coffee and still not be able to keep up. Mrs. Demas spent the entire class zooming from one end of the blackboard to the other scribbling down elaborate formulas, rapidly sketching out diagrams of the digestive tracts of reptiles, and firing off scientific terminology. Watching her ping-pong across the room was like watching speeded-up footage from Wimbledon. By the end of each class I had neck strain from looking back and forth, and my friend Gary Cutick would throw down his pen in exhaustion. "Forget it," he'd say. "Who can keep up with this nut?"

"I'm not a nut, Gary Cutick," Mrs. Demas would call out without even turning around from the blackboard, where she was engaged in diagramming the complete nervous system of an iguana. "I, like you, am a mammal. Now pick up your pen."

As our biology teacher, Mrs. Demas was required by the New York City Board of Ed to teach us a unit on human reproduction and sexuality. As jaded and oversexed eleventh graders, we thought this requirement was beyond stupid, and so did Mrs. Demas.

"I'm not going to waste valuable class time reminding you how babies are made when half of you are already dry-humping in the hallways," she announced. Hearing her say the words "dry-humping" in her high, knitted grandmotherly voice made all of us titter and squirm.

"Oh suddenly, you're all uncomfortable?" said Mrs. Demas. "You think no one sees you, necking in the hallways every day? Well I do, and let me tell you, it's bad for your education. You boys, you kiss your girlfriends before class, then you get an enormous erection, and you can't think about anything else for the rest of the day."

Now no one was laughing. We had all developed a sudden interest in the floorboards.

"I'm a biologist. And I know better than any of you the risks involved with having sexual intercourse," said Mrs. Demas fervently. "In the end, there's only one way to protect yourselves. It's just one little word. One little word with just two letters. Can anyone tell me what that word is?"

For a moment, no one said anything. Then Louis Tedesco raised his hand.

"Go," he said. "G-O. Go."

"No, not 'go,' Louis," said Mrs. Demas, ignoring the symphony of hooting he'd inspired. "The correct word is 'no'—N-O—no. Not go. As long as you say 'no,' you'll save yourselves a lot of heartache."

She looked at all of us plainly, with something that bordered on pity. "Do not be ashamed of virginity, class. Embrace it. Take pride in it. Repeat after me, 'I'm proud to be a virgin. I'm proud to be a virgin.'" She pumped her fists back and forth vigorously, as if she were leading a marching band. "I'm proud to be a virgin," she chanted. "I'm proud to be a virgin."

"Easy for *her* to say," Gary muttered under his breath. "It's not exactly like she's beating them off with a stick."

As teachers went, Mrs. Demas might have been one of the sharper knives in the drawer, but God only knew where she got the idea that horniness and patience were in any way compatible, especially in us teenagers, who, as we all know, were not exactly renowned for our impulse control to begin with. Being told to "wait until marriage" was like being ordered to hold our breath for twelve years: it was physically impossible. I was so overheated and agitated myself, I was sure I'd spontaneously combust by eighteen.

Granted, my budding sexuality had not begun auspiciously. Back in junior high school, I'd been enrolled in a seminary run by the New York Quaker Society. Quakers, my mother had reasoned, were pacifists. With the exception of Richard Nixon, they were calm, wise, meditative people—people ideally suited, she believed, to handle the tsunami of melodrama known as my puberty.

The summer before I'd started seventh grade, I lost pounds and pounds of baby fat, turning from "round" to "petite" in a matter of months. When I set foot in the Friends' Meetinghouse that September, I found myself among the smallest girls in my class. Yet while the peacenik, abolitionist Quakers might have worked miracles on the Underground Railroad, they proved to be no match for a lunchroom full of twelve-year-old boys. Soon, I was getting teased all over again.

"Hey, Flatsy," Nathaniel Eggers hooted across the lunch room, holding up a Popsicle stick. "We found your long-lost twin here!"

"Why is Susan Gilman a 'carpenter's delight'?" Nelson McClintock called out. "Because she's thin and flat as a board and has yet to be screwed!"

"Susan is a pirate's treasure," announced Carter Rowe, pausing to reload mustard into the end of his straw. "Why? Because she's got a sunken chest! Get it? Get it?"

Oh, I got it all right.

I had no breasts. I couldn't even fit into a training bra. Those useless, 32-AAA bits of lace—designed mostly to humor anxious, pubescent girls anyway—flopped around my waist. Only my mother seemed to think this was okay.

"By the time I was eleven, I was a 32-D. It was awful," she groaned. "I used to carry all my books pressed against my chest, trying to flatten it down. Thank God you don't have to go through that."

She didn't seem to realize that while other kids my age were preparing for confirmations and bat mitzvahs, I'd developed a relationship with God that consisted solely of begging for breasts. *Please, just a 32-A or B. It doesn't have to be much. Just enough to put an end to what passes for wit in the seventh grade cafeteria.*

By the end of eighth grade, I was also the only girl who hadn't gotten her period. Anytime someone stormed into the bathroom, flung down her backpack, and moaned desperately, "Oh, shit. Does *anyone* here have a tampon?" I became secretly convinced that I had cervical cancer.

It was only when I was fourteen, and already in high school at Stuyvesant, that I, too, could finally tear into the girls' bathroom with a look of knowing distress on my face.

"Please, does anyone here have an extra tampon?" I'd plead, trying to contain my pride and glee.

"Sorry," one of my classmates would say, stubbing her cigarette out on the window ledge, "but I've stopped getting my period ever since I went on the pill."

———————

One morning at the beginning of my sophomore year, I arrived at school late. Only my friends David and Andy were still hanging around outside.

"Hey, kiddo," said David, rumpling my hair.

To compensate for having no discernible figure, I'd adopted a funky "individual" style that I'd actually stolen wholesale from Diane Keaton. By wearing oversized men's shirts and antique vests, I managed to camouflage my immaturity while earning the respectable nickname of "Annie Hall" among my classmates. I was essentially a flower child in drag, but what did I know? I liked to think that I'd developed a persona that was "cool," "artsy," and "sophisticated." A lot of the hottest alpha boys, however, just called me "little sis" and "kiddo" and all those other degrading euphemisms which meant, essentially, that they found me entertaining but unfuckable. I was somewhat popular, I supposed, but popular like a soft drink or a Casio watch.

Now I put down my book bag and gave David the usual hug hello. "So, kiddo, you going to English?" he yawned. Then, suddenly, he paused. "Wow," he said.

"What?"

He squeezed me and sort of patted me down. When he pulled back, he looked slightly astonished.

"Andy," he said. "Come over here and say hi to Susie."

"What? Oh. Hey, Suze," Andy said. He walked over and gave me his usual bear hug, too. Then he went rigid. "Whoa," he laughed. Then he held me tighter. "Whoa ho."

"What?" I said.

Andrew grinned not at me, but at David. "Someone's growing up," he chuckled.

By fifth period that day, Andrew had hugged me twice again in the hallway. "Yep," he said happily each time. "Still there."

His friend Mark, who usually completely ignored me, sauntered up to me in the hallway, too. "Hey, Susie," he grinned, slapping my hand as if we'd been co-conspirators all year. "How's it going, babe?" Then he, too, gave me an enormous, doting hug.

After Geometry class, Ira, another fantastically popular boy, came up to me. "Someone told me you really need a hug today," he said, embracing me warmly.

"Me too," said his friend, Adrian, softly. "Wow, that is amazing," he said after disengaging. "Thanks."

"Hey, Susie-Q," said Jeremy, a popular *senior* boy, no less, "Did I hear that somebody needs a hug?"

Everywhere I went, from the biology lab to the auditorium to gym, boys I barely knew were coming up and offering to hug me out of what they insisted was a profound concern for my happiness and welfare. It was like someone had sounded a dinner gong over my head or—from the way some guys were acting—an enormous dog whistle. Meanwhile, girls were starting to glare at me. My classmates Nancy and Margo pointedly snubbed me when I said hi in the bathroom.

"I don't know who the hell you think you are now," my friend Erica said after school. "But stay away from my goddamn boyfriend."

As soon as I got home, I called my friend Vanessa at boarding school and burst into tears, recounting every interaction to her in minute detail—the strange, amazed looks from my guy friends, the sudden, seething anger from girls—the spooky, unsettled feeling of being a monkey-in-the-middle, the unwitting punch line of some big group joke.

"Oh, Vanessa," I sniffled. "Can you figure out what's going on?"

"Well, I can't be sure," Vanessa said, "but it sounds like what's going on is that you probably need a bra."

I cradled the phone with one shoulder, unloosened my pink satin tie, and peeked down the front of my oversized shirt. It was true: for the first time, I couldn't see clear to my feet.

When Michelle got home from school, I dragged her out into the stairwell. "What do you think?" I said anxiously, gathering up the extra material of my shirt and pulling it tight against me. "Have I grown?"

Michelle lit a cigarette, shook out the match, and appraised me coolly.

"Girl," she said after a moment. "Your tits are enormous."

I flushed with embarrassment. "No. C'mon," I said. "Really."

"I'm serious. All of a sudden, you've got these really big-ass breasts."

"Nuh-uh," I said.

"You don't even know it because you're still walking around in those baggy Annie Hall get-ups. But I'm telling you, you've at least doubled in size since the summer."

"So, like, I've finally caught up?"

"Caught up? Oh, you're way beyond 'caught up,'" Michelle laughed. "What the hell have you been doing? Taking growth hormones?"

I shrugged. "Praying?"

"Well, stop praying," Michelle laughed. "Look at you. You've proved there's a God. And let me tell you, He has one sick sense of humor."

Before going bra shopping, Michelle thought it was a good idea for us to get really, really stoned first. Even though I usually avoided smoking pot because it made me paranoid and almost suicidally depressed, this time it seemed like a really good idea. Wanting breasts was one thing, but actually getting them the way I had was profoundly distressing. It was sort of like wishing for a puppy, then waking up one morning with a pit bull.

There were some girls I knew who were brought up to view their bodies as power tools. "With tits like those," my friend Dani's mother told her, "you can have anything in the world." But I'd never felt any command over my body, any sense of its potential for dominion. I tended to regard it, instead, as a kind of novelty store whose inventory was constantly changing—a curiosity of sorts that occasionally amused or offended the public. While I hadn't been thrilled with my role as everyone's cute little sister at school, it was at least something familiar, comfortable, nonthreatening. Big bazooms catapulted me into a whole new social stratum charged with competition and sexuality—where boys would behave like rabid dogs and girls would view me hostilely just for stepping into a party.

"Listen to me, this is a beautiful thing, okay?" Michelle said, putting her arms around me. "Don't worry. We'll fix you up nice. Now here," she said, handing me a joint roughly the size of a tampon. "Take another toke and think to yourself, 'It's not just a bra, why, it's *lingerie.*'"

When we finally stumbled off the escalator at Macy's, I was so stoned, I was practically catatonic. But this was okay: with all of its flesh-colored rubber, restraining straps, and eerie, empty bodices, a bra department can be a fairly sinister place even when you're not fried out of your mind.

"You're still tense. Why are you tense?" said Michelle. "Look, I'm ordering you not to be tense, okay?"

She grabbed a giant, pointy bullet bra off one of the racks and stuck it on her head like a pair of ears. "Give to da Easter Bunny," she yipped, then hopped around the underwear display like a rabbit. I slid down on the floor and started laughing like a lunatic. Then I reached up for a black bra, draped it over my eyes and shouted, "Hey. Who turned off all the lights?"

"Bunny, bunny, bunny," said Michelle.

At this point, one of the salesladies decided it was in everyone's best interests to pick me up off the floor and hustle me into a dressing room as quickly as possible.

"Let me guess," she deadpanned. "You're here for your first bra."

She was a rotund woman in a tight apricot sweater and big plastic glasses hanging on a chain around her neck. Her name tag read "Barbara."

"Wow. 'Barbara.' That's almost like being named Bra-Bra, isn't it?" Michelle said. "How lucky are you? Bra-Bra and you're selling bras? I mean, it wouldn't be nearly as funny if you were, like, in the lawn mower department."

I could tell by the way Barbara ignored this that she was used to all sorts of imbecilic behavior and that ours was not impressing her. Pinning a measuring tape quickly around my torso, she announced, "You're a 36-C. You'll do best with an underwire. I'll bring you a couple of styles. Any particular color?"

"Pink!" I nearly shouted. "Hot pink, baby pink, pink-pink!"

"Of course," Barbara said dryly. "To match the color of your eyes."

By the end of sophomore year, my body had become like a creation of science fiction, a mad doctor's concoction that spins out of control and accidentally takes on a life of its own, growing to full maturity in a matter of seconds, sprouting appendages, swelling and erupting with muscles and flesh that expand to the point of bursting. In the six months after Mick Jagger himself had declared my breasts officially large, I grew yet another bra size, shot up three inches in height and went up two and a half shoe sizes. Although I dieted furiously, my jeans became inexplicably tighter. Sometimes I had to excuse myself from Geometry, go to the bathroom, and sit in a stall with my pants unzipped for a few minutes to ease the strange aching pressure I felt on my hip bones, straining outward against the fabric as if they were being jacked apart by machinery.

No longer was I "Fatso," "Flatsy," or even "Lil Sis" and "Kiddo." Oh no. Now, whenever I walked into history class, my friend Victor climbed up on top of his desk, pointed at me, and shouted like an ecstatic hillbilly, "Why, look, boys! There's gold in them thar hills!"

By age fifteen, I'd inhabited four different body types. I'd been chubby, skinny, flat-chested, and voluptuous. From this, I'd learned a crucial lesson: size didn't matter. No matter what kind of figure you had, someone always felt compelled to dream up some sort of asinine and degrading nickname for you.

———————

Once I had breasts, however, it seemed that boys wanted to play with them. Better yet, I wanted them to. The same hormones that had caused my body to go into overdrive were doing the same thing to my libido. I felt feverish, almost dizzy with longing. I walked around Stuyvesant High School and the whole of New York City in a fugue of perpetual arousal, writhing inside my skin, tingling, emboldened and ambitious with yearning.

In the past, my mind had been occupied with occasional, semi-useful thoughts such as: *If you make decorative covers for all your book reports, you may be able to create the illusion of actually having read the books.* Or: *By moving the bathroom scale to where the floor warps and climbing onto it after you pee, you can knock a half-pound off your weight.* But now, besides becoming famous for as-yet-undetermined talents, almost all I ever thought about was sex. The moment something even remotely reminded me of fooling around, it was like hearing "Billy Don't Be a Hero" on oldies radio—it inevitably took up permanent residence in my head for the next seven weeks, and I couldn't concentrate on anything else.

In school, I'd arrange my face into something I hoped approximated interest, then spend entire class periods staring off into space and reliving some torrid episode in which I'd made out with Mark in the hallway during Ronit Simantov's Sweet Sixteen.

"Jesus, what's wrong with me?" I asked my friend Jeff one day. "I think about sex constantly. It never lets up."

"Welcome to my world, sweetheart," Jeff said grimly, clomping me on the back. "And let me tell you: it's a bitter, bitter place."

Having a liberal, hippy-dippy upbringing has its drawbacks, but restraint, sexual repression, and guilt are not three of them. Boys wanted to fool around with me, and I wanted to fool around with them, and we all ended up feeling like we'd just won the lottery.

I loved fooling around. I loved the buildup to the very first kiss, then the frantic, semi-inept scramble of it. I loved the mounting adrenaline, and the way boys looked at me with astonishment, with reverence. The way their fingertips burned into me, branding my skin with the memory of it.

But it was also funny. Sexually, boys were about as complicated as a Pez dispenser. You showed them a nipple, they got an erection. It was Pavlovian, not exactly the stuff of higher primates. When boys were aroused and you fooled around with them, they were reduced to babies. Naked in their hunger, greedy in their needs, they whimpered and begged, then became prostate with gratitude. *Oh please. Oh yes. Oh mama,* they moaned, crumpling to their knees. Yet afterward, they strutted around purporting to be these great studs, masters of the bedroom, steely with virility. "Oh, man, did I get some this weekend," they bragged to each other in the hallway at school, as if they'd stolen or won something—when really, of course, we girls were merely being *charitable.* After all, we were at least as horny as they were.

This was another discovery, in fact: most of my girlfriends felt at least as overheated as I did.

"Augh. Don't you wish we could make out for college credit?" said my friend Jill.

Every time Jill or I hooked up with somebody, we immediately had to tell each other about it in painstaking detail. We were obsessed: *first he was like, then I was like, then he said, then I went . . .* The majority of fooling around we did took place fleetingly and clandestinely, in the urban equivalent of the back seat of a car: in stairwells, on park benches, in apartments where someone's parent was expected home imminently. Since this was in the Teenage Dark Ages when no one had pagers, cell phones, or e-mail yet, my friends and I actually had to call each other on the family phone and communicate to each other in code.

"Hey. Can you talk?"

"Um. We're just, uh, finishing dinner."

"So just say the first initial."

"Okay. M."

"Michael? Michael Barlow?"

"Uh huh."

"That guy from your chemistry class?"

"Yuh uh. Can you believe?"

"How far?"

"Um—hang on a second. No, Ma, I don't want any more chicken, thanks. Um—"

"Just give a number."

"Well, sort of two. Between two and three."

"Between?"

"You know, *on*—"

"But not *in*?"

"Exactly!"

"Ohmygod!"

———————

Occasionally, as I mashed against walls and wriggled out of my bra, I worried that I'd get branded a slut. But then, after having been called Fatso, Flatsy, Skinny Bones, and Kiddo, "Slut" actually sounded pretty terrific to me. Who, after all, called girls "sluts"? Boys who wanted desperately to fool around with them, and other girls who were jealous. "Slut" was the height of flattery, when you really thought about it.

Oh, how I loved the idea of being considered wild—a sexual tempest, a roiling tidal wave of desire, a paragon of erotic expertise. "Wow, that Susie Gilman," I imagined the boys at school saying. "That girl is a volcano."

There was only one small problem: how could you be a volcano when you were still a virgin?

Of course, no matter where you grow up, if you're female, you somehow get the message that there's only one way you're *really* supposed to lose your virginity. Teenage boys, of course, are encouraged to approach sex like shoplifting—*who cares who, what, or where—grab it whenever you can!* But girls still get the idea that there's a *right* way to lose it, and a *wrong* way.

The right way is with a guy you're totally, completely in love with, and who is so totally, completely in love with you that he'd be willing to die for you—or at least do the next best thing and marry you.

The wrong way to lose your virginity is, of course, every way else.

Even in hipper-than-thou New York City, in the pre-AIDS 1980s, Endless Love was still held up as the Gold Standard for Virginity Loss. And yet, almost every one of my friends—God bless 'em— opted to lose her virginity the "wrong" way. In fact, in the hundreds of virginity stories I've heard over the years, exactly three women I've ever met actually lost their virginity on a proverbial bed of rose petals to their worshipful One True Love. For the rest of us, when it came right down to it, Boredom, Curiosity, Horniness, and Inebriation pretty much won out.

"Getting it over with" ranked much higher, in the end, than romance. "Well, I don't know, I was at this party, the guy was cute, and I just thought, 'Why not?'" my friend Judy shrugged. "Besides, we were on top of a pool table. How cool is that?"

With so much expectation and gravitas attached to virginity for so long, a lot of girls I knew just said: *fuck it,* and proceeded to have sex for the first time with as little ceremony as they put into getting a haircut. More than a couple of my friends lost it to guys at "the parents are away" parties out in Brooklyn and Queens, where they fumbled through the act hastily in a paneled rec room while "Stairway to Heaven" blared over the stereo and other drunken kids pounded on the door yelling, "C'mon. Hurry up in there. Tony wants his bong!"

Yet literary aspirant and drama queen that I was, I wanted to lose my virginity in a way that was special—or that would at least make for good copy. On numerous occasions, I'd had the chance to have sex in a stairwell or on the rooftop of someone's apartment building. But how would that sound? In the likely event that Hollywood one day turned my life into a made-for-TV biography, I didn't want to be known as the glamorous, world-famous something-or-other who lost her virginity under a heating duct. I didn't want to "just get it over with" with one of the cute, swaggering, beer-chugging guys at my school, who'd inevitably spend the next Monday morning high-fiving his friends in the hallway and bragging to everyone while treating me, personally, as if I had the plague.

But what if, by the end of senior year, I was the only virgin left in the entire Tristate Area? This actually struck me as a distinct possibility. And I was certain that, for the rest of my life, my sexual status as a sixteen-year-old would remain my only memorable and defining quality. *Oh yes. Susie Gilman,* my classmates would say at my twenty-fifth high school reunion. *That pathetic girl who was still a virgin at graduation.*

At night, I'd lie awake, watching the lights of the city play over my ceiling, trying to imagine what sex really, actually felt like. I'd been to third base by then (whatever *that* was—apparently, it's still being debated), but intercourse itself still seemed so far away somehow, so abstractly momentous.

"Tell me," I begged my nonvirgin friends. "What does it feel like?"

I thought they'd be able to explain to me the exact sensation of having a boy inside you. I had the idea that during sex, you experienced some great shivery, physical epiphany that transformed you on an almost molecular level into a more sophisticated, more evolved human being.

But all my friend Judy could say was, "What did it feel like? Like I'd impaled my twat on a hockey stick, that's what it felt like."

The problem with wanting to lose my virginity to the "right person," however, was that I had absolutely no idea who this might be. I had plenty of boyfriends—cute Frisbee players I regularly hung out with in the park—but none of the all-consumptive, gushy, monogamous love I saw portrayed in made-for-TV movies. When my friends Gabi and Melissa sat on the steps after school, describing their "perfect guy" and "ideal relationship," it occurred to me that, while I had easily mapped out in my mind half a dozen elaborate scenarios in which I'd win the Pulitzer Prize before college, I had only the vaguest idea of what my "perfect guy" might be like. Other than looking like either a young Mick Jagger or an alive Jim Morrison, my "perfect" guy, as far as I could tell, had only one distinguishing characteristic: the ability to read minds. In the scenarios I imagined, he was able to divine all my romantic fantasies and secret longings almost telepathically, then effortlessly fulfill them. He'd be forever appearing on my doorstep with armfuls of roses, declaring his love for me over the school PA system, and making snow angels in the yard beneath my window (in the imaginary house I also happened to live in). To that end, my only concept of an "ideal relationship" consisted of a guy telling me I was beautiful about a thousand times a day and winning stuffed animals for me at amusement parks.

My friend Jill had an actual steady boyfriend named Kyle. Kyle came over to Jill's apartment after school several times a week, sometimes staying for dinner or watching college football with Jill's dad. Over the summer, he joined her family for weekends at their beach house in Fire Island, and conferred secretly with Jill's mother about what jewelry to get Jill for her sixteenth birthday. He saw Jill every day at school, and once when she got really drunk, Kyle held her hair back for her as she threw up in the bathroom.

I'd sooner stab myself in the head with an ice pick than let a guy get that close to me. Although I pined away for "a serious boyfriend," the thought of actually bringing one home made me physically ill. My home life was atrocious. My mother and I fought constantly. We had arguments that were prototypes for parents and teenagers everywhere, based largely on my mother's fascistic belief that our house was not a hotel, and my reasonable insistence that I was old enough to stay out until 2:00 A.M. on weekends.

"As long as you're living in my house, you're subject to my rules," my mother would shout. "Do you understand me?"

"Well, whoever said I wanted to live in your house, huh?" I'd scream back. "I never asked to be born. I never asked to live here. I never asked to have you as my mother with your STUPID, INSANE, TOTALITARIAN CURFEWS. All my other friends get to stay out AT LEAST an hour later than I do!"

"YOU DON'T LIKE IT HERE? THEN LEAVE!"

"FINE! I WILL!" (At this point, I'd dramatically yank a duffel bag out of the closet and start stuffing my underwear into it.)

Not coincidently, most of my girlfriends had equally lousy relationships with their mothers; we were constantly telephoning one another in tears or turning up on each other's doorsteps. One weekend when Vanessa was home from boarding school, I arrived at her apartment with my duffel bag.

"Oh, Susan. How very nice to see you," Vanessa's mother said sweetly, opening the door. "Are you all right?"

"Yuunnhh," I started to sob. "I just had a fight with my mother. She threw me out again."

"Oh, sweetie," said Vanessa's mom. "I'm so sorry. I would invite you in for a nice cup of tea, but as you can see," she gestured down the hallway of the apartment, where I could see Vanessa hurling clothes into an opened suitcase on the rug, "I'M THROWING VANESSA OUT THIS VERY MINUTE!" she shouted.

"YOU'RE NOT THROWING ME OUT!" Vanessa hollered. "I'M LEAVING!"

"SO GO!" yelled her mother. "TAKE YOUR BLOODY THINGS AND GO!" She turned back to me. "Ever so sorry, Susan," she said cheerily. "Perhaps next time."

Yet like most teenagers, of course, I believed that my family alone was straight out of "Ripley's Believe It or Not." No doubt, if I brought my boyfriends home, my father would wind up telling them one belly-flop of a joke after another, while my mother would walk around in her favorite novelty T-shirt that said "Don't Let the Turkeys Get You Down," and ask them what their zodiac sign was.

Worse still, what would guys discover if they really saw *me*? What if they thought my record collection wasn't cool enough? What if they saw I still had a dollhouse stored in my closet? What if they noticed that my inner thighs touched and I had to keep flipping my hair to keep it from falling flat? Whenever I was with a boy, I assumed that if he knew the "real me," all he'd see was the former outcast: *Fatso, skinny bones, flatsy. Eeeewww.*

Whenever a guy liked me, his desire for me almost instantly branded him a loser. I was as merciless on boys as I was on myself; I could forgive them nothing. A guy could be sweet, doting, and intelligent, but God help him if he met me at the movies wearing a dorky terry cloth shirt and a puka shell bracelet. God help him if he sweated too much, related an inane joke he'd seen on TV, or ordered a silly-sounding cocktail. I couldn't bear to be around anyone as imperfect as myself, as vulnerable, insecure, or unfinished. A boy's humanness mirrored my own, and I couldn't stand the sight of it. Fooling around for a night was one thing, but I wanted—no, I needed—anyone I slept with to be commanding, sophisticated, and more than a little unreal.

Three of my so-called boyfriends were high school seniors who'd gone on to college. Such age and distance, in my mind, gave them special cachet and worthiness: they were, after all, older men! Whenever they came back to New York during school breaks, I mentally auditioned them.

Keith was a photographer, a free-spirited Frisbee player. I adored him, and sometimes, when we walked around Greenwich Village and did the I-Ching together, I believed he was my soul mate. But for soul mates, we had an awful lot of parents constantly walking in on us, and then he always headed back to college.

Jeremy was gorgeous and an excellent kisser, but had the irritating habit of tweaking me on the nose playfully, then chiding, "Virginity isn't an incurable disease, you know," which invariably made me feel like I was six years old and sitting on the knee of some perverted Santa Claus.

Then there was Jake, who had all the charm and dazzling good looks of a young presidential candidate and just about as little sincerity. Whenever he saw me, he'd stagger backward and clutch his chest dramatically, feigning a heart attack. "Whoa, Susie," he'd gasp. He'd then proceed to use lines on me that he'd clearly picked up from movies. Seeing as I myself was a creature of self-invention, this actually impressed me. Unlike most of the guys I knew, whose idea of seduction was to say, "Hey, wanna check out the stairwell?" Ivy League Jake would take me to wine bars and order for us both in French. Then he'd lean over the hurricane candle, entwine his fingers in mine, and say, coyly, "So, what are your thoughts on Nietzsche?"

"Oh, I absolutely love him," I'd purr. "Especially his earlier films."

Best yet, Jake had about a zillion other girlfriends and a sexual appetite that bordered on Attention Deficit Disorder. He was someone I could become completely infatuated with—without any threat of prolonged, actual contact.

One weekend when he was home, he encouraged me to visit him at college. "You'd love university life," he said magnanimously. "With your mind and your body, you *deserve* university life."

I don't think he expected for a minute that I'd actually take him up on his offer, but little did he know: I'd made up my mind. So, in fact, had my friend Jill. We'd decided to lose our virginity on the same night so we could compare notes afterward and talk about it incessantly. "Ohmygod," we squealed to each other in whispers over the phone, "how totally cool would *that* be?"

After the requisite lies-to-parents and logistics were all worked out, I surprised Jake in his dorm room in New England on Valentine's Day in subzero weather. Conveniently, I neglected to mention to him that I was still, in fact, a virgin, because the weekend, in my mind, was about being fabulously sexy and passionate, which as far as I could tell were qualities that almost by definition required people to misrepresent themselves. As I liked to see it, Jake and I were two brilliant, sophisticated lovers having a weekend tryst that might kick off an epic, decades-long affair that would span several foreign cities and perhaps even cause an international scandal, but that would never, under any circumstances, run the risk of him having to meet my parents or see me in my sweat pants.

And so.

What is there to say about losing your virginity that hasn't been said a zillion times before? Probably nothing. Assembling a bookshelf from IKEA requires greater dexterity. From everything friends had told me, I was expecting obliterating pain, and when this didn't happen, the relief I felt was as good as pleasure. Jake was probably as skilled and valiant as any nineteen-year-old lover could be, but to tell you the truth, I wasn't paying much attention. I was too busy thinking about how cool it was that he'd lit candles beforehand and put on Ravel's *Bolero*—just like in the movie *"10"* with Bo Derek! *This is it,* I kept thinking. *I'm losing my virginity.* Then I'd look at Jake's Indian bedspread, at his muscular shoulders, at his art history books, and the illuminated dials blinking on his stereo and think: *Okay, now remember every single detail of this night, because you're losing your virginity.* What was I planning to do? Tell my grandchildren about it one day? Apparently so.

I'm losing my virginity! I thought ecstatically.

I'm losing my virginity!

"Do you like this?" Jake asked at one point. "You seem a little distracted."

"What? Yeah. No. Great. Whatever," I said.

I'm losing my virginity!

Had I been doing this in an ancient culture, I thought, I might have been considered ruined for the gods. I might have been forced to become a concubine. I might have been stoned to death, or banished from my village, or sent off to a nunnery. Why, I might have been deemed unmarriageable, or cursed for bringing shame upon my family. I'd be branded a fallen woman, a harlot, a Jezebel.

Wow, I thought excitedly. *Wait till I tell my friends about this.*

It was close to midnight on Valentine's Day, and I was crossing a threshold, permanently altering my status in the world: just as my friend Jill was doing at that very moment, just as billions of lovers had done before and would certainly do again. This was the moment that all my speculating and desire had come down to. It was, in its way, poignant and beautiful, but it was also really no big deal.

Maybe that was the reason that sex received so much hype, it occurred to me later. It was actually one of the simplest acts to perform. As I myself had proven, any idiot could do it. It was the easiest club in the world to get into, but you never knew it until you became a member yourself. And so, people tried to make it elite. My friends and I had yearned to be in it, and in the end, we lost our virginity more for each other and ourselves than for any of the boys we were actually with. We lost our virginity for the glamorous creatures we hoped to become, for the privileges we imagined we'd enjoy, for the experiences we longed to understand and master.

"Are you all right?" Jake whispered when it was over.

"Yeah. Absolutely. Great," I said, smiling at him in the candlelight. Though what I really wanted to say to him, of course, was, "Hey, now that it's over, mind if I borrow your phone?"

Chapter 8

My Brilliant Career

IT'S A TRIBUTE to my father that he never took much of what I said as a teenager to heart, but saw it instead as an endless source of entertainment for him and his friends. My senior year of high school, I came up with a brilliant career plan. It was so brilliant, in fact, that I believed it required me to leave school early and go downtown to his office to tell him about it.

Instead of becoming something dreary like a federal prosecutor or a brain surgeon, I announced, I was going to become a belly-dancing astrologer. My days would be spent alternately reading people's horoscopes and delivering Bellygrams. Bellygrams, along with strip-a-grams and singing gorillas, were at that moment one of the newer and more imaginative ways to humiliate your loved ones on special occasions.

"Think of it," I said. "I'll be my own boss. I'll never get bored. And I'll get to subvert the patriarchy."

"Subvert the patriarchy" was a term I'd recently picked up from one of the many feminist texts I'd been reading. As far as I could tell, it meant any activity that disrupted men's business-as-usual.

By delivering Bellygrams, I imagined, I'd be called upon to regu-larly surprise corporate CEOs for their birthdays. By interrupting their meetings with shareholders, climbing on top of conference tables, and gyrating wildly, I figured I'd be disrupting business-as-usual every day—in a gold lamé bikini, no less. Plus, I'd acquire killer abs, free up my afternoons to do people's astrology charts, and possibly arrange to sleep late. What more could anyone possibly want from a career?

"See, Dad?" I said. "I've got it all figured out."

Earlier that month, my father had shelled out roughly three million dollars in application fees for various colleges I'd applied to. Nevertheless, as soon as I finished explaining my plans to him, he declared them "ingenious."

"And the fact that you've never taken a single belly-dancing class in your life should in no way stop you," he proclaimed, pounding his desktop with conviction. "You go full speed ahead."

"Really?" I said.

"Absolutely," my father enthused. "I mean, who needs another doctor or scientist or do-gooder in this world? I say, bring on the dancing girls. In fact," he said, "it's such a good idea, I think we have to share it with your Uncle Arthur."

He reached over, pressed a speed-dial number, then said, "Arthur? You ready for something? Listen to my kid's latest career plan." Then he motioned for me to talk into the speakerphone. When I finished, he said, "Isn't that great, Arthur? Isn't that just too much?"

"Oh, it's too much, all right," said Arthur's disembodied voice. "A feminist belly-dancing singing telegram with a side business in the occult. Who could want more for their daughter?"

"I mean, you can't make this stuff up, can you Arth?" my father said.

"No," Arthur said, "you certainly can't."

"Hey," I said, frowning. "You two aren't just humoring me, are you?"

"Of course not," said Arthur. "What makes you say that?"

"We're just being supportive," said my father. "In fact, you know who else I think would be really supportive? Your Uncle Fred. Let's call him next."

My father, I realize now, was only too used to my histrionics and politics. In first grade, when Christopher Kleinhaus led the boys in a rousing chorus of "Boys Rule, Girls Drool" I'd come up with the witty rejoinder, "Girls Smart, Boys Fart," which I'd proceeded to chant around the house for weeks afterward. In grade school, annoyed that history only seemed to be about men, I made a point of reading hundreds of biographies of famous women, then sprinkled my dinnertime conversation with statements like, "Well, Phillis Wheatley, the black American poet, and Elizabeth Blackwell, the first woman doctor, probably didn't eat their vegetables either."

To me, it was always a foregone conclusion that girls were at least as good as boys. How could we not be? For starters, we were prettier. And we had better clothes.

My parents, to their credit, encouraged me. In an act of supreme masochism, they even bought me the single of Helen Reddy's "I Am Woman," knowing full well I'd play it no less than eighty-seven times in a row on my portable record player. And when I had to get glasses in sixth grade, they consoled me by saying I looked exactly like "a miniature Gloria Steinem," even though, as we were all well aware, my resemblance was actually a lot closer to R2-D2.

Once I reached high school, however, my father seemed to regard my feminism with a growing sense of bemusement. Whenever I sat at the dinner table, reading aloud from *Ms.* magazine and informing him that he and my brother were patriarchal oppressors, a big grin would seep onto his face.

"What? What's so funny?" I'd say.

"Nothing," he'd chuckle.

"Well, good," I'd say, "because there's nothing funny about clitoridectomies and workplace discrimination, you know."

"I'm not saying there is," said my father. "I just think it's cute how you call me a patriarchal oppressor, then fifteen minutes later, you hit me up for money so you can go to the movies."

Though I hated to admit it, he did have a point. I'd been so busy studying how oppressed I was that I'd somehow never gotten around to liberating myself from my five-dollar-a-week allowance.

Granted, to save for college, I'd spent summers working as a mother's helper, providing unsuspecting families with my imaginative idea of child care. And during the school year, I juggled baby-sitting gigs, where, for a whopping 75 cents an hour, I rummaged through people's record collections and cleaned them out of Diet Pepsi and Triscuits. But now, I realized, it was time to get a real job. A job that paid me with a check, not laundry quarters. A job that gave me a modicum of independence, dignity, and, most of all, feminist credibility.

Since the McDonald's and Burger King in my neighborhood pretty much doubled as outpatient facilities, I applied to work at Häagen-Dazs.

"Why do you want to work at Häagen-Dazs?" the bored-looking manager asked, reading off a laminated script.

I considered responding: *To overthrow the patriarchy, of course.* But instead I answered, "Because I totally love Häagen-Dazs."

I said this hoping to demonstrate my expertise and enthusiasm for the product. Instead, I ended up giving him the distinct impression that I'd spend every spare moment on the job drinking chocolate milkshakes in the supply closet—which was exactly what I'd been planning on doing, actually.

Blacklisted by Häagen-Dazs, I proceeded to have several equally fruitless interviews at David's Cookies, Yogurt, Yogurt!, and a place called the Nut Hutch until finally landing an after-school job at a gourmet coffee bar called Shuggie's. By that time I'd wised up and told the owner that, while I, personally, would sooner drink lighter fluid, I had no political objections to serving coffee to other people.

Shuggie's was one of several food outlets inside the atrium of a midtown office building. Decorated from floor to ceiling in bone-white ceramic tile, it had about as much ambience as a giant urinal. Nevertheless, it did a brisk business selling specialty coffees, baked goods, and something called "gourmet minute-meals" to legions of frazzled and churlish office workers.

My job was to stand behind the counter—a space just slightly narrower than an economy class airplane seat—and fill orders at a breakneck pace alongside a crew of other servers. Until then, the totality of my food service experience had consisted of making peanut-butter-and-jelly sandwiches for screaming toddlers. At first, I worried I was under-qualified, but it soon became clear that most people in the throes of caffeine withdrawal are pretty much indistinguishable from three-year-olds. Certainly, they have the same pathetic lack of patience, manners, and reading skills. At Shuggie's, a huge illustrated sign above the counter read:

WHAT IS A MINUTE-MEAL?
1 HOMEMADE SANDWICH + 1 SIDE SALAD + 1 BROWNIE.

In case you missed this, smaller replicas of the sign flanked the two pillars at the entrance and were laminated onto the counter. Yet nine times out of ten, customers barged in, planted themselves directly underneath the sign, squinted up at it, then said after a moment, "So, like, what exactly is a minute-meal?"

My first day on the job, I punched in my time card and tied on my apron with a flourish of pride. Ironically, while I'd always felt contempt for uniforms, just seeing a classmate in a paper hat had never failed to impress me. Occasionally, I'd run into kids from Stuyvesant at their after-school jobs at Papaya King or Blimpie's. Standing behind counters in their regulation outfits, they never looked like the goof-offs who sat in the back row in trigonometry amusing themselves by clipping ballpoint pens to their lips. Rather, they seemed suddenly transformed into authority figures, into fine young men and women capable of shouldering great responsibilities and making fresh sandwiches.

Now, I thought triumphantly, I, too, was a member of this elite workforce. I was competent, payable, charged with duties that extended far beyond the menial demands of my high school. I was Working Woman: Hear me roar.

"Okay, any moron can do this job," said Mercedes, the aspiring dancer-actress who'd been assigned to show me the ropes. "The only skills you might ever need are crowd control and anger management."

As Mercedes showed me how to refill a napkin dispenser, she said, "When people wait on an ice cream line, they're waiting for a treat. So they're happy, they're thinking, what flavor should I get? They don't mind the anticipation. But a coffee line is for drug addicts. And drug addicts are assholes."

She motioned toward a pudgy man with a tweed blazer and a salt-and-pepper beard who'd just bellied up to the counter.

"Take this piece of work. Thinks he's King Henry the Eighth. He's here all the time. Observe." Mercedes slapped down her dishrag and sidled over to the register.

"Yes?" she said.

"This is what I want," the man bellowed, not looking at her, but past her. "I want a large coffee with lots of half-and-half. But *heat* the half-and-half separately, will you, in that microwave over there? Set it for five seconds, then stir it, then heat it for another five seconds. Otherwise, the cream clumps. Last time someone did it for me here, they did it wrong and the cream was like cottage cheese. It was disgusting. Who puts cottage cheese in coffee? So heat the cream. Then *add* it to the coffee. And then, *before* you put on the lid, add one packet of Equal."

Mercedes looked at him. "So, like, wait," she deadpanned. "You said you wanted coffee?"

Potty-mouthed, sarcastic, and embroiled in petty melodramas, my fellow co-workers could not possibly have been more appealing. In addition to Mercedes, there was Alicia, a bass player who went to an "alternative high school" and wore so much black eyeliner she appeared to have been beaten-up permanently. Alicia worked quickly and sullenly, murmuring under her breath, "I swear to fucking God, if that guy asks me one more time what a minute-meal is, he's going to learn how to use it as a rectal suppository."

Timothy, the fourth horseman of our little Apocalypse, was studying to become a hair stylist. "Tah-dah," he announced the first day he walked in. Snapping his fingers as if they were castanets, he pivoted around to model his newly peroxided hair and matching goatee. "So what do you think? Am I a California cabana boy or simply an albino Vincent Price?" Then he froze and gasped in mock horror. "Oh my god," he cried. "Could I possibly be *more* gay?"

"Timothy, this is Susie," Mercedes said, introducing us.

Timothy proffered his hand disdainfully. "Timothy Cashmere," he announced. "The bold and the beautiful."

"Susie Gilman," I replied. "The subtle and chaste."

"Oh," Timothy grinned wickedly. "I like you."

Surrounded by such madcap cohorts made me feel like we weren't working so much as *performing*. In the caste system of midtown Manhattan office buildings, of course, we were practically Untouchables—second only to janitors and bike messengers, really. And yet, we remained convinced that we were actually vastly superior to everyone else. With their asphyxiating neckties, constricting panty hose, and pasty, haggard faces, our customers clearly held dull corporate jobs that wore away at their soul like iron filings. So okay, we might have been mopping floors and spilling coffee on them for minimum wage. But ultimately, we were headed someplace far bigger and more spectacular than theirs—to college, to beauty school, to the Broadway stage. Their jobs were like terminal illnesses. Ours, we bragged to one another, were merely temporary.

My first week, I almost couldn't wait to get to Shuggie's. I loved telling my friends after school, "Sorry. Gotta run. My shift starts in twenty minutes." How grown-up did that sound? To boys I had crushes on, I casually let it drop where I worked. "It's right near Grand Central Station," I said offhandedly. "Stop by and I'll hook you up with a killer brownie."

Once I was on the job itself, I was swept up by the newness of it. The chronic, frenzied thrum behind the counter energized me, and the smell of freshly brewed coffee and baked goods almost gave me a contact high. A vast menagerie of humanity paraded in and out all afternoon, and I watched it with immense interest. The gum-cracking secretaries who gossiped about their love lives and manicures. The disheveled old woman who wandered from table to table pressing expired grocery coupons into the hands of bewildered strangers. The hordes of Japanese tourists who seemed delighted by the Lilliputian size of our minute-meals. The high-strung, chain-smoking security guard who regularly came in bug-eyed and beat jazz riffs on the countertop. The only people utterly lacking in visual interest were my bosses. Louie and Ida Shuggie were a paunchy, middle-aged couple who had been together so long that they'd started to look alike. Their faces were two collapsed puff pastries decorated with bifocals.

While everyone else ran around like maniacs, Louie Shuggie sat at a table in the corner sipping an extra-large café mocha and breathing through his mouth with audible *pfuffing* sounds. Once in a while, apropos of nothing, he'd glance at the mermaid tattooed on his forearm, as if to make sure it was still there, before calling out, "Did anyone check the coffee levels?" But otherwise, his one talent was to wait until the 3:30 P.M. coffee rush—when we had customers lined up out the door and the kitchen took on the feel of a sauna—to grab one of us by the wrist, hand us his empty cup, and mew, like a baby, "A little more mocha, please?"

While Ida didn't seem terribly inclined to help out either, she hovered over us like a gargoyle, calling into question every Styrofoam cup and plastic fork we discarded.

"What's wrong with these coffee stirrers?" she'd say, picking wooden sticks out of the trash.

"Mercedes used them to unclog the drain."

"So?" Ida said. "Rinse them off. It's not like wood grows on trees, you know."

Years of chain-smoking had left Ida's voice froggy, giving it a gruff, reptilian quality that carried over to her entire personality. "Who left this dishrag on top of the microwave? Get it out of here," was pretty much her standard greeting. As a feminist, I tried to give her the benefit of the doubt, seeing as we were both sisters in a Male Chauvinist World. But the truth was, except for Louie himself, I was hard pressed to find a more charmless person.

Ida seemed to have two all-consuming preoccupations. The first was "cuteness." While for most of us, "cuteness" was an admirable quality, for Ida, it meant anyone who annoyed her—which was pretty much everybody.

"That plastic wrap distributor, he thinks he's real cute," she'd say, stamping out a cigarette. "Charges us for twenty cases, then only delivers eighteen. Well, he'll get what's coming to him."

"Getting what's coming" seemed to be Ida's standard punishment for anyone who was "cute."

After badmouthing all the people in the food service industry who thought they were "real cute," Ida inevitably turned her guns on us. To hear her tell it, our entire staff was nothing but a bunch of seasoned degenerates. "I don't want any of you wisenheimers getting cute with me, either," she'd glower, pointing at us with her cigarette clamped between her knuckles. "If you so much as *think* about helping yourself to anything here that's not yours, you'll get what's coming to you so fast it'll knock your teeth out. Got that?"

Alicia just looked at Ida stonily, but I had to avoid eye contact with Mercedes and Timothy to keep from cracking up. Ida's obsession with honesty amused me to no end given how much Shuggie's lied to its customers about the food that it sold. The "homemade" cookies were shipped in from a bakery out in Red Hook, while the "fresh" chicken salad and cole slaw were loaded up with so much MSG that eating them bordered on an out-of-body experience. The "seasonal" fruit salad came in cans the size of paint drums; it was our job to doctor it up by picking out the dead-giveaway maraschino cherries and replacing them with cut-up days-old bananas and apples. The only truly homemade thing at Shuggie's was its freshly squeezed orange juice, and this was on the menu only because, two years ago, the Shuggies' daughter, Rhonda, had gone on a juice diet.

"We plunked down four hundred bucks for this industrial-sized juicer, and then she gave up after only three weeks because she claimed it was turning her skin orange," said Ida. "I told her, 'For Chrissake, Rhonda, it's not the fruit that's turning your skin orange, it's that bronzing creme you use.' But oh no. She thinks she's cute, my daughter. Would she listen? No. So now she's still fat, her skin is still orange, and I'm stuck with the goddamn juicer."

The other subject that seemed to obsess Ida was virginity.

"Don't give it away, girls," she lectured us at the end of every shift as we hung up our aprons and primped to meet our boyfriends. "Get a ring on your finger first. I am telling you. Your hymen for a diamond."

When Mercedes and I snickered, she barked, "Don't get cute with me. Take it from one who knows. Men won't pay the cow if she gives milk for free."

"Oooh," said Timothy delightedly, raising his hand. "Who wants to field *that* one?"

"Shut up, Timothy. I'm not talking to you," Ida said. "I'm giving the girls here some valuable advice they're not going to hear from those ridiculous, hairy-legged women's libbers out there."

Mercedes nudged me and whispered, "Right. Because we all know how well Ida's advice works for her."

For a moment, I didn't get it. I was chewing over the remark about "hairy-legged women's libbers." I'd always shaved my legs, and what did leg hair have to do with wanting equal treatment under the law, anyway? I had the urge to stand up, hoist up my pant legs, and declare, *Well, Ida, I so happen to be a women's libber, and my calves are silky smooth, thank you very much.*

"What's that?" I said.

"Please," Mercedes said. "If he hasn't hit on you yet, it's only because he hasn't had the opportunity."

"Who?"

Mercedes motioned with her chin toward the table where Louie sat, scraping whipped cream from the bottom of his cup with a coffee stirrer, cocoa powder freckling his bifocals.

"No!"

"Mm hm," Mercedes said. "Every day, when he says he's going to check the inventory, he's really just sitting in the stockroom, waiting to ambush any girl who goes back there. So watch it."

"Ew. You have got to be kidding me," I said. "He's a rapist?"

Mercedes a gave a contemptuous little laugh. "Please, the man can hardly breathe without a respirator. He just comes up behind you, wraps his arms around your waist, and goes 'Gimme just one little kiss?' in that same awful baby voice he uses when he wants another mocha."

"That's disgusting," I said. "I'll kill him."

"No you won't," Mercedes said. "You'll be too busy laughing. He's just pathetic."

Still, I wasn't taking any chances. To apply for the job at Shuggie's, I'd worn the most winning outfit I owned: a black miniskirt, a pink button-down blouse, and black cowboy boots. When I asked Louie if he needed any references, he just looked me up and down, then shook his head. "Nah," he wheezed.

At the time, I'd simply chalked this up to his perceptiveness: clearly, here was a man who knew competence and intelligence when he saw it. Stupidly, I assumed the world would always be judging me by my own values, not by its own prize-winning set of perversions.

Looking around the restaurant, I realized that, except for Timothy and Eduardo—the Colombian dishwasher who was kept hidden away in the back—everyone on staff was a striking young female. In our slightly snug Shuggie's T-shirts, we were like the Playboy Club of gourmet coffee bars.

"From now on, I'm coming to work in sweatpants," I told Mercedes. "I, for one, will not be treated as a sex object."

The next week, I came to work wearing a track suit, and Louie did, in fact, notice.

"Hey, what happened to you?" he said. "Last week, you were such an attractive young girl."

I told him that working in food service with my skin exposed seemed like an invitation for health code violations.

"Besides," I couldn't help adding, "last time I checked, a woman's looks didn't have anything to do with her ability to brew coffee. I expect to be valued for my mind, not my body."

"Oh, great," Ida called across the counter. "Now you'll never get a husband."

Yet by late afternoon, she had another young woman to badger. The Shuggies' daughter, Rhonda, returned from vacation. Rhonda, it turned out, worked on the service line as a "counter manager."

Having heard Ida's description of her, I expected Rhonda to look like an obese tandoori chicken. Instead, a trim, tanned young woman fairly bounded into the coffee bar as if she'd just spent a rigorous day on the tennis courts.

"Hey, Ma. Hey, Timothy. Hey, Eduardo," she sang out, hugging everyone hello. "I'm Rhonda," she announced, then gave me a perfunctory hug, too. Her hair, I noticed, had been teased and moussed into a sort of mushroom cloud above her head, then dyed the color of overcooked spaghetti. Through her polo shirt, I could feel her ribs and the knobs of her spine. When she drew back, it was clear to me, too, that she'd had a nose job. While she had sleepy, hooded eyes like Ida's and thick, giblet lips like Louie's, her nose was minuscule, a pert gumdrop that gave you a view straight up her nostrils. Its shape and proportion were all wrong for her face. It reminded me of collages my brother and I used to make, where we'd cut out pictures of people's features from magazines, then paste them onto pictures of other faces for amusement. To me, most nose jobs usually wound up drawing more attention to a person's nose, not less; as soon as I realized someone had had their nose "fixed," I couldn't stop staring at it, trying to edit the old nose back in.

Rhonda must have noticed me staring at her because after a few minutes, she touched her nose and said proudly, "You like? It's a Dr. Rosenthal original. The best in Syosset. You won't believe it, but I was actually born with Dad's schnoz. This one was a Sweet Sixteen present from Moms." She put her arm around Ida and gave her a little squeeze.

"I thought it would help her find somebody suitable, but apparently not," Ida said to me.

"Oh, Mom," Rhonda said with a laugh. "Give it a rest, will you? I'm workin' on it, okay?" Then she turned to me. "Seriously, I've still got his card somewhere, if you're interested. He does boob reductions, too, you know."

On both Tuesdays and Thursdays, it was my turn to stay late with Timothy to help close up the restaurant. That evening, as I headed back to the kitchen with a tray of dirty cutlery for Eduardo, Timothy grabbed me by the elbow.

"Oh, I wouldn't do that just now," he sang. Lifting the tray out of my hands, he stashed it under the microwave, then directed me back to the counter.

"What's wrong?" I said.

"Let's just say Rhonda likes Colombian coffee," Timothy said, grinning. "And at this very moment, she's giving her milk to it for free."

"You're kidding," I said. "Right here? In the kitchen?"

"Yuh-uh," he said gleefully. "And let me tell you, Eduardo is the third Latino dishwasher she's hired this year. She goes through Hispanic boys the way our customers go through paper napkins."

Other times during our shifts, Rhonda came up beside me and whispered, "Tell me if you see Ma coming back here." Then she leaned over the utility sink and drank water straight from the faucet to wash down a Dexedrine or a couple of black beauties. As soon as Ida's back was turned again, Rhonda gestured to the pile of baked goods displayed on the countertop. "Oh, look, Susie, aren't those brownies broken?" she'd say loudly, winking. She'd lift up the plastic cake dome and gouge two brownies in half with her thumbnail. "Well, we can't possibly sell those now, can we?"

Pulling out the crumbled pieces, she'd shove one in the front of her apron and another directly into her mouth. "Here," she'd whisper, giving me the other two sections, then motioning toward my pocket. Whether I was supposed to eat it or hang on to it for her was unclear.

By the end of the third week, the full, chest-crushing drudgery of food service work had descended on me. I'd pretty much mastered everything there was to know about sticking a minute-meal into a paper bag, and all the colorful characters who'd kept me so entertained my first week were now nothing but an endless parade of irritants. It was amazing to me how quickly my gratitude and excitement deteriorated into resentment. The smell of coffee permeated not only my clothes but my hair, and by the end of my shift, my whole body began to feel like it was suffering from repetitive stress injury. Then, while we mopped the floors, stacked chairs, and scrubbed the urns—and Ida lectured us about preserving our virginity in formaldehyde—I tried to avoid Louie's attempts to grope me behind an enormous carton of Sweetheart drinking straws while his bulimic, pill-popping daughter fucked the dishwasher in the utility closet.

"So, sunshine. How's the job?" my father asked, as I flung down my bookbag and dropped onto the couch. I'd had no idea how hard it was to stand on your feet all day or work for somebody else. At least with baby-sitting, you could sprawl on the sofa and be left alone.

"I'm becoming a Communist," I said.

"Oh, that's good," my father said. "Now your grandmother will finally have someone to drink with."

Years ago, my grandmother had become a Communist for much the same reasons, I suspect, that kids today get their eyebrows pierced. While other people lost their jobs or betrayed their country for their Trotskyite beliefs, my grandmother's commitment to Communism pretty much consisted of knocking back several martinis at a cocktail party, then hoisting her dress up over her head and yelling, "Hey, everybody, look! I'm a Communist!" Other than its shock value, only the "party" part of the "Communist Party" seemed to hold any appeal for her.

"Yeah. Right, Ma. Sure you're a Commie," my father would say, rolling his eyes. "You hate authority, you hate the working classes, and you hate anyone telling you what to do. Who the hell are you kidding? If the Communists ever took over, you'd be the first person they shoot."

But now that I, myself, was technically a proletarian worker, my grandmother's politics suddenly made more sense to me. After all, it was we food service peons who did all the real work at Shuggie's. The owners just sat around on their asses, reaping all the profits and drinking decaf mocha all day.

"If you ask me, Dad," I said, "the government *should* control the means of production. They *should* seize the assets of the bourgeoisie. I mean, capitalists *are* nothing but a bunch of parasites. You should see the way Louie Shuggie carries on, making all of us wait on him for minimum wage, while his wife does nothing but yell at us. Karl Marx was right. 'Workers of the world, unite.' That's what I say."

"That's good, sweetie," said my father. "Make sure to tell that to all the people you plan on belly-dancing for."

Soon, in fact, I did become involved in a truly proletarian enterprise: the burgeoning black market of the office building's food court. Most of the other restaurants in the atrium were staffed by underpaid high school students, too. As soon as our bosses' backs were turned, we bartered just about anything edible we could get our hands on: brownies, pita pockets, chocolate-covered pretzels, egg rolls, bratwursts.

Amazingly, none of us honestly thought we were stealing. Although we weren't so naive as to think our bosses might share this opinion, we never dreamed of lifting money from the till or filching supplies to sell on the street. In giving away a coffee or a yogurt, we were simply showing off. For the first time in our lives, we had some minute sense of sovereignty, some currency in a world beyond high school. We alone had the ability to slip free brownies to our peers! We had status; we were flexing our muscles. And let's face it: we were flirting. A lot of those cookies were our idea of foreplay.

Granted, it's easy to be generous with things that aren't yours, but we told ourselves they were ours, really. After all, didn't we make those sandwiches? Didn't we unpack all of those pretzels by hand?

Ironically, never again in our working lives would we be so delighted to help each other out. As my peers and I got older, and began to assume jobs with real influence and responsibility, we tended to become more guarded with our favors. Phone calls went unreturned, résumés got buried on desks. Years later, when my first book was published, I began receiving e-mails from people I hadn't heard from in years, emerging from the ether to ask if I could possibly recommend them to my agent or give their manuscript to my publisher. And I'd often think, with some degree of resentment, *Why should I help you?* But at the very same moment, I'd pick up the phone and try to ingratiate myself to someone I hadn't spoken to in decades, casually asking them if they wouldn't mind passing a review copy along to their editor. In response, I'd usually hear the same chilly, noncommittal annoyance from their end of the line. Somehow, we were all more openhearted and generous when we were just scooping ice cream.

One day when I came in wearing my glasses as well as sweatpants to work, Louie looked at me with open disdain. So did Ida.

"How do you ever expect to catch a husband, dressed like a hockey player?" she asked.

"What makes you think I want a husband, Ida?" I said blithely, opening a napkin dispenser. "Gloria Steinem calls marriage 'breeding in captivity.'"

"Oh please," Ida said, lighting a cigarette. "Spare me the women's lib crap."

"It's true," I said. "They say you're either a feminist or a masochist, you know."

"Oh do they?" said Ida. For a moment, she studied me, looking me up and down as if I were a prime cut of beef. "So," she said, taking a drag on her cigarette. "You really think you're equal to any man?"

"Sure. Of course," I shrugged. "Why wouldn't I be?"

"Okay, then," said Ida. "From now on, it's your job to refill the orange juice dispenser."

Refilling the orange juice dispenser was the hardest job at Shuggie's. It required you to carry an enormous vat of fresh-squeezed juice in from the kitchen, climb a footstool, and pour it into the top of the machine. When completely full, the three-gallon juice vat weighed, by my estimation, no less than 438 metric tons. Usually, Timothy or Eduardo did it. Now Ida informed them that they were to refrain from helping me.

"Let's see if her muscles are as big as her mouth," she said, leaning against the tiles and fanning her cigarette smoke.

Each day, as I struggled to hoist up the juice vat, I repeated, as loudly as I could, "Sisterhood is beautiful! Equality under the law shall not be abridged or denied on the basis of sex! Workers of the world, unite!"

"Amen to that," Timothy hooted.

Ida just rolled her eyes. "You know where workers of the world unite?" she said. "The unemployment line."

Clearly, the Shuggies already knew what it had taken me several weeks to discover: I was nothing special. Like any other unskilled, minimum wage worker, my position could be filled in a snap by any number of high school girls willing to work for bupkus and dress like a streetwalker.

Each day, Rhonda pawned off on me an increasing amount of half-eaten bounty. I began to worry that when enough cookies, brownies, and minute-meals went missing, Louie and Ida would notice and begin their version of the McCarthy Witch Hunts. In their search for the culprit, the first person they'd look to would undoubtedly be the smart-ass women's libber who claimed not to care about her appearance, who thought she was real cute with her politics, and who'd stupidly made a point of bringing in a copy of *Fat Is a Feminist Issue* and leaving it by the cash register in a misguided attempt to reach out to their bleached-blond diet-crazed daughter. In giving me the once-over, they'd find exactly the evidence they were searching for: the leftover cookies, the half-eaten brownies, the picked-over minute-meals bulging in my apron pocket. And then, what would I do? Point the finger at Rhonda?

Yet one afternoon, we were busier than usual—it was a breezy spring day—and the counter felt positively besieged. Even Louie and Ida felt compelled to press themselves into service. The line of customers extended out the door and seemed to repeat itself like a Möbius strip of humanity. We kept dashing back and forth to the kitchen to restock. We were out of bags—no, we needed napkins! Someone get more napkins! And quick, more Sweet'n Lows! And more fruit salad, too! The frenzy made Timothy, Mercedes, and me positively giddy with adrenaline.

Suddenly, everything struck us as inordinately funny. "Yoo hoo. Handsome, over here!" Timothy whispered as we watched a guy pick his ear with a coffee stirrer. Then a woman came in wearing an unflattering power bow and we quickly rechristened her "Bozo."

We got so busy whispering snide, sidelong comments to each other that I guess we forgot to pay attention to what we were doing. Timothy accidentally hit the liquid soap dispenser so forcefully that some of the soap squirted across the tile floor, and before he could wipe it up, I slipped on it. At the moment I slipped on it, I just happened to be carrying one of the enormous aluminum vats filled with freshly squeezed orange juice.

"Oh," I cried.

For an instant, the entire coffee shop seemed to freeze. And then, all the customers on line appeared to take a collective step back and gasp as three gallons of freshly squeezed orange juice flew up into the air.

At that precise moment, Louie was standing with his back to me. He'd just rung up a sale. In a moment of absurd, almost supernatural choreography, the arc of juice crested brightly like an orange rainbow, then splashed down at the exact moment that the cash register sprung open, landing in the money drawer with one enormous, ejaculatory splatter.

It drenched everything.

Orange juice flooded the troughs of nickels, dimes, pennies, and quarters. The paper money slots were swimming in juice; you couldn't even see the bills, only rectangular pools of orange, with bits of pulp floating around on the top. Juice streamed down the sides of the cash register drawer, dripping steadily onto the tile floor like a citrus fountain. The buttons on the register were sticky-wet. The countertop surrounding it was one giant orange puddle. Two enormous stacks of paper bags and napkins beside it were sopping. And so, of course, was Louie. The entire front of his green Shuggie's apron appeared to be lacquered to his chest with orange juice.

For a moment, nobody said anything. As I hoisted myself woozily up off the floor, everyone sort of collected around the juice-flooded cash register drawer and stared down into it. Slowly, Louie reached in and pulled out a matted stack of five-dollar bills that were so wet, they practically came apart in his hands. He looked down at them, stunned, and for a moment, he appeared about to cry.

———————

Whenever people get fired in the movies, it's symphonic; the pressures on them build steadily, hurtling toward some imminent disaster, until a boss shrieks, "Jensen! That's it! You're fired!" Then Jensen either whips off his apron and stalks out of the store yelling, "That's okay because I quit!"—or, if he's a professional of some sort—does the walk of shame through his office holding a single file box and a houseplant while everyone in the entire office gathers around him and looks on.

At Shuggie's, it was nothing remotely like that. After Timothy and I cleaned up the blitzkrieg of orange juice as best we could, we finished out our shift as usual. Only afterward, as I was hanging up my apron and punching out, did Louie came back into the storage room. For once, I didn't flinch. "So," he wheezed wearily, stroking his mustache. "Just how much longer were you planning on working for us?" When I told him just another week or two, he nodded. "I think that's probably best," he said.

It wasn't really a firing, but still: I didn't tell my father. I could envision only too well the look of incredulous delight on his face, followed by the gleeful phone calls to his poker buddies. "Arthur," he'd begin, "wait'll you hear this." With each new telling, my story would gather momentum, until the orange juice became a veritable Halley's Comet, a gargantuan citrus meteorite slamming down into the cash register. Inevitably, phone calls for me would start coming in. "So, Susie," my Uncle Fred would say, "I hear you're the new spokeswoman for Minute Maid?"

I felt disgusted with myself. But, as teenagers are wont to do, I quickly blamed my incompetence on the Shuggies. Something like that was bound to happen, I told myself, given how they treated their workers. With their penny-pinching, their psychodramas, their reactionary sexism, how could they possibly expect me not to get distracted?

Had I been older, perhaps, I might've been able to see it differently. Had I been wise enough to actually piece together the fragments of the Shuggies' lives that I'd been privy to, I might have recognized a family portrait far more heartbreaking than contemptible. But it never occurred to me to wonder: what disappointments, what tragedies, what bad luck stories could've possibly led Louie and Ida to become the people they were? A restaurant like theirs was never a hobby. Why were they running such a backbreaking, thankless business when most people their age were retiring? Why were they spending seven days a week in a humid little food stall, nickel-and-diming suppliers and high school kids, counting every napkin and coffee lid, all the while secretly, desperately trying to resuscitate the strained, sexual game-playing of their youth?

New York City wasn't a small prairie town where a woman named Darlene could waitress at the same waffle house for twenty-five years. Even people who spent their whole lives in food service in Manhattan moved on to bigger, better restaurants. What must it have been like for the Shuggies—or even for Rhonda, for that matter—to see everyone on their payroll moving on, the kids going to college, the actresses landing roles Off Broadway, everyone bouncing off them like a trampoline, leaping higher and then away, contempt and relief bright on their faces?

Of course, it never occurred to me to be so reflective. A few days after I'd turned in my apron from Shuggie's, the fiasco with the orange juice suddenly began to strike me as incredibly funny. It was possibly the most slapstick thing I'd ever done.

The proverbial last laugh, however, was on me. Two weeks later, I received my first and only paycheck. It had been printed out by a payroll service on computerized, watermarked paper, and the hours on the pay stub corresponded exactly to those I'd recorded meticulously in the back of my trigonometry notebook. Yet the discrepancy between my "gross" and my "net" pay was so large, there had to be a mistake. Either that or it was the Shuggies' idea of some vicious parting joke.

I took it down to my father's office. "I think we've got a lawsuit to file," I announced, dropping my paycheck ceremoniously on his desk.

He picked it up, and reviewed the list of deductions with me: federal, state, city, and something onerous called "FICA."

"Nope. Looks right to me," he said.

"You have got to be kidding," I said. "That's almost 35 percent less than I'm supposed to have gotten. That's practically not much more than I earn baby-sitting. Where the hell did it all go?"

My father looked at with astonishment. "To the government," he said.

"The government?" I fairly spat. "The government took all that money?"

He smiled. "Them's taxes, baby girl."

"No fucking way!" I shouted. "Who told the government they could take all my money like this? That's robbery!"

Just then, my father's secretary buzzed over the intercom. "Mr. Gilman, your wife is on the phone," she said.

"I worked my ass off for that money!" I cried. "They have no goddamn right to take it like that. Who told them they could do that? I'm not even old enough to vote yet!"

My father chuckled and said to his secretary, "Tell my wife I'll call her back. Tell her I'm watching our daughter turn from a Communist to a moderate."

"I'm going to sue those thieving bastards," I shouted. "I'm going to launch a class action lawsuit against the IRS, and the federal government, and the—"

"Whoops. Wait. I think she just went straight to conservative," my father laughed.

Then he quickly dialed my Uncle Arthur, pressed the button on his speakerphone, and leaned back in his chair luxuriantly. The sun was setting above the Hudson, and coppery light played over his bemused face as he and Arthur listened raptly to my rant and chuckled. But I was too riled up to care. My paycheck was an outrage. The world was unjust. I was going to fight for what was mine, dammit. I'd learned a thing or two about working for a living. Now just let anyone try to pry the pennies out of my hot little feminist's hands. I was revising my opinions. I was hatching new plans.

Chapter 9

How Clever Are We?

DID YOU KNOW it's possible to survive nuclear fallout by eating miso soup for breakfast?

Neither did I. But the year I went away to college, my mother discovered macrobiotic cooking, whose devotees seemed to believe you could cure everything from radiation poisoning to excessive ear wax by avoiding dairy products.

A number of my friends found that once they headed off to college, their parents developed irritating hobbies, too. There was some excessive indoor gardening, some criminal needlepoint, even a recreational interest in prescription pharmaceuticals. More often than not, these hobbies also entailed taking a long, meaningful drive to Sears, then converting my friends' bedrooms into useful sewing rooms and dens, replacing their canopy beds and prized beer can collections with modular furniture, wicker baskets, La-Z-Boy recliners.

The first Christmas I arrived home from college, I found a pyramid of Plexiglas containers in our kitchen stocked with dried grains, fermented soybeans, and organic yeast. At first I thought it was a collection of specimen jars, or perhaps a decorative handicraft made by some mentally retarded child using dried peas and pinto beans. But no. Apparently, I was looking at our dinner.

My brother, who'd been waiting up for me, could barely contain himself.

"Oh, wait'll you see this," he squealed as I walked, stunned, through the kitchen. "She's really done it this time. Open the fridge. Open the cabinets. Guess what we're eating for breakfast tomorrow? Did you say 'miso soup and buckwheat groats'? Mm. Yum. Why, how ever did you guess? Miso soup and buckwheat groats is exactly right. Here at Chez Gilman, we now eat miso and buckwheat groats for breakfast, lunch, and dinner."

"Explain, please," I said, eyeing a landslide of dried seaweed packages cascading off the top of the refrigerator.

"Macrobiotic," he practically sang. "That's right. This time, Mom's gone macrobiotic. Or as I like to say, 'macroneurotic.' Soy paste. Boiled kelp. Tofu pudding. Endless discussions about how you can use bean sprouts to cure hepatitis. But wait," he cried. "It gets better. Check out the living room."

Our living room—once groaning with bookshelves, overstuffed furniture, and milk crates full of yellowing magazines—was completely empty, except for a pile of gray foam mats piled neatly in one corner.

"John," I said slowly. "John. Where's the sofa?"

"Oh, that little thing? That's in your room. All the living room furniture is now in your room. To go with our new, healthy, macrobiotic lifestyle, Mom's turned the apartment into a Japanese exercise studio. Yup. That's right. Twice a week at 4:00 P.M. we get to see seven fat ladies groaning on the floor. By the way," he said, "good luck finding your bed. I think it's underneath the bookcase."

"Augh. I so do not want to go home for Spring Break," I moaned to my friend Henry the next semester. It was the end of midterms, and Henry and I were in the student lounge pounding away on dueling electric typewriters in what had become a kamikaze-like attempt to complete all the papers we'd smartly put off writing until the last possible minute.

"Tell me about it." Henry stubbed out his cigarette. "My stepmother wants me to come back to Dallas and clean out my bedroom so she can turn it into a dog run for her three fucking Pekingese. Then, she wants me to escort someone's dumb-ass niece to a cotillion. That means I'll get to spend an entire weekend at a country club watching a drunken girl in a bubble dress throw up behind a pillar. Oh boy," he said. "Can't wait for that one."

I rested my forehead on the top of my typewriter. Henry was one of my best friends at college. He played the curmudgeon to my diva, and we liked to think of ourselves as terribly outré and witty. We had been awake for what felt like 457 continuous hours, whacked out of our minds on coffee, cough syrup, cigarettes, No-Doz, Pez, Fritos, and donuts.

"Seven days of listening to how lepers can heal themselves eating fermented tofu," I groaned. "Can't I just go home to your house for Spring Break?"

"You mean Belfast?" Henry snorted. Henry came from a wealthy Texas oil family known for its horses, alcoholism, and flamboyant meanness. Although his parents had divorced over a decade ago, time had done nothing to diminish their very active hatred for each other. Henry's father took malicious pleasure in regularly hauling Henry's mother into court to reduce her alimony payments. Henry's mother responded by routinely reporting her ex-husband to the IRS, then jetting off with Henry in tow to live in Rome, Sydney, and Monaco, where she collected and discarded husbands the way some women might handbags or commemorative spoons. To follow Henry's succession of stepfathers, you basically needed a program. "No, *Alessandro* was the art dealer," he'd correct. "*Alejandro* was the bullfighter."

Now Henry set his coffee cup down on the table like a gavel. "Hot damn," he said. "Why didn't I think of this sooner?"

Instead of going home for Spring Break, Henry suggested, why didn't we both drive down to North Carolina? His girlfriend from home and my boyfriend both went to Duke University. If we ignored the speed limit, we could make the run from Providence, Rhode Island, down to Durham in less than twenty-four hours.

"Think of it," said Henry. "Not only will we royally piss off our parents, but we'll also get laid."

At college, horniness was pretty much a full-time occupation. You could read all the Schopenhauer you wanted, but eventually, every late-night intellectual discussion over a Domino's pizza devolved into sex talk. My hall mates and I were seventeen and eighteen years old, but we liked to think of ourselves as erotic experts, brimming with sexual *savoir faire*. "Come on in," my friend Lisa would say blithely when I knocked on her door. "I'm just putting cornstarch on my diaphragm."

Both Henry and I secretly worried we weren't getting it nearly enough. The few pathetic liaisons we'd had at college had been even more pathetic than we'd talked them up to be. I'd dated only two guys, one of whom turned out to have a steady girlfriend, the other of whom announced, after three impassioned evenings, that he "just wasn't into women with serious breasts."

"*Serious breasts.* That was the phrase he used," I said to Henry. "You want to go near that one?"

"Hell, at least you've been dumped by two people. I've only had one reject me," Henry said, gnawing at a fingernail. For all his Texas swagger, Henry was a surprisingly delicate boy. He was cherub-faced and built like an Irish wolfhound—slight, sinewy, taut with nervous energy. His skin was milky white, like tracing paper. The girl who'd rejected him had stood him up on his birthday in order to go out with the best friend of JFK Jr.

As soon as we finished our last midterm, Henry and I loaded up his silver Toyota Supra as quickly as possible. Everyone else was heading home for Easter. They were squeezing themselves onto Amtrak's *Yankee Clipper* train that lurched along the Northeast corridor stinking of overheated hot dog buns. They were flying home standby. They were sharing rides in hatchbacks crammed with dirty laundry. Henry and I made a point of "casually" ambling through the hallways, asking if anyone had extra condoms.

"That's right. Rub it in, you lucky bastards," said our friend Burr.

We could barely contain our glee. Settling in to Henry's sports car with a bag full of birth control, Diet Pepsi, and Twix, we felt like out-laws, renegades, sexual mercenaries.

Now, as Henry gunned the engine, I shouted, "We're flying!"

"Shit. This is nothing. Hang on." Henry jammed down on the accelerator. The Supra growled and we careened down the highway with a burst of propulsion.

"Next stop," he called out, "Poontang, North Carolina."

I stretched back and propped my legs up on the dashboard, letting the wind ravage me. The moment Henry and I hatched our plan, I'd telephoned my boyfriend, Jeremy. It was 5:30 in the morning but he was wide awake in the kitchen with some of his fraternity brothers, building a yard-long bong out of a piece of industrial tubing they'd removed from the dishwasher.

"Whoa. You're coming down? When?" he shouted. The Ramones' "I Wanna Be Sedated" was blasting insanely in the background.

"After my last midterm," I shouted back. "But I won't get to your place until, like, 3:00 A.M. tomorrow. Is that cool with you?"

There was a pause. "Only if you don't wear any panties," he yelled.

And so, now, I wasn't. Sitting bare-assed beneath a silver miniskirt in a matching silver sports car that smelled like shoe polish and onion rings, I felt positively sensual, feline, and heady with confidence. I was a wild woman—chafing a bit, perhaps—but unleashed in all my reck-less glory. For I moment, I actually believed I was the only girl ever to go on a road trip, too. It seemed to me like women so rarely tore off down the highway in a blaze of adventure. Then again, this might've been because none of my New York friends or I had a driver's license. And urban hillbillies that we were, we were actually proud of this fact, too: So what if we couldn't drive a car? Cars were for people who lived in the suburbs. Besides, the only thing we ever really associated with driving was the phrase "vehicular manslaughter."

Henry had expected Interstate 95 to be a parking lot, but we zoomed across Connecticut without a hitch. Since he was from Texas and I was from New York City, both of us were chauvinists. People from other states, we believed, were inferior simply by virtue of their geography. As we stood on line for the bathrooms at the Friendly's outside New Haven, we elbowed each other knowingly. Look at these New England bumpkins with their beer bellies, their souvenir sweatshirts, their whiny, scabby-kneed children. These were small-town, "average Americans," leading pathetic lives of ordinariness and quiet desperation. As opposed to us, of course. We were merely driving 1,200 miles in seventeen hours for the sole purpose of getting laid. How clever were we?

Henry and I hadn't let our parents know we wouldn't be returning home that evening. Now that we were already on the road, it seemed that Friendly's was as good a place as any to issue our little declarations of independence. Neither of us was under the illusion that our families would be thrilled.

Henry went first. I leaned against the bank of pay phones and watched him dial. He cradled the receiver with one shoulder and picked at his cuticles.

"Hello, sir," I heard him say after a moment. "Well, no. Actually . . . North Carolina . . . Kitty's down there . . . the one I took to the prom . . . Yes, I realize . . . Well, no, I didn't know it's black tie . . . well, she didn't say . . . sir, I didn't promise." Glancing at me, Henry winked, then pantomimed slitting his throat.

Henry's father, Henry Charles, Sr., kept Henry on a tight leash. Despite his fortune, he paid Henry's tuition in installments only after receiving proof that Henry was maintaining a 3.8 grade average. Each month, Henry was also expected to send home a detailed finance report, explaining each of his expenses. These included every cup of coffee and package of cigarettes he purchased.

I myself was on financial aid. Three times a week, I worked in the university kitchen, scouring racks of humid dishware, scrubbing down tables, and serving plates of inedible turkey tetrazzini to my classmates on the dinner line. While some people considered this degrading, it seemed no worse to me than what Henry had to go through each month, adding up every receipt for chewing gum and Wite-Out.

A moment later, Henry hung up. "Well, there's one parent pissed off." He began kicking the heel of one of his boots against the toe of the other, then forced a laugh, a sort of high-pitched guffaw. "At least Dad was drunker than shit, so maybe he won't remember." He handed me the phone. "Okay, princess. You're up."

I hunkered in the corner with my fistful of laundry quarters.

"Sweetie," my mother said. "Are you at Penn Station yet?"

"Um, no," I said. "The Connecticut Turnpike."

"Oh?"

"It's in Connecticut," I said.

"I realize that."

"Guess what?" I said, deciding to attempt enthusiasm. "It turns out that my friend Henry's girlfriend goes to the same school as Jeremy. So we're driving down to Duke."

"Right now?"

"Isn't that great?" I said. "I mean, what are the chances?"

"But I thought you were coming home tonight. How long are you going for? Not the entire week, I hope?"

"Probably," I said. "I guess."

"Well," my mother said, clearly displeased. "Where are you going to stay?"

Although I'd anticipated this question, once my mother actually asked it, it hung in the air like a wrecking ball. It was one thing, I realized, to promote the idea among my peers that I was this fabulous nymphomaniac. It was quite another, however, to promote it to my parents.

Some girls probably never admitted it. They simply got married, had children, and their parents lived with the happy illusion that their daughters were virgins until their wedding night—much the same way a lot of us daughters harbored the same illusions about our parents. On the other extreme were girls like my friend Dani, who "accidentally" left her birth control pills on the edge of the sink for her mother to find. Or Judy, who got pregnant in tenth grade. Some of my friends mentioned it almost casually, the way you might announce you'd gotten your period or flunked geometry. But in high school, I'd gone to great lengths to conceal any inkling of my sex life from my parents. Whatever freedoms they granted me, I was sure, were based on their illusion that I was a straight-A goody-goody.

Now, I was on a road trip staged to announce otherwise. Yet hearing my mother's voice, I was amazed how quickly my bravado dissolved; it was like Weetabix in milk. I twisted the metallic snake of the phone cord around my knuckles, willing myself to the truth.

"I'm staying with Jeremy," I said finally. Then I added, for emphasis, "It's not like I haven't before, you know."

There was a pause on the other end of the line.

My mother cleared her throat. For a moment, I had the sensation of standing too close to an enormous bell that had just sounded; the reverberations felt palpable, physically jarring.

"Well," my mother said distractedly, after another second, "I'm annoyed you didn't let me know sooner. I just cooked up a big pot of brown rice and seaweed, you know. And I just put out fresh towels. And I just. Oh. Well. Fine."

With that, she hung up.

Back on the road, Henry and I carried on as if we'd pulled off a jewel heist. We were positively punchy, vibrating with anxiousness and relief and incredulity over what we'd just done.

When we reached the glittering Mecca of New York, *my city,* as I liked to call it, I bounced up and down in my seat like a lunatic. "Oh, New York," I cried, pointing dementedly out the window at the skyline, resplendent in all its cubist overkill. For a moment, I flashed on my mother. I was barreling past her over a bridge less than ten minutes away. Somewhere in the nestle of skyscrapers, she was leaning over our dinner table, removing the place setting she'd lovingly put out for me just hours before. I felt a stab of sadness, then forced it away. "My sweet, shining city. Don't worry, New York," I called out as we crossed the Triboro, "I won't abandon you. I'm coming back, New York, I promise."

"Oh for fuck's sake. You're crossing a bridge, not emigrating," Henry said.

"Humph. Easy for you to say, seeing as you don't live in a *real* city, Scarlet," I sniffed. "You don't mind if I call you 'Scarlet,' do you?" I added. "You know, given that you're Southern. And a redhead. And a little, you know, fey."

"Oh, that's good. That's very good," Henry grinned, keeping his eyes fixed on the road. "Just keep it up, you over-breasted Yankee nymphomaniac."

I clapped my hands delightedly. "Over-breasted Yankee nymphomaniac" actually sounded pretty good to me. "I can take it, you know," I informed Henry. "Seeing as I'm from New York City and all. The Center of the Universe."

"Yeah, well just wait till we get you over the Mason-Dixon line, Ms. Noo Yawk."

I rearranged myself in my seat. "Why, the South, I bet it's just so cute," I cooed. "With all those dilapidated plantations and lynch mobs walking around."

Henry began whistling. "I'm just going to let you go on," he said cheerily.

"Why, I'll bet there'll be little shotgun shacks," I said, warming to the task. "With guys named Jethro and Willie Ray sittin' on the porch, talking about how, one day, they're fixin' to fix the rusted car in their yard. And there'll be some prissy little grandmother, too, complaining how General Sherman burned down the grain silo and stole the family silver."

"Keep talking," said Henry.

"And then," I said rhapsodically, "we'll stop at some quaint little country store, where two proprietors named Doc and Maw will say, 'Well, howdy, stranger. If you're lookin' for some good, down-home cookin', Lurleen over there makes just about the best pecan waffles ever you tasted in all of Virginny.' Boy, I just can't wait to see that South," I said.

"You about finished?" Henry said with some amusement.

"I reckon I am," I said, settling back contentedly. "*Reckon*. That's what y'all say in the south, too, isn't it?"

When we actually crossed the Mason-Dixon line it was dark. If there hadn't been a small billboard, I wouldn't have noticed. The Interstate was one long, mind-numbing stretch of asphalt, dark on either side except for an occasional warehouse or industrial park. We'd been traveling for over eight hours by then—we'd hit a lot of traffic passing through New York—and both Henry and I were starting to curdle from sleep deprivation and artificial stimulants. Strewn with Twix wrappers, cigarette butts, Coke cans, and McDonald's bags, the Toyota began to feel like a giant ashtray. Since neither of us liked country & western music or Baptist preachers—just about all there was on the radio—we were pretty much left to Henry's music collection, which consisted precisely of three tapes, Duran Duran, Thomas Dolby, and Kraftwerk, all of which I loathed. Nineteen-eighties music, to me, was manufactured and lazy. If you were going to be a musician, at least you could play your own instruments.

The Toyota's ventilation system seemed to alternate between chilly and smelly, and I began to think that not wearing any underwear for a seventeen-hour car trip had been a mistake, too.

"Oh happy day," said Henry, lighting another cigarette, then gesturing to the car in front of us going ten miles below the speed limit with its left blinker on. "We've got Grampa here taking his car for a walk."

Just south of Washington, we pulled over to a gas station. Henry bought a cellophane cone full of pink and yellow daisies for Kitty, which he propped up on the floor of the back seat in an empty Mountain Dew bottle he'd filled up with water.

"I hope these'll keep. You don't think they're too withered?" he said, nibbling at the cuticle on his thumb. "I wanted roses, but these were all they had left." Then we walked over to a phalanx of pay phones by the roadside to let our paramours know we'd be late. It was eleven o'clock at night. The wind was hot and relentless. Cars tore by on the overpass, making it difficult to hear. On Jeremy's end of the line, there was a ball game on in the background, which didn't help any.

"What did you say?" I shouted.

"I said, 'What?'" he said.

"I said, 'We're going to be even later!'" I yelled.

"Are you really coming down here?"

"We're in Virginia," I shouted. "Go to bed if you have to."

When we got back in the car, Henry said, "Kitty's at the library now, but her roommate says they'll leave the door propped open with a knee sock. Fucking hell. This is what my sex life has come down to," he said. "A knee sock." He started up the Supra and swung it out of the station with a jerk. "The things you go through for poontang."

I laughed. I'd seen a picture of Kitty, and "poontang" was not a word she brought to mind. In the photograph, she was standing primly in a mint green evening gown with silk gloves pulled to her elbows and her head turned demurely to one side. It was hard to imagine Henry going out with her. At this particular moment, he was wearing a shredded "Adam Ant" T-shirt and combat boots.

Henry was an only child, and sometimes when I looked at him, I could see in his face his parents battling for his soul. One day, he'd walk around unshaven and flinty-eyed in cowboy boots. The next, he'd be foppish, almost fussy, in an antique silk vest and ascot. He'd dress preppie for a football game, then put on eyeliner and hair gel to go clubbing. For the trip down to Durham, he had on his Road Warrior costume, replete with a leather jacket and safety pins.

We drove for a while in silence, trapezoids of silver light sliding across our faces from time to time from the oncoming traffic, which was thinning out considerably. I followed along on the map as we passed turn-offs for Manassas, Richmond, Norfolk, green exit signs pointing off into a void. We were hurtling deeper and deeper into the

South. Except for a school trip to D.C., this was the farthest I'd actually ever been from home. And yet it was all the same: a repeat of shrubbery, guardrails, wind-tossed trees, the dark road sliding beneath us as if the car were devouring it. Then Henry steered the Supra down an access ramp and into an industrial parking lot. He cut the engine quickly, stopping us with a jerk. "Voilà," he said.

Around us were nothing but abandoned rigs, enormous, ghostly eighteen-wheeler trucks, and huge metal shipping containers in what looked like a graveyard for cargo. Sodium lights overhead bathed everything in ghastly orange fumes. In the distance was a squat concrete building with steam billowing out behind it. You could hear the hiss and rasp of its ventilation ducts. It seemed to throb like a heart, like the centralized nervous system of some alien organism. It was well past midnight. Except for an occasional vehicle tearing past on the freeway, there was no evidence of life. Even the saplings at the far edge of the lot looked skeletal.

"C'mon," Henry said, unfolding himself from behind the steering wheel.

"Where are we?" I climbed out of the car awkwardly and tugged at my silver skirt, which was beginning to look more and more like an accordionized gum wrapper. It was misty outside. The air was leaden with the smell of wet soil and gasoline. A thin film of moisture coated everything.

"You wanted to see the South," Henry said, starting across the lot.

I squinted at the structure ahead. "What's that? A substation?"

"No. The Jarratt, Virginia, truck stop. C'mon. Coffee time."

I had to trot to keep up with him, and as we drew closer to the building, I noticed a small neon sign reading "FOOD, DRINKS" sputtering in the window. Every other second it hissed and crackled, then half the letters blinked dark, so that it spelled out "FOO, DRI" instead. The building was massive, much bigger than it had looked from the parking lot, and eerily windowless. Though it would make a fine morgue or secret munitions plant, it didn't look like any place you would ever want to eat.

"You're kidding," I said.

Henry swung the door open and grinned. "After you, Ms. Noo Yawk," he said. Ever since Maryland, I noticed, his Southern accent had grown more pronounced, ripening with languor. "Well, thank yew ma'am," he said to the toll booth attendant. "Y'all have a good evening."

Inside the entrance a small boutique had been set up. Instead of selling the usual for-the-road mints, cigarettes, and plastic flashlights, it had racks upon racks of ornate cowboy boots. Stetsons hung from the ceiling, twirling lazily like mobiles. Finely crewled leather belts hung down the walls. In a corner by the cash register, a walrussy-looking man sat on a stool beneath a sign that said "O-K Corral Apparel. Custom Made." He was chewing gum absentmindedly and staring out at the parking lot. In one hand he had a pair of bright green dice that he kept shaking and releasing out on the countertop without once glancing to see what he'd rolled.

Henry led me through two fire doors and suddenly we were in an enormous room blazing with artificial light. It was the kind of light you find in casinos, designed to simulate daylight and sterilize time.

We were in a cafeteria the size of an airplane hangar. A countertop snaked through the room, and hundreds of truckers sat along it on orange vinyl stools, hunched over cups of coffee and tucking into plates heaped with pancakes and sausages. At every bend of the counter stood waitresses in peppermint-striped uniforms and harsh makeup, with hairdos that seemed to have been whipped up out of a frozen custard machine. Toward the back of the room was what looked like a glass-enclosed deejay booth displaying a splashy sign: "WQJR: Travis, Conway, and Wayne Every A.M.!" Beneath it, a makeshift photography studio had been set up. A man who looked like a televangelist stood rod-still in front of a white backdrop while a blonde in a red polyester suit and stilettos patted his face with a powder puff. A photographer in suspenders paced back and forth between two light stands, smoking and flicking his ashes on the floor and looking generally irritated. The room hummed with activity, and yet everyone seemed oblivious to what was going on around them. The truckers chewed blearily. The waitresses refilled coffee cups mechanically. The man being groomed for his close-up looked embalmed. In New York, I was used to all kinds of bizarreness. But this was surreal.

"Henry, let's go," I said.

"Whatchew tawkin' 'bout, woman? This here place is right homey," Henry announced, his drawl now in full bloom. "Yew jes' sit yerself down and order me some coffee. Ah need a piss."

With that, he turned and sauntered into the men's room. I stood there, alone in the unforgiving light. A trucker whose forearms were scrolled with tattoos glanced casually over in my direction and nudged his buddy.

In addition to my silver miniskirt, I had on little pointy black elfin boots and a black rip-necked sweatshirt pulled seductively off one shoulder *Flashdance*-style. With my fingerless lace gloves and one enormous rhinestone earring, I'd felt pretty proud of myself fourteen hours earlier, preening in the mirror back at college, convinced that I looked like a star in my own MTV video. Now, standing in the middle of what was, essentially, the National Trucker Convention, it suddenly occurred to me what a mother lode of bad judgment this had been.

I slipped past the truckers as coolly as possible, then hoisted myself onto a stool. "Hey, sugar," a waitress drawled. "What kin ah git fer yew?"

Hearing her address me like that made me utterly tongue-tied. Surely the moment I opened my mouth, the entire room would realize I was a Yankee and elect to string me from a tree.

"Two coffees to go puleese," I said with a slight inflection. I didn't know who I thought I was kidding.

Henry seemed to be taking his sweet time in the men's room. Casually, I surveyed the cafeteria and tried to pretend that I was perfectly used to hanging around truck stops at two in the morning dressed like a prostitute.

Back in New York, I'd spent countless afternoons with a notebook, spying on various people and inventing stories about their lives. On any given Saturday in Central Park, the city pretty much spoon-fed characters to you. A fat woman in a purple caftan would shuffle by with a cat on a leash, followed by two Hispanic men in identical white leather pants. It was easy to divine characters from people who on some level, I realized, saw themselves as characters already, who put themselves on display in the hopes that they'd be someday immortalized. But the truckers in Jarratt, Virginia, were of an entirely different ilk. Their faces were like no faces I'd ever seen. They were like furrowed fields and scorched earth, full of turbulence and erosion. I could not begin to imagine who they were or what their lives were like. Watching them, I suddenly felt a very long way from home. There was a whole, vast, unknowable world out there that could swallow me instantly. I was completely out of my league.

Henry sauntered out of the men's room just as the waitress handed me the coffees.

"You okay?" he asked. "You don't look too good."

"Just don't leave me like that again," I said in a low voice, motioning toward the door. "Can we just get out of here now, please?"

"Why? You uncomfortable?" he said with some concern.

I nodded.

"Well, goddamn it," he bellowed in his Texas twang, loud enough for an entire group of truckers to hear. "If I didn't know any better, I'd reckon someone'd put *semen* in those dispensers instead of liquid soap. It sure as hell looks like it, and it sure as hell smells like it. Here, you're from New York. You're the expert. Smell my finger," Henry boomed, thrusting his hand in my face. "Sniff. That's semen, iddin't it?"

Out in the parking lot, he couldn't stop laughing. "Oh my Lord. I wish I'd brought a movie camera. The look on your face. I've never seen you so freaked out in my life."

"That wasn't funny," I hissed, though it was, in fact, funny.

Henry cackled and shook his head. *"Henry, get me out of here. Henry, stop it right now.* Oh man. That was priceless. What's wrong, Ms. Noo Yawk?" he laughed delightedly. "Southern hospitality too much for you neurotic Yankees to handle? *Neurotic.* That is what y'all say in the North, isn't it?"

"Okay," I said. "Touché."

After that, we were pretty much played out. It was ridiculously late. Even Henry was sick of his tapes, so we drove on in silence. I was ready to be at Duke already, ready to tiptoe into Jeremy's room and slide in beside him.

Jeremy had been two years ahead of me in high school, where he'd been a Frisbee champion as well as captain of the track team. In one of the school musicals, he'd played Tarzan leaping around the stage hammily in a loincloth while girls in the audience screamed ecstatically. He was silly, but he knew it, which only made him more adorable. Playful, good-looking, and up for anything, he was hard not to like. Every time he came home from college, he'd called me up as if he'd only seen me yesterday. "So what do think, Susie-Q? Margaritas and a make-out session on Friday?" I was secretly amazed he went out with me.

By the time Henry and I arrived in Durham, it was 4:30 A.M. The sky had downgraded from black to inky blue, and it was raining slightly as we pulled up outside Jeremy's fraternity house. Henry got my bag out of the trunk, carried it up the steps to the porch, then waited while I felt around under the mat for the key.

"Do I look okay?" I asked him. "Not too exhausted or puffy?"

"Nuh-uh. You look great. What about me?" He adjusted his jacket, squared his shoulders. "Not too psycho?"

"No. Totally cool. Kitty's going to love the flowers and the song."

Henry had brought his guitar along. He'd written a song for Kitty, which he'd sung for me a cappella on the ride down. It was actually pretty good.

We glanced at each other on the darkened porch. We'd been together almost seventeen hours straight, but it seemed like much longer. Just the morning before, we'd been sitting before our type-writers in the student lounge, but recalling it now was like looking through the wrong end of a telescope.

"Well," I said. "Maybe you want to get together for dinner in a couple of nights? The four of us?"

"Sure. That would be good," said Henry. "Well. Okay."

He turned and hurried down the steps.

"Don't do anything I wouldn't," I called after him.

"Well, that leaves me plenty of options," he teased. Then he swung down into his car and was gone.

Inside the darkened fraternity house, Jeremy had left a piece of paper taped to the banister: "Susie—Up. 1st Door Right." The house was an old Victorian, and I could tell it hadn't been kept up. Every step creaked underfoot, and paint flaked beneath my hand on the banister. Before entering Jeremy's room, I felt in my bag for a brush and ran it vigorously through my hair. Then I eased the door open slowly. As soon as I stepped inside, I nearly banged into a ladder. I hadn't realized Jeremy had a loft bed. When I'd envisioned arriving, I somehow imagined him sprawled on a king-sized mattress and pulling back the covers seductively, with a flourish. Now there was a shifting and thumping overhead. Jeremy leaned over the edge of the loft sleepily, his hair standing straight up with static, his eyes barely open. "Hey," he croaked faintly. "You made it."

"Uh huh," I said hoarsely. I was suddenly overwhelmed with exhaustion. "I'll be up in one minute, lover," I whispered. Then I set my bag on the sofa beneath his loft, plunked down beside it, and proceeded to fall asleep.

———

Later that morning, Jeremy nudged me awake. He stood over me fully dressed with a knapsack slung over his shoulder and an apple in one hand, clearly on his way to class.

"I was going to let you sleep," he said, "but you've got a phone call."

He helped me off the sofa and led me across the landing to the common room. One of his fraternity brothers stood by a wall phone, holding out a receiver.

"Chem test," Jeremy whispered. "Back in an hour." As he disappeared down the stairs, I took the receiver and put it to my ear. For some reason, I had a terrible headache.

"Hello?" I said groggily.

"Mornin', princess." It was Henry. "So," he exhaled, "you about ready to go?"

"Go where?" I said.

"Back to Providence," he said. "Kitty broke up with me."

"What?"

"When I got to her dorm room this morning, there wasn't any knee sock. She got out of bed and told me to sleep in the lounge. She said she didn't want to see me anymore." Henry gave the same helpless guffaw he had the day before, talking to his father. "My fucking luck," he said.

I sat down on the floor beneath the phone and tried to get my mind around what he was telling me. "Well, why—I mean, if she didn't want to see you, then why did she have you come all the way down here?"

Henry snorted bitterly. "Here's the real kicker. The really beautiful part. She said she, quote, 'respected me too much' to break up with me over the phone. She said she wanted to wait and do it in person."

"You're kidding," I said.

"Apparently not," Henry said caustically. "She respects me enough to want to look me in the eye when she kicks me in the teeth. So," he exhaled trying to sound chipper, "how are you doing? Get any action yet?"

"I've barely seen Jeremy. Last night I was too tired, and now he's got a chem test."

"Then I'm guessing you're not quite ready to leave yet," Henry said miserably.

I knew that as his friend, I should tell him it didn't matter—that we should just go. But horniness didn't tend to bring out any of my better qualities.

"Look," Henry said after a moment. "I have one more night before they kick me out of the lounge. But frankly, I don't think I can take it here much longer."

As soon as Jeremy returned from class that morning, I eased his knapsack off his shoulder and told him we had to work quickly. "You won't believe it," I said, pulling him against me playfully and unzipping his jacket. "But Henry's girlfriend just broke up with him."

"Really," Jeremy said, staying my hand. He sounded genuinely interested.

"Yeah, she locked him out of her room as soon as he got there," I giggled, nuzzling his neck. "She said she wanted to break up with him in person. Can you believe that?" I reached for Jeremy's fly, but he grabbed my hand again. A strange look passed over his face then, like the shadow of a cloud sliding across a field.

"What?" I said.

Carefully, Jeremy disengaged himself, then paced a few steps and sank down on his couch. He sighed and fixed his gaze on the floorboards.

"Look, I thought maybe once you came down here, once I actually saw you in person, maybe I'd feel differently," he said uneasily.

"But the fact is," he continued, "I simply respect you too much to do this over the phone."

———

Twenty minutes later, Henry pulled up to the house in the silver Toyota while I stood on the porch trembling. Out of some perverse sense of gallantry, Jeremy insisted on escorting me to the car and holding the door for me as I settled in. "You're a great girl, Susie," he said gently, setting my bag on the back seat and kissing me perfunctorily on the cheek. "Try not to take this too hard." Then he actually went around to the driver's side and shook hands with Henry as if they'd just completed a business transaction. I felt like a mental patient, like a rejected game show contestant, like some public official who'd just been indicted and was being led away in handcuffs before a crowd of onlookers.

"Well goddamn it," Henry said, as soon as Jeremy was back inside. "I can't believe we drove twelve hundred miles to get dumped. Hell, we could've just stayed at school for *that*."

I tried to smile, but at that stage in my life, the only default mode I had was crying. I should have ordered Henry to drive the Supra straight through the front porch of Jeremy's fraternity house, but instead I sat there, drenched in shock, weeping from the campus all the way to the waffle house downtown where Henry stopped to have us fuel up for the long drive back. I couldn't eat. I just sat in the booth with the fork limp in my hand, shielding my eyes from Henry while tears and mucus ran down my nose in highly attractive spindles.

"He said he wasn't into me anymore," I choked. "He said I was 'overly sexual.' Those were his words. But he's only the second person—" I threw down my fork and sobbed baldly. Henry got the check and hustled me out.

I cried from North Carolina to Virginia, and from there all the way to D.C. In my head, I began hearing not only Jeremy, sitting on his couch, thoughtfully outlining for me a concise list of my shortcomings, but everyone else in my life who'd ever rejected me. I heard the boy back at college who wanted un-serious breasts. I recalled the guy at Stuyvesant who said "Making out with you is one thing, *going* out with you is another." I heard Nathaniel Eggers nicknaming me "Flatsy" and every guy in New York who'd ever said "I'll call you," then suffered an amazing paralysis of both his index fingers and his vocal cords.

Then, horrified, I thought of our friends back at school. Wait until everyone in our dorm heard how Henry and I had driven seventeen hours—arguably one of the longest booty calls in recorded history— only to be ceremoniously dumped by our lovers. After all our boasting and carrying on, I could only imagine what was in store. All Burr would have to say was, "Hey, anyone want to take a road trip?" and everyone on the entire hall would crack up. We were going to be punch lines for the rest of the semester.

I knew that the drive back would be brutal—long, deflated, tedious. I knew that the pain of rejection would linger, forming a fine little keloid scar on my ego, making me second-guess myself anytime I flirted with a guy, as if the first year of college didn't fuel my insecurity enough. And I knew that strangely, inexplicably, I wanted to go home, to be surrounded by people whose pathologies were at least familiar and predictable to me, the bunny slippers of weirdness. When Henry and I pulled into the Vince Lombardi Rest Stop on the New Jersey Turnpike at daybreak, I knew that I would reluctantly eat half a banana split for breakfast, then slide off the stool and wander back to the pay phones. Sheepishly and humiliated, I would dial. And as I listened to each ring, my heart would constrict wildly with nervousness, with shame.

What I did not know was that when she answered, my mother would say simply, "Well of course, sweetie. What time will the two of you be here?"

I did not know that even before we crossed the Hudson, my father would move the sofa and the bookcases back into the living room. That my mother would run out to Key Food to stock up on steak and roast beef, stuffing virtually half a frozen cow into the refrigerator. "Well, Henry is from Dallas, so I assume he doesn't know from vegetables or miso soup," she'd say brightly.

I did not know how elegantly my family would smooth themselves out for the occasion.

I did not know that Henry would not be repulsed by them at all. Rather, he'd be charmed, even impressed. "Boy, your folks are cool," he'd say. "For starters, they're sober."

And I did not know that for the entire week we stayed with them, not once would my mother mention that you could cure emphysema with soy beans. She would simply sit beside me at the edge of my bed, quietly stroking my hair. The sex lives of their children, parents might not want to know. But heartbreak, they understand.

PART III

Reality Says "Hello"

Chapter 10

Picnic at Treblinka

SO HERE WAS THE PLAN: after graduating from college, I'd return to New York City and walk around Midtown radiating talent and intelligence. Dazzled by my aura of competency, the editors of the *New York Times* and *Vanity Fair* would dash out of their offices and run down the street calling after me, "Stop! You're a genius! We've got to hire you!"

In no time, I'd be mentioned in the gossip pages of the *New York Post* as a "hot young novelist." *New York* magazine would profile me as "one of those under-thirty Wunderkinds who make you question what you've been doing all your life." *The New York Review of Books* would declare me simply "a revelation."

Instead, of course, after finding only two want ads for proofreaders (5+ yrs. exp. nec.) and absolutely none for writers who'd written political "prose poems" for their college newspaper, I lay around despondently in my bedroom for a month reading back issues of *People*. Until that moment, my life had been as pampered and well supervised as that of a laboratory rat. Now, suddenly, as a college graduate, it was just me, alone, facing the Void of All Eternity. Me, alone, facing the Void of All Eternity plus my student loans, which came in a deceptively cute little coupon book designed to make me think that, at 9.25 percent interest, I'd been getting some sort of bargain.

Eventually, I mustered up enough effort to carpet-bomb the publishing industry with my inventive idea of a résumé. This resulted in a handful of interviews—mostly for trade journals with names like *Sheetrock Weekly* and *Kitchen Appliance Gazette*. When the editor of *Aluminum Siding Times* asked me, "So, what entices you about aluminum siding?" I had to resist the urge to reply that it seemed like a topic you could write about regardless of how much recreational medication you happened to be taking.

Much as I told myself that every writer had to begin somewhere, and that a paycheck was a beautiful thing, given the starting salaries I was being offered, this seemed like a stretch. At $265 a week before taxes, my paychecks would not only *not* be beautiful, they'd be things you wouldn't even want to look at without the benefit of grain alcohol.

In the end, it turned out that only one newspaper was willing to hire me anyway. And this was primarily, I suspect, out of morbid curiosity.

If I'd thought *Shippers and Truckers Daily* or *The Paper Fastener Picayune* were lethal, *The Jewish Week,* at first glance, didn't strike me as a whole lot better. It was a musty-looking publication full of grainy photographs of octogenarian philanthropists and fuzzy-faced rabbis. "Torah Portion of the Week" was one of its regular offerings, along with something cryptic called "Federation Appeals Update." What *The Jewish Week* did have going for it was that it was, in fact, a bona fide newspaper—in addition to "hard news," there were features, movie reviews, and entertaining personal ads that began "Enough with the Dating Already, Make Your Mother Happy" and "Frum Mensch Seeks Kosher Cutie."

When I arrived for my interview, Sheldon, the managing editor, leaned back in his chair and looked at me wryly. "So," he said, tossing aside my meticulously Xeroxed résumé. "What do you know about Judaism?"

The truth was, I knew about as much about Judaism as I did about aluminum siding. For most of my life, I'd been under the impression that Judaism had been created by three "lost tribes"—the Coins, the Levi's, and the Israelites. The Coins, as I understood it, had become bankers, the Levi's blue jeans manufacturers, and the Israelites modern-day Israelis. Do not ask me where I got these ideas. It wasn't until a born-again Christian clued me in that I learned there'd actually been *twelve* tribes of Israel, not three. Apparently, this wasn't any secret, either: it was right there in the Bible for anyone who bothered to read it.

Sitting in Sheldon's office, surrounded by his journalism awards, I realized it was one thing to feign interest in hand-blenders and Sheetrock, but quite another to fake expertise in an entire religion.

"To be honest, I don't know a thing about Judaism," I said plainly. "The only time I ever set foot in a synagogue was to attend Lloyd Goldfarb's bar mitzvah in eighth grade. And mostly I went because his parents were taking us to see *Beatlemania* afterward."

"I see." Sheldon exhaled. At that point, I expected him to end the interview and usher me out the door. Instead, he made a little tent with his fingers and said affably, "So in other words, you wouldn't be approaching your subject matter with a lot of bias."

That my ignorance could be in any way construed as a selling point had never occurred to me. Yet somehow, I felt an almost pathological need to be candid—if not to sabotage my case outright. The truth was, I wasn't exactly keen on writing for a Jewish newspaper.

Ever since making my grand debut as an archangel in the sixth grade Christmas pageant, all I'd ever managed to learn about Judaism was that people could kill you for it for no good reason. As a result, I tended to regard it as a kind of genetic deformity. Whenever someone actively embraced their Jewishness, I couldn't help but think that they were some sort of moron.

What was there for Jews to be proud of, I wondered. Christians had inspiring cathedrals and interesting saints. They had Christmas, and Easter bunnies, and suntanned ministers in ice-cream-colored suits with their own TV shows. They had numbers and certainty. Granted, heaven and hell seemed to me like transparent attempts at crowd control. But all we Jews seemed to have was Israel and the Holocaust. Christians were visited by angels, Jews by the Gestapo. It was no contest.

I warned the editor I'd been educated in Presbyterian and Quaker schools. "Not only that, but I sang in the choir," I confessed. "My family has a Christmas tree that we don't even pretend to call a 'Chanukah bush.' My mother quotes this guru named Baba Ram Dass. We spent a year following a Maharishi, another doing Buddhist chanting, and another being macrobiotic, which, believe me, is kind of a cult. So you see," I concluded haplessly, "I'm really not Jewish at all."

"That's funny," Sheldon laughed. "You sound pretty Jewish to me."

"Really?" I said, trying to hide my displeasure at this news.

"Sure. Who else puts their kids through all that? You don't see Catholics sending their kids to synagogue just to 'expand their horizons.' Look," he said, "if I want a religious expert, I'll hire a rabbi. Until then, we pay $22K and 80 percent of your medical. When do you want to start?"

My first day on the job, I was given my own desk, computer, press card, and stapler—all the trimmings I associated with world-class journalism. After rearranging my office supplies several times, I practiced whipping out my press card with authority. Then I called my father and made him call me back so he could listen to my professional-sounding voice mail message: *Hello, this is Susan Gilman, staff writer for* The Jewish Week *newspaper.* After that, however, the thrill and novelty pretty much wore off, and I settled down to demonstrate to my editor just what a terrible choice he'd made by hiring me.

Although I harbored fantasies of being a cutting-edge journalist, writing with great insight and acumen about the substantive issues of the day, I somehow could not get past the fact that I was working for such a totally dweeby newspaper. Whenever I went to happy hours or to little networking parties with my friends, someone invariably hooted, "You write for *The Jewish Week*? My grandmother reads that."

In the meantime, my friend Giles—a fact checker for *The New Yorker*—got free backstage passes to see R.E.M. Julia, an editorial assistant I knew at a trendy start-up called *7 Days,* got review copies of Bret Easton Ellis books and advance-release CDs by the Hothouse Flowers and Prince. Another girl, Belinda, a gofer at *Vogue,* went to press parties at the Rainbow Room, where she was able to shovel three pounds of jumbo shrimp into a Ziploc bag in her purse. The only freebie at my job was a pamphlet called *The Manischewitz Guide to Kosher Wine Tasting,* an oxymoron if there ever was one.

New York City is arguably the most competitive city in the world. Never mind the professional ambitions: People race to be the first person to cross the street! The first person in the elevator! The first person at the dry cleaners! It's the Urban Living Olympics. All around me, other college graduates were pushing their way to the front of the bar and flaunting their new business cards from the *New York Times, Sassy* magazine, *The Village Voice*. How had they landed these jobs? And how had I missed them? Although I told myself that I was the only twenty-two-year-old I knew with a real byline, this wasn't very comforting. Dancing at the Limelight, nobody was going to be reading the heart-rending obituaries I wrote. When people asked where I worked, I answered *"Jew Week,"* hoping they'd mishear it as *Newsweek* and be really impressed.

"I can't believe I spend my days writing about Jews," I moaned to my friend Jill. "How fucking un-cool is that?"

"What are you talking about?" Jill said. "Susie, you're Jewish. I'm Jewish. Loads of our friends are Jewish. And we're all cool."

"Yeah, but we're not Jewishy Jews," I said. "We don't run around in those creepy beards and yarmulkes, or act all JAPPY, talking in Long Island accents and waving around our gold jewelry."

Jill sat back on her sofa and stared at me. "Listen to you," she said after a moment. "I can't believe how anti-Semitic you are."

"*We* don't say *oy vey* all the time. We don't keep moaning about the Holocaust and Israel, or go on about what victims we are," I said.

Jill laughed. "Neither you nor I know a single person like that," she said. "Where on earth did you get the idea that that's how Jews really behave?"

"I don't know," I shrugged. "The media?"

Back at my job in the media, I had such contempt for my employers that I didn't bother even pretending to have a work ethic. Expected in the office by 9:30 A.M., I waltzed in around 9:50, then went downstairs to buy breakfast. Scheduling hair appointments and aerobics classes for noon, I stretched the concept of "lunch hour" to new limits. And since the workday technically ended at five, I made sure to be out the door by exactly 5:01 P.M. "Shalom y'all," I'd holler, leaving the other reporters scrambling to meet the deadlines. The way I saw it, the only real purpose of my stint at *The Jewish Week* was to help me cultivate a far groovier freelance career and highly important social life. One of my editors, Steven Schloss, told me he practiced counting to one hundred every day keeping track of my personal phone calls.

"But what I can't figure out," he said, "is when do you have time to make them? It's not like you're ever here."

After work, I'd often go meet my friends at a bar, where we'd all sit around complaining about how our bosses never gave us any responsibility. Ugh, the Xeroxing, said Julia. My database was programmed by idiots, said Kim. "I have a college degree," Maureen groaned. "How exactly does that translate into 'envelope stuffing expert'?" But while I joined in the chorus of entry-level grievances, I secretly could not believe that I had not, as of yet, been fired.

As I'd learned the hard way, reporters were not supposed to wear miniskirts to Holocaust memorials. Nor were they, under any circumstances, to refer to rabbinical students as "co-eds." Also, if you handed in your story late, and the proofreader didn't catch that you'd misspelled the word "cult" with an "n" instead of an "l," well, there'd be no end to the grief for everyone.

One day, I was assigned to conduct a lunch interview with a high-powered rabbi who had just flown in from Israel. The features editor, Roberta, went over the questions with me so I'd appear to know what I was talking about.

"So, how did it go?" she said afterward.

"Augh, it was great," I said. "The lobster ravioli was amazing."

"You ate lobster ravioli," she said.

"Not just any lobster ravioli. In a sherry cream sauce with chives," I said. "And chocolate mousse for dessert."

"With the top Orthodox rabbi in Israel," said Roberta.

"Well, actually, he wasn't hungry," I said. "He just had tea."

"Excuse me a moment, please." Roberta walked into the managing editor's office. A moment later, I heard Sheldon shout, "GILMAN, GET IN HERE."

I came in to find him standing red-faced behind his desk.

"Gilman, did you really order lobster ravioli for lunch with a rabbi?" he demanded.

From his tone, I knew I'd done something wrong, though I couldn't imagine what. All I could think to say was, "It was the house special."

"You know, Gilman, what you choose to eat on your own time is your own business," Sheldon said, almost spitting with anger, "but when you're representing *The Jewish Week* and you're in the presence of an Orthodox rabbi, who is doing you an enormous favor by granting you an interview, don't you think it behooves you to keep kosher?"

"Lobster ravioli in cream sauce isn't kosher?" I said.

He looked as though he was about to have an aneurysm.

"What do you think?" he said.

"Well. You seem pretty upset, so I'm betting it's not," I said brightly.

"Why is it not?"

Kosher, I recalled vaguely, had something to do with milk and meat. "The cream sauce?" I guessed.

"No. The lobster. Shellfish isn't kosher, Gilman."

"You're kidding," I said.

"Not kidding," said Sheldon.

"Really?" I said. "Are you sure about that? Not even in Chinese food?"

Sheldon called out to the bullpen, "LIPPY, GET IN HERE."

Lippy was another staff reporter. He was modern Orthodox, which meant that while he didn't dress traditionally, he observed the Sabbath and a zillion other religious restrictions. These included abstaining from drinking, gossiping, and gratuitous cursing. How he'd survived in a newsroom was completely beyond me.

Though Lippy was kindhearted and intelligent, I tended to avoid him. Devoutly religious people made me irritable. Instead of compelling me to become more pious, their rectitude and moral certainty just made me want to act out even more. Around them, I often had the impulse to writhe around orgiastically on top of a pool table and pour Sangria on my tits—if only to balance out the universe. I got the urge to be yin to their yang, sinner to their saint, Godzilla to their Bambi.

Now, Sheldon announced that, until further notice, Lippy was going to serve as my de facto rabbi. "I'm not saying you have to teach her Kabbalah," he said to Lippy, "but at least make sure she knows not to order lobster ravioli again in front of Rabbi Turkletaub."

Lippy clamped his hands over his mouth to stifle a laugh. "You ordered lobster ravioli in front of Rabbi Turkletaub?" he said to me.

"How was I supposed to know it wasn't kosher?" I said irritably. "Christ, I ate matzo for Yom Kippur this year. What more do you people want?"

The next week, Lippy took me to lunch at a restaurant on Broadway that tried to disguise the fact that it was kosher by devising overly clever names for its sandwiches like the Bruce HornesBeef and the Tina Tuna. Having endured years of health food, I expected the meal to be yet another exercise in inedibility. Instead, I was presented with an overstuffed fresh turkey sandwich (the Cluck Norris) and a bowl of free pickles.

"Hey, not bad," I said, digging in. "This actually tastes normal."

"The human sacrifices come later," Lippy said dryly. "With dessert."

With his yarmulke, his 1950s eyeglasses held in place with elastic, and his pants pulled up to his nipples, Lippy was nebishhood incarnate, a caricature of nerdiness, the poster boy for anti-Semites everywhere. Even though he'd been nothing but generous toward me, I felt it was my duty to inform him of this.

"Okay, Lippy," I said to him over our third lunch together. "I get the whole 'Torah' thing now, and how Jews regard it as divine law and blah blah blah. But just where, in the Bible, does it instruct us to dress like dorks?" I waved my hand in his general direction. "I mean, the high-water pants, the pocket protector, the yarmulke stuck on your head with a bobby pin. Why don't you just wear a sign taped to your ass reading 'Kick me, I'm Jewish.'"

Lippy grinned, then scratched the underside of his chin. "Actually, I was going to suggest that you tape a sign to your backside saying 'Vain, superficial, misguided feminist.' But then," he said philosophically, "I realized your miniskirt pretty much says it for you."

I had to admit: Lippy was no dummy. No matter how many inane or purposely offensive questions I peppered him with—*Why don't Jews just call it a day and believe in Jesus? Why can't synagogues print the Torah in English so people can actually read it?*—Lippy answered me calmly and intelligently. Even when I sent him a sympathy card on his fortieth birthday, he refused to be provoked.

"I've got to give you credit, Lippy," I said finally. "I'm impressed with your patience."

"Jews have been waiting almost six thousand years for the messiah," Lippy said. "You think one little *schmendrick* like you is going to faze us?"

As a journalist, Lippy told me, it was always good to develop an area of expertise that you could parlay into your own "beat." Since my one talent at the paper seemed to be infuriating our readers, I decided my specialty would be to give our conservative and elderly readership regular heart attacks.

Luckily, this was not difficult to do. Much to my surprise, there was no end to the number of Jewish freaks and renegades running loose with the rest of the yahoos in America. Sorting through press releases I'd previously ignored, I discovered a Jewish doctor who'd spent twenty-five years taking peyote on various Indian reservations and discussing the Kabbalah with Hopi tribes. I discovered a satirical Yiddish heavy metal band called Black Shabbos that sang songs like "Reggae Rabbi (He Eats Bagels with Dread Lox)." I discovered a pregnant lesbian rabbi, a black hip-hop artist who ran a sideline business drawing portraits of Hasidic rabbis, and a biker gang called the Star of David Motorcycle Club created by beefy Harley-Davidson aficionados as the Jewish alternative to the Hell's Angels.

Soon, I did in fact have a niche, unofficially known among my fellow reporters as the "freak beat," which seemed to entertain them no end. "Hey, Susan," Lippy liked to call across the bullpen, "I just heard that a group of transgendered Communist rabbis are going to be skateboarding across Jerusalem in support of human cloning. You want to cover that?"

My editor Sheldon, however, was less amused. "So what if you met a bunch of Jewish call girls?" he'd say with exasperation. "How is the fact that they're Jewish news?"

"Well," I said, "most people don't think of Jewish girls as prostitutes."

"So what are you proposing? That we run the headline *Hey, Jewish Chicks Are Hookers, Too!* No dice, Gilman. The day a group of Jewish prostitutes brokers peace in the Middle East, we'll run a story about them. Until then," Sheldon said, "I'd like to see you write a story for a change that does not begin with someone trading in their bar mitzvah money for a box of bondage equipment. Call me crazy, but it would be nice to have an article from you once in a while that we could actually publish."

He didn't seem to care that I was finally taking an interest in my work. I loved going out on assignment, interviewing different people, and hearing their colorful, often heartwarming stories—especially when I could schedule interviews in a way that allowed me to sleep late. And after my first year as a cub reporter, I had to admit I was starting to see Judaism in a more favorable light. Jews—it seemed—did more than eat pickled herring and argue about paying retail. And Judaism was actually more than a state of perpetual victimhood. As religions went, it even had a few moments of stunning common sense. For example, I discovered, Jews didn't believe in original sin. In Judaism, you never had to excuse yourself for living, and you could think about any despicable, depraved thing you wanted to, provided you didn't act on it.

Moreover, Jews seemed to believe that literacy was next to godliness. No spiritual leader should spoon-feed ideas to you; rather, you were required to read, study, and think for yourself. Bookish as I was, I liked the idea of a religion that required you to do extra homework, even if I, personally, had absolutely no intention of ever doing it.

For me, though, the one real appeal of Judaism was that no other religion or culture seemed nearly so tolerant of smart-asses. What others considered blasphemy, Jews tended to regard as a poor attempt at comedy. How else to explain my continued employment?

Yet just as I was beginning to hit my stride as Susie Gilman, Jew Girl Reporter, I got a call from my friend Giles at *The New Yorker*. "Guess what?" he said, trying to sound nonchalant. "I just got my own column." *The New Yorker* was adding a new nightlife section to the front of the magazine. Hip, literary, and supremely talented, Giles had been tapped by the editors to write it. When he said, "Want to come out and celebrate? My treat," I felt like lopping off my head with a paper cutter.

The next week, my friend Julia called from *7 Days*. "You won't believe this," she said breathlessly, "but I just interviewed Kevin Bacon."

At that moment, I was working on a piece Sheldon had assigned me about a new girls' religious school that had opened in the basement of a town house on West 73rd Street. The school had only seven students, and while the rabbi who'd founded it was full of lofty plans, all the girls cared about were boys. Said the one student who'd deigned to go on record, "Torah, Schmorah. If I don't get a date in the next three weeks, I'm out of this dump."

As Julia told me about her interview with Kevin Bacon, my stomach felt like someone had run it through an industrial juicer. How was it that my friends were living out my dreams, while I was stuck writing about single-sex yeshivas?

As I walked home through Times Square, blazing with newsstands and gargantuan billboards, the whole city seemed to mock me, to set up a tantalizing display of other people's celebrity and accomplishments in order to underscore my own obscurity. In New York City, in the entire world, I was an absolute nobody. Why, most of the time, I thought miserably, you couldn't even find *The Jewish Week* on the newsstands; better to rifle through the magazine rack at your local geriatric hospital. And while my peers in, say, Bangladesh or Afghanistan might have told me to cry them a river, all I could see were other people's bylines, other people's fabulous literary careers, other people hurtling toward greatness.

———

The next morning when I stumbled into work late, Sheldon poked his head into the bullpen and yelled, "GILMAN, GET IN HERE." Setting down my coffee and donuts, I figured this was it: my first post-graduate firing. Armed guards, no doubt, would be summoned, and they'd stand as sentries beside me as I untaped my Doonesbury cartoons from the side of the file cabinet.

Instead, when I walked into Sheldon's office, he leaned back in his chair with his hands clasped behind his head and said, "Poland."

"Poland?" I said.

"How'd you like to go there?"

"Forever?" I asked.

Sheldon laughed. "For a week. To cover a story."

An event was being planned, he explained, called March of the Living. Three thousand Jewish teenagers from around the world were going to converge in Poland for a week to learn about Jewish history and the Holocaust, followed by a week in Israel, where they would learn about the Jewish state. Since Lippy knew Hebrew, he was covering the Israeli leg of the trip. Since I knew nothing, Sheldon thought it might be a good idea for me to cover the Polish leg, where I could join a legion of three thousand other know-nothings and, in his words, "finally learn something." I'd leave at the end of the month.

"What do you say?" Sheldon asked. "You ready to become a foreign correspondent?"

Never one to pass up a golden opportunity, I said, "Well, I don't know. Can I do a stopover in Paris?"

In preparation for such an overseas assignment, any smart, enterprising young reporter would undoubtedly get busy reading up on Polish and Jewish history. Telling myself I wanted to maintain the utmost objectivity, I instead did nothing but brag to my friends and plan the vacation that I had, in fact, wangled for myself in Paris beforehand. My best friend Michelle had introduced me to a guy with an apartment near Sacre Coeur. Didier wore leather pants and managed a French rock band, and when he offered to let me stay with him, neither of us had any illusions I'd be sleeping on his sofa. Since there weren't a lot of female "new journalists" I could draw on as role models for my assignment overseas, I'd looked to the doctor of gonzo journalism himself for guidance about writing about the Holocaust. "How would Hunter S. Thompson prepare for visiting a bunch of concentration camps?" I wondered. Since transporting firearms, cocaine, and ether were out, getting laid in Paris seemed as good a preparation to me as any.

In the end, this proved better planning than I could've imagined. Although the organizers of the March of the Living had managed to arrange for three thousand teenagers to tour Poland for a week, they'd somehow forgotten to pick me up at the airport. When I arrived at Warsaw's international airport from Paris at nine o'clock at night with my press credentials and my word processor, neither the soldiers brandishing machine guns nor the Politburo agents at the tourist counter had any idea where I was supposed to go. Had I come straight from New York, I probably would've freaked. Instead, I was now flushed, bowlegged, and slightly drunk. "Well, okay. Whatever," I shrugged to the tourist agent, pointing to phrases in my pocket English-Polish phrasebook, "Just stick me in a taxi and take me to your biggest hotel."

In 1990, Poland was still technically part of the Soviet Eastern Bloc. With only two accredited tourist hotels in Warsaw, I figured if I just showed up at one of them, I was bound to bump into someone. Bouncing through the streets of Warsaw in a jury-rigged taxi, I was amazed how gloomy the city was; the entire place seemed to have been lit by one 40-watt lightbulb. The boulevards were impassive blocks of concrete high-rises. None of the stores were open; the streets were eerily empty, sickly red and green traffic lights blinked into the darkness for no one. Only a few dim bands of neon occasionally illuminated the tops of buildings. It was like a city in the middle of an air raid, or after a neutron bomb; all the infrastructure remained, yet the people had vanished. I wouldn't see another place so bleak until I went to Detroit three years later.

Warsaw's top tourist hotel had all the charm of a legion hall after an Elks dance. When I asked the receptionist whether my contacts had checked in yet, she smiled uncomprehendingly. "You wait for the lobby?" she said, then pointed toward the bar. "Maybe you like drink of the vodka."

In a stark, paneled room, local men, none of whom appeared to be under seventy, sat smoking and staring blearily at an old television set bolted to the wall. Their faces were like crumpled butcher paper, and their clothing looked salvaged, a mishmash of canvas coveralls, thread-bare sweaters, and plaid polyester shirts. The only woman was the bartender, with sloppily bleached blond hair and a no-nonsense look that suggested she'd spent all day at target practice. When I walked in, nobody said anything or even acknowledged my presence. They were all transfixed by the television. Overhead, Madonna was on-screen, singing, "C'mon and Vogue" in a black velvet bustier. For the next two hours, I sat on a folding chair with the rest of the lumpen proletariat, shivering in the unheated bar and watching MTV. *Wow, I thought delightedly, so this is what it's like to be a foreign correspondent. If only my friends back home could see me now!*

Eventually, the March's organizers showed up and checked me into the hotel. The next morning at breakfast, I ran into Shimon, a freelance photographer for *The Jewish Week.* A former tank commander in the Israeli army, Shimon had traded in the barrel of a gun for that of a Nikon. Sauntering around Warsaw in his flak jacket with camera bags slung across his chest like a bandolier, he was cocksure and charming, a sort of Jewish picture-snapping Rambo. I called him the "anti-Lippy," which seemed to amuse him. He didn't have Lippy's sense of humor, though. Shimon was thirty-eight years old with a wife and two kids, and anytime I called him "Old Guy," he got really annoyed.

"Hey, you made it," he said. "I've been here two days already. Let me tell you. This whole country is a shithole. The hotel staff? Imbeciles. And the march we're on? A zoo. The organizers have no idea what the fuck they're doing. They've got three thousand Jewish teenagers running around the Polish hotels like maniacs. But what do I give a shit?" he said. "The Polish zlotys are trading at something like six thousand to the dollar. Last night, I had a steak dinner with wine for two-and-a-half bucks."

Shimon and I headed into the hotel parking lot, where a tour bus was waiting. "I've already staked out seats for us in the front," he said. "There's no place reserved for press. You didn't happen to bring a flask, did you? With these little maniacs, we're going to need it."

As we settled into our seats, Shimon gave me a copy of the week's itinerary to review. It read like a vacation package designed by Joseph Goebbels. Monday: Majdanek concentration camp. Tuesday: Treblinka concentration camp. Wednesday: Warsaw ghetto. Thursday: travel to Kraków. Friday: Auschwitz and Birkenau concentration camps.

"Are they kidding?" I said to Shimon. "I thought this was a Jewish heritage tour. All we're seeing here are death camps and ruins."

"Yeah, well. Welcome to our heritage," Shimon said, opening a canister of film with his teeth.

Around us, scores of Jewish teenagers carried on like teenagers, flirting, pinching, giggling, playing grab-ass and keep-away with each other's sweatshirts and baseball hats.

"Roxanne," a girl in a pink sweater and matching leg warmers shrieked from the back of the bus, "toss me the Pringles?" Behind us, two beefy boys crammed into their seats, then put on Walkmans and cranked up the volume until their headphones emanated dueling bass lines. "Yo, man, I want the window," another boy laughed, playfully shoving his seatmate across the aisle.

"Yo, get off me."

"No, you get off me."

"You gonna say uncle? Say uncle, man."

"I'm not saying uncle. You say uncle."

"You guys, cut it out," a girl yelled. "You're making me spill my nail polish."

"What the hell is this," I said to Shimon. "'Camp Concentration Camp'?"

"Listen to you," he laughed. "What were you expecting, a garden tour and the ballet?"

I supposed that I was.

The first stop on our whirlwind tour of Nazi atrocities was the Majdanek concentration camp, set on the outskirts of a bucolic Polish village. Indeed, some of the picturesque little houses seemed to have a fine view of the crematorium across the fields—or rather, they would have had a fine view, had the crematorium, like most everything else in the camp, not been torn down and cleaned up. A few neat barracks had been left standing, though, and inside were displays of canisters of Zyklon-B, the poison used in the gas chambers. There were also piles and piles of Nazi loot, old clothing and luggage taken from the victims, as well as the tattered and disintegrating uniforms they'd been forced to wear. The barracks were dark and stinking of mildew and clay, yet outside, it was balmy; the sunlight was dusty with pollen. Fields around the camp glittered in the breeze. You could hear sparrows chirping and the steady hum of insects. It was surreal and disorienting.

In another section of the camp stood a huge, stony memorial above what appeared to be an enormous mound of crushed seashells. These, we discovered, were actually human remains: bone bits and ashes left over from the crematoriums. This was pretty much a conversation stopper, and even the kids eating potato chips seemed to pause in mid-bite. Isaac, one of the boys I'd been interviewing along the way, kneeled down to get a better look.

"They just don't seem real," he said softly.

I'd read books by camp survivors Elie Wiesel and Primo Levi; I'd visited a Holocaust museum and seen movies like *Sophie's Choice*. But now that I was actually at a concentration camp, it was, perversely, like seeing a celebrity in person—or, perhaps more aptly, Charles Manson. After viewing pictures and footage of them for years, it was hard to comprehend that they were actually standing in front of you.

Around me, some of the teenagers started to weep or say fevered prayers in Hebrew, but I found myself feeling devoid of any emotion whatsoever except for a strange, free-floating anger directed not just at the Nazis and Poles, but at the March's organizers and the entire world. Why was this the very first stop on a Jewish heritage tour, I wanted to know. Surely, there had to be more to our past than this. Do not tell me that this is *everything*.

"So, what do you think?" Shimon said as the group solemnly proceeded out of the camp. "I'll say one thing. There's no better way to shut up three thousand teenagers."

"What do I think?" I said irritably. "I think I want to go for one of those two-dollar steak dinners and a bottle of wine, that's what I think."

"It's Tuesday, so it must be Treblinka," I groaned as I climbed aboard the bus the next morning and eased myself carefully down into the seat next to Shimon.

"Fucking hell. Are you as hungover as I am?" he asked, massaging his forehead.

After we'd returned to Warsaw, Shimon and I had skipped the "debriefing" at the hotel and gone out to dinner instead. The restaurant overlooked one of the few ornate buildings in Warsaw, a monstrosity Stalin had commissioned that resembled a grotesque wedding cake crowned with a hypodermic needle. Shimon and I were two of only four customers in the restaurant. Heady with the power of our expense account, we ordered vodka cocktails, then half the menu and two bottles of wine. The bill came to a whopping $6.47, and Shimon and I drunkenly vied to pay it. When we left an additional six-dollar tip, the waiters fell all over each other thanking us. "God, He blesses you, Mr. and Mrs. America." Their gratitude was heartbreaking. The whole nation seemed picked-over, a wasteland of concrete. Even the vowels had been looted from the language.

"This world is one cruel, unfair, fucked-up motherfucker," I told Shimon after dinner as I slid down onto the floor of the hotel elevator and leaned my head back against the simulated wood panels. I wasn't quite sure how I made it from the elevator to my room, but I had a good idea that I'd crawled.

Now, the tour bus sat idling in the parking lot. "Augh. Can we go already?" I said impatiently. "The exhaust fumes are making me nauseous." The driver was standing by the side of the bus, languidly smoking a cigarette.

"Boy, that's a first," Shimon smirked. "I guess now that we're not going to be killed there, nobody can be bothered to drive us to a camp."

Treblinka was so pristine, it looked more like an art installation than a concentration camp. Indeed, the entire site had been demolished by the Nazis in the wake of advancing Allied troops, so the only structures now were memorials. Jagged rocks, each engraved with the name of a town whose population had been annihilated, were scattered around the woodsy site like a haphazard graveyard. Seeing it without knowing the historical context, you'd have absolutely no way of divining what had actually happened there. You might think it was another Stonehenge, a miniature Easter Island. A few kids seemed to be under just this impression: they sat down beside one of the memorials and began passing around chicken salad sandwiches.

"Oh look," I said sarcastically. "What a great place for a picnic. Or, better yet, a fashion shoot. Here," I said, striking a pose beside a chunk of granite with the name "Bialystok" etched on it. Bialystok had been the town my grandmother had come from; all her relatives there had been killed.

"Get one of me like this." I tucked an arm seductively behind my head. "For Grandma."

Shimon looked at me incredulously. "You're insane," he said.

"Why not?" I said bitterly. "Everyone else here seems determined to pretty things up."

Just then, Jonathan ran over to me. Jonathan was one of the kids I'd chosen to track throughout the March, recording their impressions and experiences. He was a sixteen-year-old punk rock aficionado and sci-fi enthusiast from San Francisco. Out of respect for the trip, he'd pinned a yarmulke to his dyed-blue-and-purple hair. "Hey, Susie," he said breathlessly. "Are you ready for the height of sickness? Check out the souvenir shop."

Amazingly, while authorities hadn't bothered to put up detailed plaques or exhibits explaining what had transpired at the camps, they had managed to build a souvenir kiosk. In case you're ever in dire need of a concentration camp commemorative *tschotchke,* you'll be relieved to know that, at least when I was there, Treblinka sells key rings, change purses, and souvenir bookmarks.

"What, no snow globes?" I cracked.

"Yeah. Why not?" Jonathan said with mock annoyance. "I mean, they could have little ovens inside, and fake ashes instead of snow."

"I see there are no Nazi lawn trolls, either," I sniffed.

"Hey," Jonathan called over to the bored-looking woman behind the counter. "Do you have any bumper stickers that say 'Honk If You Love the Führer'?"

"Communists." I shook my head. "They know nothing about merchandising."

"Un-fucking-believable, isn't it?" Jonathan handed me his camera. "You have to take a picture of me here. Otherwise, people back home will think I'm making this up."

"Ohmygod. Look at these," I cried, motioning to a rack of post-cards. The cards had attractive shots of Treblinka on a sunny day, some with a montage of close-ups and long views of all the memorials. "Okay," I said. "Hands-down, this wins."

We each bought some, along with the airmail stamps thoughtfully provided at the cashier's window.

"Augh, this is so great," Jonathan said, writing hurriedly. "I just hope people realize I'm being ironic. How's this? 'Dear Mom. Here I am at Treblinka. As you can see, it is very pretty. The people are friendly. I am having lots of fun. That's all for now. Bye.'"

"Oh, that's brilliant," I said, then handed him mine. *Greetings from Sunny Treblinka! Having a Wonderful Time,* I'd written. *P.S. Wish You Were Here.*

"Are you okay?" Shimon said when we climbed back on the bus.

"Of course," I snapped. Ever since Jonathan and I finished our post-cards, we couldn't stop making caustic remarks and laughing—if laughing is what you'd call the shrill, mirthless asthma that seemed to have overtaken us. My ribs ached and my breathing was irregular. "Why wouldn't I be okay?" I said acidly. "I'm a professional journalist."

That night, Shimon and I drank two bottles of wine with dinner again. When the restaurant closed, we moved on to the dreary bar at the hotel and ordered shots of industrial-strength potato vodka washed down with the Polish version of champagne, which is every bit as bad an idea as it sounds. A group of sad Polish prostitutes lingered by the elevator banks in out-of-date dresses and stucco-like makeup; the same old men who'd been there the night of my arrival remained hunched over their drinks, staring at the cheap laminate tabletop. Being awake at 2:00 A.M. in Warsaw was depressing, but given the images that were swirling in my head, I figured it beat going to sleep.

The next morning, the March of the Living toured the site of the Warsaw ghetto, now a concrete housing development that reminded me of any number of inner city projects back in the states: one ghetto echoing another. A memorial to the uprising had been constructed in a plaza nearby, an abstract sculpture of fists emerging through flames. Then, the group was taken to a dilapidated Jewish cemetery which had been mostly destroyed during the war.

"What genius figured that a Jewish cemetery would be a nice break from the concentration camps?" I said to Shimon. "I mean, what are they trying to do here, depress every kid to death?"

"No," he sighed wearily. "Make sure they realize their responsibilities as Jews. You know, support Israel. Don't marry a *shiksah*. Call your mother. That sort of thing."

The so-called highlight of the March took place on Friday. All the participants would go first to Auschwitz. From there, they'd march two kilometers to the neighboring Birkenau. This would be a replay, in reverse, of the "March of the Dead" that concentration camp prisoners often had to walk from the labor camp to their own extermination. Nobel laureate and Holocaust survivor Elie Wiesel was going to be leading the March personally.

"Another day, another horror," I moaned as I settled in beside Shimon for the ride to Auschwitz. Then I said, "Do you think, if we asked really, really nicely, they'd drive us to Dachau afterward? Because frankly, I just don't think we're getting to see enough concentration camps on this trip."

The fields around Auschwitz were flooded with hazy sunshine.

Forsythia bloomed on the roadsides. "Ugh, my allergies," wheezed a kid across the aisle. People handed around Kleenex and cans of 7-Up they'd bought at the hotel vending machines. I realized I loved and hated teenagers for exactly the same reason: only teenagers, en route to Auschwitz, would sing "We Will Rock You," then pass around an economy-sized bag of Doritos.

The great irony about Auschwitz was that now, apparently, you had to pay to get in. Near the entrance was a cafeteria/snack bar, followed by an ice cream stand. A few families were there already; parents sat at the tables, trying to cajole squirmy, petulant children into eating cut-up pieces of kielbasa and melty vanilla ice cream. There it was: *Auschwitz—fun for the whole family.* Since I'd somehow lost both Shimon and the teenagers I was interviewing, I just sort of wandered around by myself. We had an hour before the March, and as I walked up a stony path, I came upon the official entrance to Auschwitz, the famous wrought iron "Arbeit Macht Frei" gate that had mocked prisoners with the announcement "Work Makes You Free" as they staggered to their deaths. I'd seen plenty of photographs of the gate before, yet seeing it for real was almost more disturbing than anything else I'd witnessed thus far. Before I could even absorb the shock of it, a group of teenagers from the March came barreling up the path.

"Ohmygod, it's the gate!" a girl in a Day-Glo orange T-shirt and a scrunchie shrieked. "Quick, you guys, we have to get a picture!"

In a moment, four of them were posing beneath it in their shorts and baseball caps, their arms flung around each other chummily, everyone squirming and giggling. One kid made a peace sign with his fingers. "Okay," called the boy taking the photograph, "at the count of three, smile and say 'cheese.'"

"CHEESE," they chorused.

I could only imagine their photo albums back home: *Here's me and Jason at Disneyland. Here we are at the junior prom. Oh, and here we are at Auschwitz* . . . But then, strangely, I found myself tickled, almost gleeful. Hitler, after all, had hoped to turn a handful of synagogues into museums documenting "the extinct Jewish race." Instead, his own machinery had been preserved as a tourist attraction, and now here we were, the shrill, popcorn-crunching crowds, the kids with cartoon T-shirts, Instamatic cameras, and picnic lunches, as mindless and ordinary as any other group of spectators, posing beneath the defunct infrastructure of genocide, laughing and squeezing together to fit into the frame of the autofocus.

Suddenly, I felt buoyant—the best, really, that I had ever had since arriving in Poland. Oh, it was good to be at Auschwitz! Jews weren't just victims; in the end, we were victors, too! The Third Reich was gone, but all the people they'd tried to exterminate were still here, kicking around on the planet: the Jesuits, the gays, the disabled, the Gypsies, and, yep, the Jews. Here I was, a reporter on assignment, surrounded by thousands of exuberant teenagers, and the machinery of Nazism had been converted into a sort of impotent theme park. Just how triumphant was that?

I rounded a corner onto dirt paths separating blockhouses. Apparently, these were former barracks where prisoners had slept packed together like cattle. Now, except for a sample bunk room, they were largely empty. Yet after wandering upstairs, I stopped. Preserved behind a wall of Plexiglas was an enormous pile of hairbrushes and combs. There must have been a hundred thousand of them—piled nearly to the ceiling—and if you looked closely, you could see a few strands of hair in some of them.

More disturbingly, the next room was filled with shoes, men's and women's—all sizes and styles—scuffed leather, buckles, lace-ups, high heels that had clearly been danced in—and tiny children's shoes—the kind that parents used to have bronzed and made into paperweights, commemorating "Baby's First Steps"—thousands of pairs, again piled nearly to the ceiling, an avalanche of footwear, all of them bearing the shapes, the sweat stains, the imprints of their former owners.

Six million. Hearing that number, my mind always went numb. I had trouble simply visualizing a dinner party for more than twelve people. Six million was like trying to wrap my mind around the limits of the known universe: I just wasn't capable of it. But to see the combs and the shoes that belonged to people, suddenly I could picture the woman in dark green leather pumps with cracked soles, the man with a tortoiseshell comb tucked in his breast pocket. One hairbrush, one belt buckle, and for the first time, the dead became individually palpable.

Then, compounding this awfulness, in the next room were eyeglasses, a big, mangled tumbleweed of wire. I wore eyeglasses. As light came through the window, I could see myself perfectly, reflected in the display case.

I don't know how I got out of the barracks, or accidentally stumbled into the gas chambers next door, but that's where I was next. A dank, impassive, clinically tiled room—or was it merely concrete?—I couldn't quite focus. I felt disoriented and strangely light-headed. Overhead were big, flat shower heads. Were those fingernail gouges in the walls, or was I imagining things?

The first time I'd heard about the gas chambers was on the ice cream line at Silver Lake. My friend Ruthie had told me there was a man named Hitler in Europe who'd made all the Jews take off their clothes and go into a big group shower where poison gas came out of the pipes instead of water. After the Jews died, she said, they were burned in giant ovens.

I was horrified—yet stunningly, more so by the idea of being naked in public than by anything else. "So wait," I said to Ruthie. "Before the showers, they didn't even let you wear towels?"

Now, here I was, in a gas chamber myself. The horror was sonic. The room seemed to vibrate with malignancy and pain. I was out of jokes; I was utterly alone. Stepping out of the chamber proved no less devastating: adjacent to the showers was a crematorium. True to their rep, the Nazis had been efficient. The ovens were reddish brick, long and deep, with human-sized spatulas protruding from them. Even the gas chambers looked a little nonspecific, but with the design of the ovens, there was no mistaking their purpose.

Until that very moment, I realized, I'd stupidly believed, "I would've gotten out of this somehow." Until that moment, staring directly into the genocidal maw of a body-sized pizza oven, I'd somehow assumed that the Holocaust had been meant for other people— for real Jews, Jews who actually cared about their religion, Jews who had some allegiance to their people and their heritage, Jews who were earnest and pigheaded. Jews who had been weak or naive. Jews who hadn't been nearly as savvy, charming, or modern as my family was. Surely, we would have been spared. Surely, we would have figured out some way to wriggle out of it, to avoid the debasement of it all, to be granted an exemption from a fate reserved for six million others. Surely, in trying to kill us, the Nazis would at some point have realized that they were making a terrible mistake. Look: We had a Christmas tree. I'd sung in a choir. The last time I'd checked, my mother was a Buddhist.

Yet as if it could speak, as if a demonic voice had been summoned from the inferno of its past, the oven gaped before me and its message was only too obvious: Oh, Sister. Don't kid yourself. This one's for *you*.

———————

At some point, I suppose, all of us in our lives confront some unavoidable, outsized horror. Maybe it's a tumor, or a little brother playing with a gun, or a psychopath in a day care center, but inevitably, a moment comes for all of us when we realize that we cannot beat the devil on this one: we have been targeted for injustice or tragedy. And nothing in school, nothing in daily life really prepares us for this. Maybe nothing can, except art, perhaps. Or faith. All that piousness and religion that irritated me so.

At twenty-two years old, I had been ridiculously lucky. In my own neighborhood, I'd grown up surrounded by kids who had constant, firsthand knowledge of the world's prejudices and cruelties. Yet amazingly, I'd remained strangely naive. Now, staring into an oven designed specifically for me—me in my shoes and eyeglasses—I was suddenly aware of just what a moral and psychological lightweight I was, how spoiled and ill-equipped I was to cope with the viciousness of the world. What the hell did I know? I was just some ambitious little asshole from New York. Until that moment, the free fall of adulthood had seemed scary enough to me, without the horrors of the world to confront. Now, I didn't want greatness or glory. I wanted to go home and curl into a fetal position in my bedroom, then get a job replacing toner cartridges in a Xerox machine. I'd happily forfeit substance and forgo all wisdom if it meant I'd never have to recognize *this*.

I had the urge to rip open my own skin, crawl out of it, and leave it behind as I fled. Hurrying out of the crematoriums, slipping down the stony path beneath the "Arbeit Macht Frei" gate, I banged right into Shimon.

"Whoa," he said, as I grabbed on to him as if I were drowning. "You okay?"

Shimon had a faint scar over his left eye from when he'd fought in the '73 War in Israel. He'd faced the brutality of the world long ago. He saw its handiwork every time he looked in the mirror.

I sort of collapsed on him, then started sobbing like a three-year-old, emitting big, lunatic strangulated hiccups.

"Ah, shit," Shimon said. He grabbed me beneath my armpits to help keep me vertical. As I wailed, I beat my head deliriously against his flak jacket, behaving the way everyone wants to behave, of course, in front of their professional colleagues. "Okay, easy now," Shimon said. "Steady."

"I'm sorry," I said later, as I sat on the bench outside the snack bar, sniffling and wiping my nose on a paper napkin.

Shimon shrugged. "This whole trip is a little much. In Israel, they don't do this. We have one moment of silence once a year. A siren sounds, we say a prayer in our heads, and then we move on."

Move on. That suddenly sounded so wise. Shimon loaded a fresh roll of film into his camera while I slowly collected myself and opened my notebook. Together, we set out to follow the March between Auschwitz and Birkenau. For the occasion, a lot of the kids had donned bright blue March of the Living windbreakers with white Jewish stars emblazoned on the back. Even though they took their role very seriously, they were still strangely ebullient, radiating energy the way teenagers do, and I had to admit, I felt proud of them. As if cued, the sky became overcast, and a soft rain began falling as we marched past the ominous watchtowers and under the brick archway of Birkenau, where railway tracks ran, then came, chillingly, to a halt.

The day would become even more emotionally brutal before it was over. Holocaust survivors would speak of the atrocities they'd endured at that very site. Group prayers would be said, and Elie Wiesel himself would become too choked up to finish his speech. In the end, even Shimon would be weeping. It was a mass funeral for a mass grave. There was no getting around it.

———————

Later that night, after Shimon and I got drunk together for the fifth and final time, I finished typing my last dispatch from Poland on the floor of the bathroom. At the tourist hotel outside of Kraków, the only electrical outlet in my room was located next to the toilet: another peculiar vestige of Cold War culture, I supposed. The next morning, while everyone else headed off to Israel, I flew back to Paris. I faxed my articles from the post office in time for my deadline, then fell exhaustedly into Didier's bed. The day after that, I returned to New York. By then, I'd recovered enough to be disappointed that my arrival went unheralded. No paparazzi snapped my picture at the gate. I was still a Nobody, writing for an obscure ethnic newspaper. The only difference was that now I would do so with a glimmer of dedication. Amid all my bitterness and inappropriate behavior, something had occurred to me. It was noble, really, to write about nitwits, artists, dissidents, and yokels—to document Jews—or *anyone,* for that matter—who managed to live life passionately and inventively, who managed to do more than suffer or antagonize others. These alone, in this brutal world, were accomplishments enough. To the living and hopeful, attention must be paid.

I'd try to remind myself of this from time to time—even as I continued bombarding other newspapers with my fatuous résumé. Even as I still yearned to interview Kevin Bacon. Even as I sauntered into work an hour late eating a jelly donut. Even as I leaned over Lippy's desk and said, as I grinned wickedly, "So what's up with us not getting the day off for Good Friday? I mean, isn't that like a major holiday or something?"

Chapter 11

I Was a Professional Lesbian

A LITTLE INITIATIVE can be a dangerous thing. My final year as a reporter for *The Jewish Week,* I took it upon myself to write a lengthy, compassionate article about gay and lesbian rabbis. Feeling magnanimous and, perhaps, professionally suicidal, my editor, Sheldon, took it upon himself to run this article on the front page.

Gay spiritual leaders are hardly news. But back in the early 1990s, *The Jewish Week*'s idea of racy and controversial journalism was to publish a low-fat recipe for potato kugel.

"Oh, are we going to get phone calls over this one," groaned the managing editor. "Fifty readers canceled their subscriptions last year just because we changed the typeface. When we ran that article on Jewish nursing homes, we were besieged with angry letters from geriatrics complaining we'd given their children 'ideas.' Now we've got a photograph on the front page of a single, pregnant, lesbian rabbi." He tossed a copy across his desk. "I might as well just harvest my own organs with a letter opener."

Sure enough, the paper had barely been on the newsstands an hour when the phones started ringing, lighting up the receptionist's desk like a Las Vegas casino. Sheldon announced that while he would handle all the calls from irate community leaders, all those from lay lunatics, religious zealots, and freaked-out grandmothers should be directed to me. Helen, the receptionist, attempted to screen my calls. However, since I'd never managed to figure out the intercom system, this basically resulted in her shouting across the newsroom to me:

"Susan, there's a Mrs. Ida Mandlebaum on line one. SAYS SHE WANTS TO TALK TO YOU ABOUT YOUR GAY RABBI ARTICLE."

"Ooh," my ever-supportive colleagues hooted gleefully from behind their computer monitors. "Susan's in trouble! Susan's in trouble!"

"Have fun," said Steven, slinging his feet up onto his desk. "Remember, our subscription office is based in Omaha. Tell 'em they're wasting their time coming in here for a refund."

Before picking up the phone, I braced myself. Certainly, I'd gotten angry calls from readers before. But until now, these had always been due to my own ineptitude: misspelling the name of the deceased in an obituary, for example, or referring to the head of the B'nai B'rith Sisterhood as "sixty-ish" when, it turned out, okay, she was only thirty-nine. But this time, my critics would not be mollified by an apology and a simple printed retraction. I'd actually have to defend what I'd written on principle.

To be sure, there were a lot of lofty and noble reasons to profile gay and lesbian rabbis. These were people, after all, who felt such a profound love for Judaism they'd dedicated their lives to it despite the fact that the Bible condemned their sexuality. Their work was a testimony to the power of faith and to the desire to serve God. None of this, however, had been what motivated me. I'd simply written the story because the topic seemed titillating and I was sure it would piss off our readers.

As I'd compiled my research, I relished the idea of thousands of complacent, self-righteous Orthodox Jews picking up the morning paper over a steaming cup of coffee and prune Danish, then having a seizure. It hadn't occurred to me that, in place of doing this, they might simply opt to call me instead.

"Yes, Mrs. Mandlebaum," I said hurriedly. My tactic, I'd decided, was to sound offhand and distracted—and therefore, maybe, not fully accountable.

"Are you Susan Gilman?" the woman on the other end of the line demanded. Her Long Island accent was so thick that for a moment I thought one of my friends might be playing a joke on me. That I worked for *The Jewish Week* seemed to amuse my cohorts to no end. Friends were constantly calling the office, asking to speak to me, then disguising their voices as they offered up bogus story suggestions. *Hello, this is Mr. Manischeweitz from the Manischeweitz Matzo Ball Factory. I was wondering if you might be interested in doing a story about my balls. You see, they're not quite as firm as they used to be.* That sort of thing. Great wits, my friends.

"Okay, who is this, really?" I said now, reaching for my nail file. "I'm on a tight deadline, you know."

"I told you," the voice said. "I'm Mrs. Mandlebaum. And I need to know, are you the lady who wrote the story about the lesbian rabbis?"

"Why?" I said cagily.

"Because of my daughter, Brandi," said the woman, "she's smart, she's funny, she's attractive—and I'm not just saying this because I'm her mother, either. She has a degree in psychology from Brandeis and an MSW from Columbia. So I was thinking that—oh, Brandi would kill me for doing this—but, I was thinking that, are you by any chance single?"

"Excuse me?" I said.

"It's just that Brandi isn't getting any younger," Mrs. Mandlebaum sighed. "And some of the girls she's dated in the past. A housing contractor. A dance instructor. Augh. Don't even get me started," said Mrs. Mandlebaum, clearly getting started. "Her last girlfriend was a truck driver. Can you believe that? Whoever heard of such a thing? Worse yet, that no good little *gonif* broke Brandi's heart. Smashed up her Subaru, then took the VCR *and* the food processor when she moved out. I told Brandi, I told her, 'Don't date a *goyisha* dyke.' But do children ever listen? No, they do not. So when I read your article, it occurred to me. You're obviously such a well-educated, nice, gay Jewish girl. So I thought to myself 'Ida, maybe you can make a *shid-dach.*' Why not? Crazier things have happened."

"Um, Mrs. Mandlebaum," I said.

"I thought 'Who knows? Maybe Brandi and this Gilman girl will meet, fall in love, and the next thing you know, they'll do one of those little ceremonies they do nowadays, and I'll finally get to buy a dress. And then they can do a follow-up article on it, too, right in *The Jewish Week*—"

"Mrs. Mandlebaum? I'm flattered that you'd like to fix me up with your daughter," I fairly shouted. Glancing around the newsroom, I noticed all my colleagues were grinning at me like maniacs. "But I'm not gay."

"Oh," said Mrs. Mandlebaum. There was a pause. "You're not?"

"I'm sorry," I said.

"Oh, well. Naturally, reading your article, I thought . . . well." She sounded apologetic and embarrassed. For a moment, an uneasy silence percolated between us.

Then she seemed to brighten. "Well, what about that rabbi on the cover?" she asked. "The cute, pregnant one. *She's* still single, isn't she?"

No sooner had I hung up when the phone lit up again. "Susan," Helen called over, "a Mrs. Lowenthal's calling for you about the rabbi article."

"Susan Gilman," I said, picking up the receiver.

"Susan Gilman?" a woman said primly. "Is this *the* Susan Gilman who wrote the article this week on lesbian rabbis?"

"I'm afraid so," I said.

"Well, Susan, my name's Harriet Lowenthal," said the woman, "And I know this is probably going to sound really strange to you, but are you by any chance single?"

———

By the end of the day, I'd gotten no fewer than seventeen calls from Jewish mothers wanting to fix me up with their nice, lesbian daughters. This was not including the dinner invitation I received on my voice mail from a woman who described herself as a "fabulous fifty-one-years-young kosher dyke just back from three years in Nairobi." I also got a call from someone named Alma, who told me she was a "goddess-worshipping but culturally Jewish" mother of three. "I'm really bisexual," she explained. "And while some people think I'm just kidding myself, the fact is, I really do like to date men once in a while. After reading your article, I thought I should ask you out because you seemed like an open-minded-enough lesbian to handle it."

I did receive one disgruntled phone call from someone named Myron Leftcort, who told me it was a good thing Jews didn't believe in hell because otherwise that's where I'd be going—along with all the gay rabbis I'd profiled, my editor, my publisher, Noam Chomsky, Ivana Trump, Andy Rooney, the Pointer Sisters, Imus, Caspar Weinberger, Al Sharpton, and about three dozen other public figures he seemed to have some gripe with. Someone also walked in and handed Helen an angry, anonymous letter scribbled on the back of a paper placemat from a Chinese restaurant. On one side was a handwritten diatribe declaring that *The Jewish Week* was a disgrace to the Jewish people and that "lezzies and fags are abominations." On the other side were the standard little red drawings of animals and the question *What's Your Chinese Zodiac Sign?* The anonymous letter writer was apparently a Goat—he'd taken great pains to circle it and write in the margin "the best!!!"

"He's telling us we're all bad Jews while he's eating pork fried rice and dabbling in the occult down at Woh Hopp's?" Lippy laughed. "Wow. You can't make this stuff up."

Rather than being shocked or appalled by the idea that there were gay and lesbian rabbis in their midst, our readership, it turned out, seemed far more concerned that there might be someone—anyone in the Jewish community—who had not yet been set up with their still-single gay daughters.

All week long, phone calls came in from desperate mothers and exuberant dykes. Rabbis called, hoping to set me up with their closeted gay colleagues. Grandmothers called, offering to mail me pictures of their granddaughters. It wasn't people's assumption that I was gay that bothered me; rather, it was the relentless wisecracking from my colleagues.

"Maybe you should change your voice mail message," Steven suggested. "You know. *Hi, this is Susan Gilman, lesbian reporter at* The Jewish Week *newspaper. By that I mean I write about lesbians—not that I actually am one.*"

"We all knew you were desperate," said Lippy, "but using a cover story to troll for dates? Why couldn't you just use the personals like any other pathetic loser?"

"Maybe, up until now, you were straight by default," my colleague Toby suggested. "You know, maybe you've just been going out with men because you've never thought a woman would ever have you."

Even Sheldon got into the act. "Susan, I know that homosexuality is something you're born with," he said slyly, "but maybe you should try converting anyway. Because let's face it. You haven't gotten this much action since the day you walked in here."

Though I prided myself on being able to take a joke, by the end of the week, I had pretty much had it.

Some of the rabbis I'd interviewed were so scared of having their identities revealed that I'd had to promise I wouldn't just use a pseudonym for them, but a *pseudo-initial*. And I had to assign them initials that rarely appeared in English or Hebrew names, either. *Q*,* I ended up writing *(*not his real initial), knew he was gay ever since he began having fantasies about Jacob wrestling the angel in Hebrew school.* It was heartbreaking, really. Why did everyone assume that only a gay reporter could write empathetically about such a community?

"When I wrote about Ethiopian Jews, no one assumed I was Ethiopian," I said with some annoyance. "When I wrote about runaway teenagers, no one called up offering to place me in a foster home. And when I did that piece on Jewish fashion models, photographers didn't suddenly line up outside wanting to take my picture."

"Well, maybe that's because they'd already seen what you looked like," Lippy offered.

Mercifully, the next Tuesday, another issue of *The Jewish Week* hit the stands, and readers found a whole new series of articles to complain about. My stint as a lesbian heartthrob literally became old news.

———

A year later, leaving behind my disgraceful career in Jewish journalism, I moved to the Midwest for graduate school. During the summers, I returned to New York City starved for irony, bagels, and people who did not wear terry cloth sun visors color-coordinated with their track suits. While the truth was, I really enjoyed the Midwest, like most things, I enjoyed making fun of it even more. Plus, few of my friends had ever ventured farther west than Pittsburgh, so my life in Michigan made me somewhat of a novelty—albeit one like a shunt or a hairpiece.

"Oh my god. Are you all right? How do you survive out there?" my friend Nicole teased. "Quick, let's get you to a sushi bar and a museum." She then invited me to join a group of her friends for dinner at a chi-chi restaurant. Among them would be Rachel, an über-hip columnist for the über-hip *Village Voice* newspaper. Rachel was famous among the downtown crowd as a cultural critic, art expert, and lesbian activist—the Trifecta of Cool, really.

I would willingly have donated a kidney to write for *The Village Voice,* and though I tried to be very nonchalant about it, I was thrilled at the prospect of meeting Rachel and her lover, Lana. I'd been angling for an introduction ever since Nicole had become chummy with them at their synagogue. In my fantasies, Rachel would befriend me, then generously fork over her job. *Really,* she'd say, *the* Voice *needs some new blood, and with your talent, we'd be crazy not to snap you right up.*

"Come by our synagogue after services," Nicole suggested now, "and I'll introduce you."

I'd known Nicole since we were fifteen, when our friendship could have easily served as a case study in adolescent girl hysteria. Together, we'd watched *General Hospital* obsessively, danced to the B-52's in her living room like maniacs, and consumed vast quantities of Tab with frozen Cool Whip because one tablespoon of nondairy whipped topping, we discovered, had only nine calories. Every time a boy touched our breasts, we had to call each other up, pull our telephones into our respective bathrooms for privacy, and squealing, issue a Special Report. For each other's birthdays, we made personalized collages documenting every single "in-joke." Reading them, you'd have thought we were suffering from Alzheimer's: *Do you remember,* our litanies always began, *Strawberry daiquiris at Poncho Villa's? Listening to Air Supply? "Oooh, I'm driving my life away" and giving Mark kissing lessons?*

Yet a few years after college, Nicole had an experience that was hers and hers alone. One day she walked into the waiting room of her therapist's office, and met an attorney named Kay. They fell deliriously in high-octane, triple-caffeinated, whiplash love. Within the year, they'd had a commitment ceremony and exchanged wedding rings. Kay joined Nicole's temple and converted to Judaism.

"Well," Nicole's mother sighed, "we always did want our daughter to marry a nice Jewish lawyer. So okay. It's a woman. What can you do?"

Ironically, the rest of my cohorts and I were dating one inappropriate guy after another—then, stupidly, bragging about it. We were sleeping with drug addicts, having vague "uncommitted" relationships, then getting drunk on Jell-O shots and calling ex-boyfriends at 2:30 A.M. We were staggering around bars in lace stockings and leather jackets, then coming home with toilet paper stuck to our shoes.

In the meantime, Nicole and Kay had a custom-designed living room set, plans to have children, an investment portfolio, and respectable positions on the board of their synagogue. They had the most stable, promising, adult life of anyone I knew, and if you thought about their happiness long enough, it could depress the hell out of you.

———————

Having read her byline for years, I'd somehow gotten the idea that Rachel would be a haughty, anemic European lesbian who'd sit at a café smoking Gauloises while making withering pronouncements about Derrida and the death of postmodernism. Instead, she was affable and robust, with cool, red-framed glasses, brown lipstick, and a slightly goofy, asymmetrical haircut. To my great amazement, she'd actually read *The Jewish Week* newspaper. "Of course I know who you are," she said, pumping my hand vigorously. "It's one thing to write about progressive subjects for the *Voice*. But for a conservative paper like *The Jewish Week*? That takes *chutzpah*."

I couldn't help it; I beamed. I didn't expect Rachel to even know or care who I was, let alone see my antisocial impulses as anything remotely flattering. "Well," I heard myself saying, "we all do what we can to subvert the patriarchy, I guess."

"And that cover story on gay and lesbian rabbis," Rachel said, shaking her head wondrously. "That was really a coup. Lana and I talked about that for weeks."

"Thanks," I said proudly. "It seemed to make quite an impression."

"Look, I just have to ask." She leaned in toward me intently, clutching both my hands in hers. "What was it like coming out at a newspaper like that? I mean, *The Jewish Week,* with all of its religious commentaries and Orthodox rabbis. How did you tell them? Did you start with one editor, or just casually let it slip, or come in wearing a pink triangle, or what?"

For a moment, I was stunned. Then I began to laugh. "Actually, it wasn't like that at all because—"

Yet before I could finish, a woman in a Dupioni silk coat ran up to Rachel and shouted, "Sweetie! Congratulations! Donald and I are both so happy for you!"

Just the week before, Rachel and Lana had had a commitment ceremony at the synagogue. Now, Lana had suddenly materialized, and she and Rachel were engulfed by well-wishing fellow congregants. I looked around for Nicole, hoping she might be able to help set the record straight, so to speak, but she and Kay had gotten lost in the throng. Ah well, I thought, I'll clarify things over dinner.

Oddly, though, I felt tickled.

Back in college, I'd spent ridiculous amounts of time at the womyn's center, sitting cross-legged on the floor with other young, privileged, Ivy League feminists passing around a "talking stick" in order to share endless testimonials about how marginalized and oppressed we all were. In this feminist community, it was taken as gospel that lesbians were, by definition, sophisticated, liberated, and enlightened, whereas straight girls were misogynistic, spineless breeders who'd been brainwashed into wearing high heels and voting Republican.

But now Rachel, of all people, thought I was gay. How cool was that? If only all my old cohorts back at college could see me now, I thought. Susie Gilman: so hip, you'd think she was a dyke. I Can't Believe She's Not Lesbian.

Naively, I'd thought my long hair and lipstick pretty much broadcast to the world that I was heterosexual. But for all I knew, people took me to be a transsexual post-op. And this was possibly a very good thing. Talk about street cred, I thought. I could hit all the coolest girlie bars that Nicole and Kay went to, the Lunchbox and the Clit Club. No more third-tier journalism and Midwestern cheese fries for me: as a sexually ambiguous cultural critic, I could become the darling of the hard-core Downtown Intelligentsia. I imagined myself in ripped fishnets and blue lipstick, writing scathing exposés about funding for AZT, penning a column called "cliterature," reviewing performance art at PS 1. Mysterious, yet scathingly sexual, I'd walk into cocktail parties in the East Village and people would nod in my direction and whisper: *I heard she slept with Madonna.* And just think of the networking possibilities!

What was the harm, really, in *not* letting people know my true sexual orientation, I wondered. Certainly, gay people didn't always come out immediately. And while some people were secure enough to always be themselves in any given situation, I had never been one of them. In my undying callowness and naked bid to be loved, I was endlessly reinventing my personality, nipping and tucking it here and there. In junior high school, I'd bought records just because Dawn Chapnick, the most advanced new girl in eighth grade, said they were "wicked": how else to explain owning both "More Than a Feeling" and "Dust in the Wind"? In high school, I'd doctored fake IDs so I could drink underage, and at Studio 54, when Vanessa's druggie, debutante friends asked me where my family "summered," I replied blithely, "Oh, you know. Sometimes at the Betty Ford Clinic, sometimes Gstaad." Around boys I dated from Harvard, I'd tried to be erudite; around street girls from my neighborhood, I'd tried to act tough. On dates, I'd feigned interest in all sorts of nonsense—trout fishing, Civil War reenactments, foosball. My personality, when I really thought about it, was a perpetual motion machine of self-invention, a giant mood ring in a hall full of mirrors.

If I did not let Rachel know that I was not, in fact, a lesbian, I wouldn't be committing a crime. I'd just be sparing her embarrassment—and assuming a mantle of fabulousness in the process. Why, I'd be like a drag queen, except in reverse. If gay men could dress up as straight women, why couldn't a straight woman masquerade as a butch for an evening? Hell, they had "Queen for a Day." Why not "Dyke for a Night"?

And then, whenever it did come out that I had a boyfriend, well then, I figured, all of us could have a really good laugh.

"Susie, this is Bridgette," Rachel said slyly, when we arrived at the restaurant. She directed me to a delicate, Pre-Raphaelite-looking redhead in a batik sundress. "Why don't the two of you sit over there?" She pointed to the last two places across from each other at the end of the table, where a lone hurricane candle flickered seductively. Bridgette smiled at me coyly, then ran a hand through her hair. I knew the gesture all too well. It was one I'd made about a zillion times with guys I'd been attracted to on first dates. Loneliness had its own, sad perfume, and I could smell hers a mile off. It was unnervingly like my own.

I felt a bolt of panic.

"So," Bridgette said as we all settled in. "Rachel tells me you're a writer?"

"Not just any writer, Bridge," Rachel prompted across the table, "she's the one who did that big story on lesbian rabbis."

"Oh," said Bridgette. "That was very good."

"You are one gutsy dyke," Lana declared, taking a swig of ice water. "I'll say that."

"Well, actually—" I began. I had to come out to them, I realized. Immediately. Sins of omission were one thing, but leading someone on falsely was quite another.

Yet at that moment, Bridgette reached across the table to pour a glass of wine for me. Her hands shook and liquid spilled across the tabletop. "Oh, I'm sorry," she cried. "I'm a terrible klutz." We scrambled to sop up the mess with our napkins. She set down the carafe, then put her head in her hands.

"Oh, I'm just never any good at this," she said miserably. "My dad, he was an alcoholic, so I think I'm just bad, you know, at being casual about wine and stuff." Then she straightened up and attempted to smile, trying to look happy, and attractive, and secure in herself.

"Bridgette's been in recovery," Rachel said, seemingly for my benefit, "and she's been doing an amazing job of it."

"Amen," said Lana, raising her glass toward Bridgette. "To you, girl. You've been an inspiration."

I looked at Bridgette, then at the glass of wine in her hand. "You're recovering from alcoholism?" I said.

"Nuh-uh." She took a sip of wine, which seemed to embolden her. "Sexual abuse. My uncle raped me when I was fourteen." Then she set down her glass and took a breath decisively. "But I don't want to talk about the past," she said, willing herself to smile. "I want to talk about hopeful things. Love. Art. The future."

"Hear, hear," said Lana.

"So," Bridgette said, leaning toward me, "do you go out a lot?"

"Oh, Susie, before I forget," Rachel interrupted, foisting a pen and paper napkin at me. "Give me your phone number. My editor wants to talk to you about doing an article for him."

Distracted, I wrote out my number. "Which editor?" I said as casually as possible. "Leonard?" Leonard was the editor-in-chief at *The Village Voice.*

"No, the one at *Outweek,*" said Rachel. "You know, he actually dated one of the rabbis you profiled. I think he's dying to get the scoop from you. Hey, an old 'Academy' exchange," she said, studying my phone number. "You've got a place on the Upper West Side?"

"It's my mother's," I said. "I'm living back home for the summer. Listen." I took a deep breath and said, "With this *Outweek* thing. I think you should know—"

"Well, that's gotta suck," declared Lana. "Moving back home with your mom."

"Yeah, well," I said. "What can you do? Listen, with *Outweek*—"

"Are you out to her?" said Rachel.

"Well, no, as a matter of fact, I'm not," I said, seizing the opening. "I'm not, because, you see—"

"Hey, Rach," Lana called across the table. "Do you have your house keys on you?"

"Yeah. Sure. Why?" Rachel said.

"Because." Lana shot her a nudging look.

"Ohmygod. Of course!" cried Rachel. "She'd be perfect."

"Listen," Lana said, turning to me. "We've got an apartment in SoHo. It's tiny, but it's air-conditioned. And we're leaving for Holland tomorrow morning for our honeymoon. Why don't you house-sit for us while we're gone?"

She reached into her pocket and actually took out her house keys.

"Oh no," I said with some violence, though the prospect of having my own place in SoHo was almost more fabulous than I could ever stand.

"We'll be gone only two weeks, but that should give you a little respite from your mother," said Lana. "Believe me, I know what a bitch it is to have live with your family after being on your own."

"And it's a great place to write," added Rachel. "Good vibes. Totally quiet. Do you use a Macintosh? We've got a Mac."

"Frankly, we'd rather have someone in there," said Lana. "Pick up the mail, water the plants."

"You'd be doing us a tremendous favor," said Rachel.

"And if you're not out to your mom and want to bring a girlfriend back, well, you know, we're cool with that," Lana laughed.

"Here." Rachel slid her gleaming house keys across the table toward me, until, quite literally, they dropped in my lap.

"That's the thing," I said desperately. "You see, I don't have a girlfriend to bring back because I—"

"Really?" said Bridgette, perking up. "I don't have a girlfriend either." She smiled and raised her wineglass. "To lonely-hearted lesbians.

"Hey, no pity parties here," Lana laughed. "Trust me. You'll both find someone yet." Then she, too, raised her glass. "To finding Ms. Right."

At that moment, with a precision timing seen only in sitcoms, the waitress arrived.

"Good evening, lay-dees," she said perkily, removing a pad from her apron. "My name is Cassidy. And I've got several specials tonight I'd like to tell you about. First, I've got a poached halibut with a cilantro-ginger puree over a bed of organic lentils with a soy milk and white wine reduction."

I looked beseechingly at Nicole and Kay for help, but they were sitting at the far end of the table, staring raptly into each other's eyes and massaging each other's hands, their faces awash with the oblivious, caramelized look of two people irritatingly in love.

Clearly, I had to come out. But how? I couldn't just blurt "Excuse me, but I'm a heterosexual" while the waitress distributed the menus and the busboy plopped bread baskets in front of us, could I? In getting to know people, there seemed to be a window of opportunity in which you established yourselves and communicated vital bits of information. Once that window closed, things got decidedly sticky. With names, for example: if you forgot someone's name right after being introduced, it was fine to say, "I'm sorry, I didn't catch your name." But the longer the conversation went on, the harder and more embarrassing it got to correct them. Once someone confessed to you, "So they dropped the sodomy charges against this guy, and now I'm addicted to painkillers," you could not, in good conscience, reply, "Oh, I'm sorry, but what was your name again?"

Now, there didn't seem to be any opportune moments. As soon as we each had our menus, Rachel and Lana ordered a bottle of champagne. A bottle arrived at the table, glasses were passed around, more toasts were made. "To love!" "To romance!" "To same-sex marriages!"

What was I going to do? Yell, "And to straight marriages, too"?

In the wake of the toasts came laughter. A platter of bruchetta appeared, "Compliments of the chef," said the waitress with a wink.

"The chef used to date my friend Alan," Lana informed us.

"To the gay kitchen mafia," Kay cheered, raising her glass in yet another toast. What was I going to do? Refuse to toast the gay kitchen mafia—especially after free bruchetta?

Then, before I could think of some elegantly casual way to clarify things, everyone launched into a lusty debate over the merits of grilled ahi tuna with sun-dried tomato pesto versus pan-fried portobello mushrooms with wild herb polenta. I thought about subtly interjecting something corrective like, "Well, my boyfriend says sun-dried tomatoes are good for your immune system," but just how asinine would that sound? Before I could come up with something else, the conversation veered into synagogue gossip, followed by questions about journalism, to a debate about whether the Guggenheim

Museum should be expanded based on designs Frank Lloyd Wright had jettisoned before his death.

I'd never had to come out before, and sitting there, I realized just how fucking hard it was. The timing alone was exasperating, like trying to grab the brass ring on a merry-go-round. You couldn't interrupt a conversation to announce it, but presenting it as a non sequitur seemed equally awkward and lethal. Plus, how could you mention your sexuality without it seeming like any big deal? But, if it really wasn't a big deal, why mention it at all? But what about Bridgette, casting fleeting glances at me across the candlelight? And then, what if I came out and it made everyone at the table uncomfortable? Certainly, it would be a conversation stopper. But then, what if it wasn't? Then I'd look like an even bigger asshole—making a big deal out of nothing. Or, worse still, what if they thought I was telling them because I was uncomfortable with homosexuality and wanted to establish that I was "not one of them"? Or, would *they think* that *I thought* that *they* would have an issue with my being straight—that I didn't trust them to be cool enough to like me regardless of my sexual orientation? But then again, what if they really *didn't* like me because of my sexual orientation? What if they thought all straight women were mindless, self-hating wimps incapable of producing anything other than babies and needlepoint oven mitts?

For years, I'd been hoping to hang out with Rachel. Now that I was actually doing it, sitting in her inner circle, I couldn't absorb a single word she was saying because of the monologue unfurling in my own head: *They wouldn't have asked me to house-sit for them if they knew I was a heterosexual, would they? Why do I feel guilty? I shouldn't feel guilty. I haven't done anything wrong. Why, they've made assumptions about me. But I feel like a fraud. But then, what if they think I'm a freak and take back their house keys?* As the evening progressed, my distress only increased.

It wasn't lost on me that the profound ickiness I was experiencing was something that every other woman at that table had endured for a lifetime. No doubt, all of them had, at one point or another, been fixed up with a guy unwittingly. No doubt, they'd been ambushed at some bar or a party by an oblivious acquaintance gesturing eagerly, "Come on over here and meet Leonard." Surely, they'd had to withstand overtures from men while their straight friends looked on encouragingly, winking and making lewd pantomimes across the table, then pulling them off to the ladies' room for a grilling: "So? Do you like him? He certainly seems to like *you!*"

Even I'd been guilty of that. Hadn't I once tried to fix up a copy editor named Parker with my friend Maggie? "I really think you guys would be good together," I'd insisted. Now, Parker was living with Richard in TriBeCa with two cocker spaniels and a Persian cat named Stonewall.

Back at college, some of my straight friends and I had flirted with the idea of having a lesbian experience "just to see what it's like." Well, now I was truly having one, all right.

By the time the check arrived, the only thing I'd succeeded in doing was drinking way too much and developing a massive headache.

When people believe you've grown up, suffered, or loved the same way they have, they can be inordinately generous with you. Convinced you share the same religion, the same sexual orientation, or even the same alma mater, they will give you their business cards with their home phone number scribbled on the back. They will make painful confessions to you about their marriage. They will let their voices slide back into the homey, regional accents they've struggled so hard to shed. It may be flattering at first, but if their assumptions about you are wrong, ultimately it becomes mortifying. As they take you into their confidences, you watch them violate themselves. Even if you've done nothing to mislead them, you can't help but feel guilty and undeserving of their trust.

"I don't have anything against homosexuals," a straight rabbi had told me when I'd interviewed him for my article. "It's just that, why do they have to be so in-your-face?"

But coming out isn't something you simply do for your own benefit, I realized. You do it out of respect for other people, too, because you can't stand to have them bare their hearts to you unwittingly. You don't want to perpetuate their unknowingness, or see them played for a fool.

For the next two weeks, I felt like a con artist as I slept in Lana and Rachel's loft, recycled their newspapers, and dutifully collected their mail. Because what was I going to do: call them in Amsterdam, tell them I was straight, and abandon their houseplants? Yet it was hard to tell which was more uncomfortable: living back home with my mother, or ensconced in SoHo as a counterfeit dyke.

Every so often, Nicole called the apartment, "Hello, is this Susie Gilman, professional lesbian house sitter?" she teased. She was as amused by my predicament as other friends had been about my job at *The Jewish Week*. I tried to laugh along. I tried to make jokes. "Well, I'm just here straightening up," I'd say campily.

But then, I'd sit down at Rachel's desk. Above it was a bulletin board she'd decorated with Man Ray photographs, pro-choice buttons, and bumper stickers reading: Silence = Death.

I had nothing to be ashamed of, I told myself. My sexuality was nothing to apologize for. Why, plenty of great people throughout history had been heterosexual. I couldn't help the way I was born, dammit! Whom I chose to love was nobody's business but my own. "I'm straight, I'm great, get used to it," I tried chanting. But life in the closet can be gnawing and insidious, and in the end, I just couldn't shake the feeling that I was doing something horribly, horribly wrong. I was sexually ambiguous, all right, and now I felt abhorrent—a case study for an unwritten exposé: I was Susie Q*. Not her real initial.

Chapter 12

My Father the Park Ranger,
My Mother the Nun

ONE THANKSGIVING when John and I were in elementary school, our parents decided to take us to Vermont for the holiday. A colleague of my father's had purchased a farm outside Brattleboro. "You kids will get to see some real Holstein cows," our mother said. "We'll sleep in a barn and eat Thanksgiving dinner in front of a big stone fireplace. It'll be very rustic. Very Norman Rockwell."

The problem with Norman Rockwell's world, however, was that it was a bitch to get to. Driving our battered old VW minibus through the icy roads of New England was like maneuvering a giant breadbox across a skating rink. Halfway through our trip, we had an accident. Skidding across two lanes of traffic, we slammed sidelong into a guardrail on the edge of a mountain. This guardrail was the only thing between us and a 1,200-foot plunge into a frozen river, and for a moment, the minibus strained against the metal ribbing, the laws of physics willing us over the precipice. Then the bus lurched back and settled into a snowbank with a scrape.

Once my father switched off the ignition and ascertained that all four of us were, indeed, okay, my brother and I could not have been more thrilled.

"An accident! We've had an accident!" we yelled excitedly. Two summers before, our downstairs neighbors had been in a major car crash. They'd come home from the hospital with a stunning array of injuries and a truly impressive collection of medical paraphernalia. Our friend Naomi was in traction with a body cast up to her armpit. For months, she was the star attraction of the neighborhood. All the local kids vied to decorate her cast with their graffiti tags, and she received unlimited supplies of *Archie* comic books, Hostess Twinkies, and Scooby-Doo coloring books. Her exalted status as invalid had not been lost on us. "Can we go to the hospital?" we begged now as our parents climbed out to assess the damage to the fender. "Can we be in traction?"

Instead, our parents simply pried the VW bus off the side of the guardrail, then drove the dented hulk of it to the nearest Howard Johnson's Motor Inn Lodge.

"Sorry, kids," our father sighed, "but it looks like we're here for Thanksgiving. I'm not going any further without snow chains."

He pointed to the churchlike turquoise and orange roof dispirit-edly, as if Howard Johnson's was a terrible consolation prize. But to John and me, it was even better than traction. The prospect of "sleeping in a barn" had not held the same appeal for us that it did for our parents. From what we'd learned, whenever grown-ups used the word "rustic," what they really meant was "outhouse." But a motel—we'd never slept in a motel before!

"Yippeeeee!" we shrieked, dancing around the freezing parking lot. "We're spending Thanksgiving at HoJo's! We're spending Thanksgiving at HoJo's!"

As soon as our parents unbolted the door, we tore through our room like maniacs. The entire place looked like it had been sterilized and shrink-wrapped. The Formica bureau, the polyester bedspreads, the laminated headboard all gave off fumes of plastic and room deodorizer, filling the air with a chemical cheerfulness. We were drunk with it, instantly.

"LOOK," we shouted dizzily, pointing, "A COLOR TV!" (At

home we had a black-and-white portable.) "TWO DOUBLE BEDS! WALL-TO-WALL SHAG CARPETING!"

"Mom, Dad, look!" we cried, running out of the bathroom brandishing the miniature guest soaps wrapped like party favors we'd found on the side of the sink. "Free soaps!"

"Look!" we cried again, running back in a minute later to show off the doll-sized bottles of shampoo we'd found by the tub. "Free shampoo!"

We then spied a Styrofoam ice bucket atop the bureau. "A FREE ICE BUCKET," we yelled, then immediately took turns wearing it on our heads like a fez while jumping up and down on the bed.

Our parents stood by the doorway looking stunned, their glazed-over faces suggesting that they could not quite believe they'd created us—two offspring who were capable of going bazookies over a Styrofoam ice bucket and a piece of Howard Johnson's guest soap. The ice machine by the elevator amazed us. That our bathroom had not one, but *two* sinks was incredible. Best yet, however, was the Thanksgiving dinner itself. The chef at Howard Johnson's was clearly a culinary genius. Why, he'd managed to cook a Thanksgiving dinner identical to that of our favorite TV dinner. The tissuey slices of turkey came smothered in sweet, brown, gelatinous gravy—just the way we liked it—accompanied by a troika of starches. Tater Tots. Mounds of processed mashed potatoes. Dinner rolls. Not a green bean or a cranberry in sight. And afterward, Oh! None of those awful Thanksgiving pies in which vegetables tried to pass themselves off as desserts. There were simply, gloriously, twenty-eight flavors of Howard Johnson's ice cream.

"Oh, Mom! Oh, Dad!" we proclaimed rapturously as we dug into parfait glasses dripping with chocolate syrup. "This is the best Thanksgiving *ever!*"

And so we inscribed it in our annals of the family: *The best Thanksgiving ever.* Occasionally, as teenagers, John and I prompted, "Hey, remember that Thanksgiving we spent at Howard Johnson's?" Then we'd lovingly recall each detail, reliving our pleasure, our naive delight at the voluptuousness of it all. Oh, it had seemed like such an adventure, didn't it? Remember when we made a fort using the luggage rack and extra pillows? Remember playing "The Flying Wallendas" by jumping off the dresser? Remember those hot fudge sundaes for dessert?

Only years later, when we were waxing nostalgic about it again one morning, did our father audibly groan: "Augh. That Thanksgiving we spent at Howard Johnson's. Was that ever a fucking nightmare."

"Oh, it was horrible," our mother agreed. "The absolute worst."

My brother looked stunned. "What are you talking about? That was, like, our best Thanksgiving *ever*."

Our father chuckled. "For you kids, maybe," he said. "For you kids, it was the Thanksgiving when we let you run up and down the halls of Howard Johnson's playing with the ice machine."

"But for your father and me," our mother interjected, "it was the Thanksgiving when we nearly drove off a cliff."

"Boy, I will never forget hitting that guardrail," our father said soberly, staring down into his coffee cup. "I was sure that was *it*. We were going over." He shook his head. "Driving up to Vermont in that old VW. What were we thinking?"

"We were young. Young and stupid," our mother said gently.

"And remember? I had to plead with the receptionist at Howard Johnson's to take a personal check because we didn't have enough cash for the rooms?"

"And we couldn't find a garage—"

"And I got a nosebleed from the stress—"

"Oh, that blood in your beard. All over your shirt—"

"I sat in the motel lobby with an ice pack so it wouldn't scare the kids—"

"And then we had that disgusting Thanksgiving dinner—"

"That turkey was like Alpo—"

"Nobody else in the whole place except for those two drunken farts feeding dinner rolls to their beagle. And one of them yelled at you, David, when you asked her to put out her cigarette because John was just getting over the mumps, and he was congested—"

"I had the mumps?" said John.

"Oh, was that ever depressing," said our mother.

"I can't believe you guys," I cried. "It wasn't that way at all. That meal was delicious. That motel was a palace. We jumped on the beds. We watched color TV. We loved every minute of it."

Our parents laughed. "Well, *you two* did, sweetie," said my father. "And that was the only redeeming thing about the whole holiday. Otherwise . . ." His voice trailed off.

"That day was horrendous," our mother declared. "That day was criminal."

———————

Two months after I'd left home, post-college, to live on my own, our parents announced they were separating. Although their twenty-six-year marriage had oscillated between grinding frustration and festering resentment, their decision somehow still managed to come as a total shock to John and me.

"How can you guys be separating?" my brother cried when my parents called him at college with the news. "You just redecorated the apartment."

"What do you want us to do?" our mother sighed. "Stay together so your father can look at the wallpaper?"

Their marriage had stagnated, she said. They needed some time apart to "gain some perspective" and "work a few things out."

"It's only temporary," said our dad.

Yet no sooner had he transplanted his toothbrush and business suits to a furnished one-bedroom across town than it became obvious he was not moving back.

"I can't believe our parents are splitting up," I sobbed to John. "I mean, they already stuck it out twenty-six years. Would another twenty-six really kill them?"

"Did you see this coming?" John asked incredulously. "I didn't."

"I didn't either," I said. "Okay, except for whenever Mom yelled at Dad that she wished she lived alone—"

"Or those times when he said he might leave her."

"Or when she told him he was boring."

"Or when he refused to comfort her when she was upset."

"But except for those minor details—" I said.

"They seemed happy enough together," John concluded.

"Besides," I said. "Isn't marriage, by definition, supposed to be deadening and lethal anyway?"

By the mid-1990s, almost nothing from our childhood remained. The Upper West Side had become so aggressively gentrified, sections of it now resembled a cruise ship. Luxury condominiums with polarized windows sprang up, sporting awnings with pretentious names like "The Key West" and "The Montana," suggesting that they were not really part of New York City at all. On street corners where residents had once shelled out $25 for a Baggie of marijuana, they could now spend the same amount for a plate of blackened catfish. In a move that was particularly ironic, a number of bodegas run by Central American immigrants were replaced by Banana Republics.

While John and I supposed we shouldn't complain, we did anyway. Given the choice between counting our blessings and whining, we usually opted for the latter, and it annoyed us to no end that the Upper West Side had become so chic and expensive, none of us who'd actually grown up there could now afford to live in it.

Worse still were the new arrivals—snotty, suburban-bred professionals who harbored the delusion that they deserved to live in our neighborhood simply because they could pay the rent. Their sense of entitlement was galling. Twice, young stockbrokers with attaché cases body-slammed me in attempts to grab the taxis I'd hailed; at my gym, a balding Master of the Universe climbed onto my step machine and tried to shove me off because, even though he'd missed his turn, he was in a hurry, goddamn it! During my childhood, I'd dodged countless threats from black and Hispanic kids in the neighborhood, but these turned out to be nothing compared to the viciousness of white yuppies, who would physically assault you without warning over a Nordic Trac or a latte.

To console each other, John and I indulged in the archaeology of memory, regaling one another with our "insider knowledge" of what the neighborhood had *really* been like.

"Oh look," I'd say nostalgically, pointing to the new Blockbuster Video on Broadway, "remember when that used to be an empty lot and all the junkies used to nod off there?"

"And across the street was that adult movie theater that only showed Spanish porn?" John added wistfully.

"And remember that paranoid schizophrenic named Quack-Quack who used to wander around Amsterdam Avenue wearing duct tape and terrorizing all the women?"

"Oh!" we'd wail in unison, "where did everything go?"

After our parents separated, John and I had the awful, nagging suspicion that not only had the infrastructure of our past vanished, but that our entire home life had been like Thanksgiving at Howard Johnson's. Had we spent our childhood dancing around with ice buckets on our heads, thinking everything was just dandy, when really our parents were sitting there spellbound with misery? Apparently so.

We spent hours on the phone performing autopsies of our parents' marriage. "Was that why Dad took so many business trips? Was that why Mom was so moody?" It was now impossible to leaf through a family album, to look at pictures of birthday parties, of summers at Silver Lake, of the four of us grinning before our Christmas tree, without feeling queasy. Suddenly, every memory was suspect, counterfeit, a likely illusion.

"Was anything the way we thought it was?" we asked each other. "Why didn't we have a clue?"

A dead giveaway, apparently, should've been the interior decorator.

"Your parents completely redid their apartment, then announced they were splitting? Augh, that's classic," said Joshua, my boyfriend at that time. Joshua's own parents had divorced when he was thirteen, then remarried twice each by the time he'd turned twenty.

Unsurprisingly, he now considered himself an expert in marital pathology. As he explained it, there was no surer sign that a marriage was in trouble than when a couple paid professionals to reupholster their sofa and knock down their drywall. To hear him tell it, an interior decorator might as well arrive on a couple's doorstep wearing a black-hooded robe and holding a scythe. As soon as a designer started sashaying around the living room enthusing, "I'm thinking terra-cotta. I'm thinking Moroccan/urban. I'm thinking throw pillows," you could be sure the marriage was kaput.

"It's like a joint midlife crisis," Joshua explained, running his fingers around the rim of a margarita, then sucking off the salt. "Instead of a sports car and a blonde, couples install track lighting and buy a new dishwasher. Hell, my mother and her second husband built a whole new country house just before they called it quits."

Of course, neither my brother nor I had known any of this. The year our parents had decided to redecorate, all we'd thought was: *It's about fucking time.*

As an artist, our mother had always been loath to throw out anything that might, with a dab of Elmer's glue and a sequin, be converted into a decorative handicraft. And so, over the years, our apartment had taken on the distinctive look of a roadside garage sale. Virtually every room had become crammed with discarded picture frames, pipe cleaners, bolts of colored felt, acrylics, yarn, saw horses, plastic milk crates, and those Styrofoam heads used to display wigs in department stores. It was a "decorating scheme" not unlike the process that formed the Grand Canyon. One layer of debris settled prettily on top of another, preserving it for all eternity.

Our father drifted among these canyons seemingly indifferently, content just to sack out on the sofa with the sports page amid piles of our mother's Mondrianesque collages, decoupage coffee tins, and 3-D mobiles painted to look like psychedelic fish. His own idea of home improvement pretty much began and ended with picking his socks up off the floor.

Yet the year my brother left for college, our father made a sudden, stunning decision. "We're redoing the apartment," he announced. From the way he said this, there was no way of mistaking that "redoing the apartment" was really a euphemism for "getting rid of this tsunami of crap."

His adamancy was surprising.

As they'd gotten older, John and I had noticed, our parents' personalities had begun to ossify into caricatures of themselves. More and more, our mother's sensitivity and "artistic temperament" were giving way to a simple, constant state of agitation. She was like a storm system, filling our household with weather and drama, her views of the world swinging wildly between hope and indictment. One moment, she was weeping with gratitude over all the poignant beauty of our lives; the next, she was raging over their mediocrity. We lived on constant alert for the shifts in her moods, trying desperately to forecast her.

Our easygoing father, on the other hand, had mellowed to the point of inertia. Lolling around placidly in sweatpants, he spent his time at home hypnotized before the television. He'd read the paper for hours, or absentmindedly stare out the window, seemingly immune to the histrionics that the rest of us felt compelled to engage in on a nearly daily basis. Occasionally, he'd rouse himself just long enough to realize that he should be taking more demonstrable interest in our lives.

"So, Susie," he'd say awkwardly, casting about for some clear point of entry. "How's that, um, party planning of yours going?"

"What party?" I'd say.

"Weren't you planning a party? Something with champagne and ice cream that boys could only come to in drag?"

"You mean my Sweet Sixteen?" I said. "Dad, that was seven years ago."

By middle age, our parents were interacting like two components of an EKG reading, our mother the erratic heartbeat, our father the perennial flatline. It wasn't our idea of fun, but it seemed to work well enough for them.

Yet once our father decided to redecorate, he was transformed overnight into Napoleon. Our apartment, to him, was suddenly a continent waiting to be attacked, pillaged, and colonized through the strategic use of paint swatches. He didn't hire a decorator so much as *appoint* one. "Everyone," he announced imperiously, "this is Gene."

Gene was an elegant, bearded man who insisted that his specialty was decorating apartments in such a way as to make them look as if they'd never been decorated. Before my mother could even wonder aloud why we needed a decorator if all he was going to do was make it look as if he hadn't done anything, a legion of "removal specialists" arrived. On my father's orders, they spent two days carting away our prized collections of saw horses and broken floor lamps. "Out," my father commanded, as they trooped back and forth with their burlap-covered dollies. "All of it. *Vamoose.*"

"Who is this person?" my mother said with alarm. "Yesterday, he couldn't find the clothes hamper. Now, he's a fanatic who sits in the bathroom, obsessing about linoleum."

It was strange to see my father so invigorated. No sooner were the rooms cleared than carpenters, painters, and contractors arrived, clomping through the apartment in coveralls and ponytails, filling it with industriousness and the distinctly oniony smell of male perspiration. Under my father's direction, the renovations then proceeded as frantically as time-elapse photography set to the *William Tell* Overture.

Soon, every evening began to feel like Christmas morning; my parents and I hurried home from work eager to discover the latest surprise: six sleek leather chairs tucked around a new dining table. A hand-embroidered carpet unfurled on the living room floor. The beauty went beyond anything we had ever imagined for ourselves. It was hard to believe, frankly, that so much material good fortune could be visited upon us—and that my father, of all people, had instigated it. Why, when it was all done, my mother and I dared to whisper, our apartment might look like something out of *Architectural Digest.*

Yet the less our home looked like a storage facility, the more alien we felt in it. We moved around the new rooms stiffly, gingerly, like guests in a furniture museum.

"Don't sit on the sofa!" we shrieked when one of us entered the living room with a glass of Diet Pepsi. "You'll spill!"

"We'll get more comfortable with this in time," my father said with newfound authority. "It'll be better once the wall unit arrives."

For the *pièce de résistance,* he'd ordered a custom-made wall unit for the living room. To hear him go on about it, however, it was not merely a wall unit that was going to arrive, but a wall unit messiah.

"Wait till you see it," he said excitedly. "It's a brand-new design by the same company that builds wall units for the royal family of Denmark."

For as long as I had known him, my father had had almost zero interest in material goods. Any gadget harder to operate than a bottle opener was a source of anxiety for him. Designer suits, athletic shoes—my father could barely pronounce the names, let alone appreciate their status. Whenever we asked him what he wanted for his birthday, he shrugged. "Jeez. I don't know. Maybe a new pair of sweat socks?"

This custom-made wall unit was the first item I'd ever seen him get visibly emotional about.

While I struggled to present myself as someone who cared, he described in painstaking detail how it was made of a rich mahogany veneer, making it easy to clean! Bolted directly into the wall, there'd be no warping or wobbling! "It's indestructible. You can store anvils in it," he said excitedly, as if this were something we were actually contemplating doing.

For weeks, our apartment lay in wait, the renovations complete except for one naked, gaping space in the living room and a mountain of boxes, ready to be emptied. *Once the wall unit arrived,* our father insisted repeatedly, our apartment would be *clear for the first time in decades.*

The day of the delivery, he was so excited, he stayed home from work. "When you get back this evening, it'll be like you're in a brand-new apartment," he said gleefully.

"For starters, it'll be quiet," said my mother, rolling her eyes. "No more listening to your father obsessing about the goddamn wall unit."

That night, the apartment was, in fact, quiet. As my father had promised, when I arrived home from work, there were no more cartons barricading the hallways, no more stepladders and paint cans lying about. All traces of renovation had vanished.

"Hello?" I said plaintively.

I hung up my coat and headed into the living room. My father sat on our newly upholstered couch. My mother was over by the window, staring blankly out at the city.

"So. Did the wall unit come?" I asked. But before they could answer, I saw it for myself. It was impossible not to. Extending from the floor to ceiling, it took up the entire eastern wall of the apartment.

Gargantuan and liver-colored, it looked not so much like a piece of furniture as a gigantic control panel, an enormous monolith riddled with brass industrial hinges and knobs. The retractable "cabinets" were more like hatches and vaults, and the dark shutters looked impenetrable, giving it a foreboding, sinister quality. The unit was so massive, it overpowered everything else in the living room. It gave you the distinct feeling it would slam down on top of you at any minute and crush you. It was hideous: the Death Star of furniture.

My father leapt up. "Well," he said, forcing a smile. "What do you think?"

I studied it for a moment.

"Is it really bolted to the wall?" I said.

My mother gave a little cry of despair.

"I could kill Gene," she said, nearly in tears. "And I could kill you, David. It didn't look like this in the catalogue at all."

"Look, Ellen. I told you," my father said desperately. "It has lights." Turning to me, he fairly pleaded, "I told her, it looks better with the lights."

Hurrying over to the wall unit, he pushed a button on the side and small halogen bulbs embedded in the top shelves came on weakly, illuminating the uppermost cubbies like a row of shadow boxes. "See?" he said. In a court of law, he would have been accused of leading the witness. He twisted the dimmer on "high."

It was a little better, but not much.

I walked over and examined the wall unit. It was made of a sort of plastic laminate, a glossy fake wood oddly reminiscent of the halcyon furnishing at HoJo's. There was no painting it, no bleaching it, and, I saw quickly, no removing it. It was bolted to the wall, all right—an exterior wall—which meant my parents would probably have to knock down the entire building if they ever wanted to get rid of it. It was a monstrosity, a titanic eyesore, and they were stuck with it.

For a moment, we all stood there, marinating in misery. "Maybe you just need to remove some of the cabinet doors," I suggested. "You know, lighten it up. Make it more homey."

"Yes. Of course," my father said, seized with relief. "Remove some of the doors."

Immediately, the three of us got very busy with screwdrivers, removing the cabinet doors, then stocking the exposed shelves with my mother's prettiest art books and handicrafts. She positioned a couple of philodendrons in each corner so they cascaded down greenly.

"Well," she said uncertainly. "That's a little better. I guess."

"Oh, it's a lot better," my father insisted. "See, how much nicer that is? I think this will work out well, actually. I think this looks pretty good."

I didn't know who he thought he was kidding. Our efforts were the aesthetic equivalent of pinning a corsage on a robot. Yet as I watched him struggle to make the best of it, I found myself rooting for him, hoping that he would succeed in taming the oppressive wall unit—or at least in convincing my mother that he had not, in fact, made some colossal mistake.

By dinnertime, we were utterly fatigued from the physical labor and forced optimism of it all. Too tired to cook, we went to our local

Chinese restaurant and pushed shreds of shrimp lo mein around on our plates while studiously avoiding any mention of the wall unit. When we came home, I noticed, none of us made a beeline for the living room.

"Look, I think we just need to sleep on it," my father said finally. "When we wake up in the morning, it may look like a whole new piece of furniture."

"Well," my mother said dubiously. "I suppose."

"You know, sometimes these things just take getting used to," I prompted, eager to help. "We've been living amid drop cloths and boxes for so long, naturally it's going to take us a while to adjust to *real* furniture."

"Oh, that's such an excellent point." My father looked at my mother encouragingly. "Isn't that an excellent point? It'll just take us a while to *adjust*. In a few days, you'll see. We'll probably love it. In a few days, we probably won't even notice it's there." Then he smiled. "I mean, people, it's just a goddamn piece of furniture. It's not death and it's not cancer, right?" He laughed. "I mean, let's keep some perspective here. It's only a wall unit."

"That's right," my mother said mirthlessly. "It is only a wall unit, David."

Later that night, however, I found I couldn't sleep. Beyond my window, the city glittered, then grew steadily darker as lights in other buildings snapped off, like eyes shutting, like faces turning away. When the numbers on my clock radio flipped over into the single digits, I finally surrendered, got up, and headed into the kitchen for a snack. The tiny halogen bulbs on the wall unit were still on, glinting bleakly in the darkness. I almost didn't notice my father, sitting alone on the couch, staring up at the wall unit. He seemed unaware of my presence, or, indeed, of anything around him. All the florid optimism had been drained from his face; alone in the shadows, he looked worried, utterly bereft, more defeated than ever.

"Dad," I whispered, "it's only a wall unit."

Startled, his head jerked in my direction. "I know, sweetie," he whispered sadly after a moment. "It's just furniture."

But any stranger with an IQ higher than room temperature would've known that it was not "just furniture" at all. One look at my father, and they would've known instantly that as he stared at the wall unit, he was seeing a void that he believed would become the rest of his life. His frenzied redecorating hadn't been a quest for more closet space, but a desperate, naive attempt to resuscitate his own life, to renovate his marriage, to stave off some gangrenous rot. No doubt, with that damn wall unit, he'd hoped to contain my mother, to confine her volubility, to shut away years of tension behind a sleek mahogany veneer. He had tried his best, but his efforts had only resulted in this: a more permanent hideousness, bolted to his wall. Now, he was exhausted. He was out of ideas.

Anyone else would've known instinctively that, as my father gazed despairingly into the shelving, he was seeing not a piece of furniture at all, but his own, awaiting coffin.

Anyone but me would've known that, at that very moment, he was planning to leave.

———————

Divorce, we'd once thought smugly, was for other, less intelligent families. The fact that we had remained "intact"—while all around us, our neighbors were divorcing—had always been an enormous source of pride to my family. Occasionally, my mother would come home from the grocery store and announce, "I just heard that Ben and Rosalynn Schneiderman are splitting." Hearing this, our faces would break into the same triumphant look that children got whenever they snagged a seat during musical chairs. Just like these children, my family and I secretly believed that we remained in the game not because of timing or luck, but because of o   own inherent cleverness.

Sure, our mother was often seething. Sure, our father wandered around like a zombie. But at t e end of each day, we ate dinner together. We had our Sunday brunch rituals, our driving to the beach rituals, our Christmas morning rituals—and none of them ever involved the words "custody," "visitation," or "stepparent."

When our parents began divorcing, John and I found ourselves jettisoned from one demographic pile into another. Suddenly, in our twenties, we became the children of divorce, part of the other 50 percent. In a matter of weeks, our father had moved out, then moved again, then hired Gene the Decorator once more—this time to help him furnish his new bachelor pad on East 12th Street.

"Most men leave their wives for another woman. Our dad left Mom for another wall unit. Do you suppose we should feel lucky?" my brother said.

By waiting until we were grown, our parents had spared us a serial nightmare: the custody battles, the court appearances, the anxiety over whether child support and alimony would ever arrive, the possible parental vanishing acts. By waiting, our parents spared us the torture of thinking that we ourselves were to blame for the divorce. They'd spared us all traumas but one: the fact that our family had been smashed apart like a pumpkin.

Within weeks of my father's exodus, our family circle had expanded. In addition to the four of us, there were soon our shadows, four alter egos in the form of four therapists, earnest men and women with leather-upholstered furniture and white noise machines whirring away in their fern-filled foyers. In our readiness to seek professional help, we became possibly the first family to *double* in size in the wake of a separation; it was as if our parents had initiated an act of mitosis.

It was every bit as ludicrous as it sounds. Soon I was having phone conversations like this:

Me: *Hi, Dad. Listen. I'm calling because I'm upset about something, and when I talked it over with my therapist, she said I should talk to you about it directly.*

Dad: *Oh. She did? Well, listen, sweetie. Right now's not a good time. I'm actually late for my therapy appointment.*

Me: *So let me get this straight. You'd rather go to your therapist to talk about our problems than talk to me about them directly?*

Dad: *Hm. I guess I would. But that's an interesting observation. I'll be sure to bring it up in therapy.*

Overnight, we'd become clichés, a stupid caricature of New York neurotics flailing around, and I hated us for it. Once, I had worried that my family's eccentricities made us a bunch of freaks. Now, I saw that we were no different from anybody else, and this was at least as depressing. All the standard pettiness, wretchedness, and temporary psychosis that plagued every other divorcing family in America plagued us, too.

My father, for his part, behaved like a man who had just emerged from a coma. Having spent decades catatonic on the sofa, he suddenly erupted with personality, becoming a great fount of needs, opinions, appetites, and the highly irritating desire to express himself almost constantly.

"You know what I realized today when I was at Gristede's?" he said as I wandered dumbstruck through his trendy new downtown apartment, examining his love seat with its Aztec designs, his modular glass coffee table, his wicker basket filled with dried seed pods from Pier One Imports: *Was this stuff really my father's?* His black, lacquered bureau was neatly stacked with ticket stubs from Lincoln Center. There was a coaster from Caramba's! where I often went with Joshua for obliterating margaritas. Since when did my father like Yo-Yo Ma? Since when did he drink tequila?

A few weeks earlier, he'd taken my brother on a two-week whitewater rafting trip through the Grand Canyon. Until that moment, he'd never gone camping for more than a weekend—and never farther than a twenty-minute drive from a waffle house. But now, standing in the middle of his stainless-steel kitchen, he announced, "If I had my life to live over again, I wouldn't have done what I did. I'd lead a much more outdoors life. I'd live in Colorado or Utah. I'd maybe be a wilderness guide or a park ranger." Then he looked at me beamingly, as if awaiting applause.

He'd separated from my mother, he said, to save his own life. Now, he was center stage of it for the first time, basking in his own attention. Each day, he became more alive, more engaging, more thoroughly unrecognizable to me.

Early one Sunday morning, he telephoned. "I didn't wake you, did I?" he said, his voice full of pancakes and sunshine.

"Nuh-uh. I was just getting up to answer the phone," I said groggily.

"Good. Because I just had such a great idea, I had to call you immediately," he said. "What do you think of me getting my ear pierced?"

I waited for the punch line, but apparently there wasn't one.

"Okay," I said. "I'm hoping this is a crank call."

"I'm serious," my father laughed. "A diamond stud in my left ear? Or maybe a little gold hoop? How cool would that be?"

"Dad," I said. "You're fifty-two years old."

"So?" he said. "I'm a very hip fifty-two-year-old. And an earring would make me look even hipper, don't you think? I'd be, as you kids say nowadays, 'fly.' I'd be 'phat.' I'd be 'keeping it real.'"

"For starters, if you ever want to be any of those things," I said, "don't ever, ever use any of those words again. Look," I sighed. "In this world, only two groups of straight men get their ears pierced. The first are rebellious seventeen-to-twenty-three-year-olds. The second are pathetic middle-aged men trying desperately to look like them. Guess which category you'll fall into?"

"Gee. Really? You think so?" My father sounded deflated.

"You might as well just walk around with a sign tattooed to your forehead saying 'Hi, my name's David, and I just can't do enough to advertise my midlife crisis.'"

"No," said my father.

"Yes," I said. "Think 'comb-over,' Dad. Think 'toupee.' An earring is just the 90s equivalent. You might as well get a Corvette and an artificial tan."

"I'm calling your brother," my father said. "He'll think it's brilliant."

"No he won't. He'll think it's the stupidest fucking thing he's ever heard."

"Five dollars," said my father.

"You're on," I said. "And pay up's in cash."

Three minutes after we'd hung up, my father called back.

"Well?" I said.

"It was hard to hear his opinion," my father conceded. "He was laughing so hard he had to put down the phone."

Being a fifty-two-year-old man was far different than it had been only a generation ago. At fifty-two, men of my grandfather's generation had looked and acted like, well, grandfathers. They didn't plan white-water rafting trips down the Colorado River. They didn't wear blue jeans and leather bomber jackets. They didn't unabashedly discuss their group therapy over a double-skim latte.

Similarly, being a twenty-six-year-old woman was far different. In the not too distant past, an unmarried woman my age was on the fast track to spinsterhood. Now, my father and I were living at perhaps the first moment in history when a twenty-something daughter could lead a life almost identical to that of her middle-aged father. As single, urban professionals, both of us stayed up past midnight in our own little apartments watching *Tootsie* and *Diner* on video, eating Kung Pow Chicken straight out of the carton, wearing T-shirts and unisex boxer shorts we'd each purchased at the GAP. Both of us were dating, but skittish about marriage. We compared recipes and housekeeping tips. We read the same books and even listened to the same CDs: the soundtrack to *The Commitments. Ingrid Lucia and the Flying Neutrinos. The Joshua Tree.* My father would leave messages on my answering machine:

Hi, honey. Question for you. What's the name of that band I like so much with the three initials? M.R.I.?

"That's *R.E.M.*, Dad," I'd respond. "The album you like is called *Out of Time.*"

After twenty-six years, we were suddenly contemporaries, each struggling anxiously to live without my mother.

I should have been grateful. Too many fathers divorced their entire family when they left. Mine, by contrast, could call me three times in one night to report on the progress he'd made reheating spaghetti sauce. Living alone in his studio, reading travel brochures, and contemplating cooking classes, he was happier than I'd ever seen him— more generous with me, more involved in my life than ever. He was like a whole new parent. More Fun! More Attentive! Easier to Talk To! 150 Percent More Entertaining!

Unfortunately, I resented the hell out of it.

Parents, I believed, were supposed to remain older than you. While you could change—you could grow up, up, and away— parents, by virtue of being parents, were required to remain static. Ideally, they should eat the same bowl of Oat Bran every day for forty years, dress in the exact same cardigans and bathrobes they'd worn since you were three, sit in the same armchairs, bickering over the crossword puzzle every Sunday, and never once alter their recipe for meat loaf. Ideally, they should live in a time capsule, so that whenever you came home to visit, you could breathe in the familiar mustiness of your childhood, survey the anachronistic furnishings, and chuckle, "Boy, nothing ever changes around here, does it?" Their sole purpose in life was to maintain your own happy illusion of security.

When my therapist told me that such expectations were deluded, narcissistic, and childish, I stuck out my tongue, then spit at her.

The other problem, of course, was that my father's newfound well-being seemed to come at the expense of my mother's. My mother had claimed she'd wanted to salvage the marriage. Why hadn't my father? Over the phone sometimes, her voice sounded like that of a bewildered little girl. "Why didn't he want to work it out with me, Suze?" she pleaded softly. "I just don't understand."

A steady, relentless worry had entered her life like the dripping of a faucet: worry over finances, worry over bills, worry over what would happen to her as a woman in her fifties alone.

Despite her tofu and New Age sensibilities, my mother had not existed entirely in the counterculture. Like so many "good girls" of her generation, she'd trusted my father would take care of her "until death do us part." Amazingly, she'd never had her own bank account. She'd never balanced her own checkbook. Without my father standing sentry by her side, she found herself fully exposed to the contempt our culture levels at middle-aged women. Every day was riddled with petty cruelties and small indignities: the smarmy condescension of doctors: *So how are we feeling today, Mom?* The salesman who ignored her for ten minutes, then rushed to greet another customer obsequiously: "How can I help you, sir?" The young, shiny-haired bank teller who rolled her eyes and said huffily, "Tell me you've never owned an ATM card before."

Restaurants were particularly brutal. Whenever my mother took herself out to dinner, the hostesses invariably eyed her with disdain and did nothing to disguise the fact that they considered her a waste of a table. "Just one?" they said, frowning, then led her, grudgingly, to the last table in the back, the table just before the bathroom, adjacent to the pay phone corridor, directly in the path of the swinging doors.

One night, as my mother sat in a restaurant, listening to the shouting and clatter coming in great gusts from the kitchen, a man at the table beside her turned in her general direction.

He was dining with a woman, and he'd been holding forth bombastically, gesturing with a wineglass full of Bordeaux.

"I'm sorry," he said to my mother, without actually looking at her. "But do you mind? The service here tonight is awfully slow."

With that, he leaned over and put his dirty pasta bowl, along with that of his companion, on my mother's table, leaving it there for the busboy.

Dumbstruck, my mother sat looking at the congealed remains of this stranger's linguini, his plate graveled with clumps of Parmesan cheese and bread crumbs. Then she looked at the wreckage of shrimp casings clinging to his companion's plate, streaked bloodily with cocktail sauce. The man had gone back to talking, oblivious: it was no longer his problem. My mother's heart thumped wildly with outrage, helplessness. Finally, she set down her fork, too sickened to eat.

Only after she paid her bill did it occur to her what to do. "Excuse me," she said to the man as she got up to leave. He and his companion were lingering over a shared plate of tiramisu, twining and untwining their fingers seductively across the table. "But do you mind?" said my mother. With that she picked up her plate, slick with garlic, olive oil, and half-eaten fish, and set it right down in front of him.

To his credit, the man was sufficiently shamed. Blushing, he fumbled to his feet, dropped his napkin, sputtered an apology. But as my mother stalked off, his dining companion said loudly, "Wow. What a bitch."

Hearing my mother relate this story, I felt her own helplessness and rage—not only at the couple dining next to her, but at my father, too, for leaving her to a lifetime of dining alone. Unless something changed, I realized, John and I would now be left to function as our mother's surrogate spouse. We would change her lightbulbs and program her VCR for her. A few years down the road, we might very well end up shouldering even bigger responsibilities that were supposed to have been, by law, our father's: co-signing loans, perhaps, supporting her through the death of her parents, admitting her to hospitals, advising her on retirement. Until further notice, I was, at least, her date for nights out.

As I hung up her coat at a restaurant one evening, I noticed her dress was undone in the back.

"Mom, your bra is showing," I whispered.

"Whoops. What?" she said woozily. It was clear she'd had a drink beforehand—a habit which was new for her. Hurriedly, I yanked the zipper over the pale, exposed triangle of skin.

"I'm sorry. I'm used to your father doing that for me," she said quietly. "Now that I'm living alone, I can't always dress myself, you know."

Ironically, the only quality of my mother's that seemed to remain predictable was her unpredictability. Early one morning, she telephoned with an announcement. "I don't want to upset you," she said, "but I'm thinking of becoming a nun."

"A nun?" I said. "But we're not even Catholic."

"So?" she said. "I can convert. I've always been a very spiritual person. And from what I understand, nuns have a lot of fun."

The last time I'd heard the words "nun" and "fun" used in the same sentence was in third grade, when my classmate Jennifer and I had written a poem together for extra credit. We'd composed a stanza about "a nun in a habit" who'd had "fun with her rabbit," and we'd been extremely pleased with ourselves.

"I'm sorry," I said. "But just where did you get this idea?"

"A new colleague of mine, Faye, is a former nun," my mother said brightly. "She told me nuns have a really good time together. They take field trips, visit art museums. A lot of them play musical instruments. The way Faye made it sound, convents are sort of like sorority houses."

"I see," I said. "And this is reason enough to pledge allegiance to the Vatican and oppose things like birth control?"

"Look, I could become more conservative in my old age," my mother offered. "Besides, in a convent, I'll always have a roof over my head, medical care, and three square meals a day."

She paused, and only then did it dawn on me where all this was headed.

"I'll be well taken care of as a nun," she sniffed. "No matter how little alimony your father winds up paying me."

Suddenly, I understood why women jurists are tougher on rape victims than men are. Watching her enlist the services of a feng shui expert, a psychic, and a twelve-step program for support . . . listening to her brag that she'd hadn't missed a day of work, even as she fell asleep each night with the help of a few drinks and QVC blaring on the television . . . seeing her struggle to remain upbeat as her so-called friends called to report to her that they'd seen my father on a date—my heart repeatedly broke for my mother, then retreated in self-preservation. For years, my mother had been a force of nature, formidable and fierce. Yet seeing her diminished was far worse. It was too terrible, too sad. If I permitted myself to feel for her too much, I would drown in the sorrow and injustice of it. I would hate my father. I would lose all faith in love, marriage, and trust—in which I had very little faith left, anyway.

Feeling gutted, bereft, hamstrung between my parents, I refused to accept the long-term parsing of loyalties, the schizophrenic love, the careful negotiations and balancing acts that divorce extorts from its children—and that become necessary, frankly, for the rest of our lives.

Instead, genius that I was, I decided to alleviate my pain by treating both parents abominably, battering them with guilt, exhausting them with resentment. Calling them at odd hours, I'd sob, "Why are you doing this? *You're* the ones making a mess. *You* clean it up!"

"Don't tell me you're saving your own life!" I'd scream at my father.

"Don't tell me how much pain you're in!" I'd yell at my mother.

"Who cares about your goddamn happiness?" I hollered at both of them: "What about me and John? What are we supposed to do now that we don't have a family? Where are we supposed to go for the holidays?"

The first Christmas without my father was such agony that I bowed out early, selfishly, leaving my mother and brother stranded by her sad little Christmas tree, thick with the ghosts of Christmases past. Every silvery ornament, every strand of tinsel reflected our raw, gaping loss, our sense of abandonment, our amputated limb. Our mother had tried her best. It was just the three of us.

"Hey, kiddle-dees," she said with forced cheerfulness. "Who'd like a glass of sparkling cider to ring in the holidays?"

She brought out three cut-glass champagne flutes she and my father had received for their twenty-fifth wedding anniversary. All we could see when she set them down was the fourth one, missing.

"Who'd like to sing some Christmas carols?" she said, smiling painfully.

As soon as I could, I'd fled to my friend Gabi's. Her family had an annual Christmas Day bash that qualified as overkill even by New

York standards. Almost immediately, I'd proceeded to get blotto on champagne. Two university students had been visiting Gabi from Italy—they were a couple of Adonises whose names ended promisingly in "o's"—and I'd spent most of the party sprawled across their laps on the couch, giggling, enticing them to take turns feeding me hors d'oeuvres by placing them between their teeth. Of the one hundred people crammed into Gabi's apartment, I alone managed to distinguish myself as the Great Yuletide Slut. I must have done quite a job of it, too, because months afterward, apparently, her neighbors were still talking about it.

"It's gone. Everything's just gone," I'd weep aloud to no one in my little apartment at night. "Where's my family? What's happened to us?"

Often, I stayed out bumping and grinding with strangers at dance clubs, then engaging my friends in elaborate, sobbing melodramas in public bathrooms. I hung out with my high school friend Jeff at his bar, drinking until closing, then crashing on his plaid, fold-out sofa in Hell's Kitchen if only so that I didn't have to go home to the woeful messages from my parents on my answering machine. *Hi, honey. It's me. Just wanted to chat. Oh. Well. Guess you're not there. I'm going to therapy in a little while . . .*

Most evenings, I called my brother at college in tears. "You won't believe what it's like here," I sniffled. "Dad's talking about getting his ears pierced. Mom's thinking of becoming a nun. Everyone's going crazy."

John had little patience for any of it. "Look, Suze," he said flatly. "You've just got to deal with it." As if to underscore his point, the R.E.M. song "It's the End of the World as We Know It (and I Feel Fine)" played repeatedly in the background. "Duuude," I could hear his roommates shouting across the hallway.

"Mom and Dad are adults," John said irritably. "So are you and I now. If they want to go their own way, that's their decision. You've got to be a grown-up about this. Their separation shouldn't affect us."

That spring, however, when he came home for Spring Break, he immediately got into an enormous fight with my mother. After punching a hole in one of her closet doors, he wound up downtown at my father's new bachelor apartment, where he proceeded to yell at my dad insanely and call him "a fucker." By midnight, he was standing on my doorstep in hysterics. He spent the remainder of his break immobilized on my couch in his pajamas.

"I'm glad to see you're being a grown-up about this," I couldn't resist crowing. "Because really, their separation shouldn't affect us."

My brother laughed bitterly. "What are you talking about?" he said, downing a glass of Yoo-hoo and wiping his mouth on the sleeve of his bathrobe. "All four of us are in excellent shape."

Eventually, our mother decided against joining a convent. "You know what I found out?" she said incredulously. "Nuns aren't allowed to have sex."

"No," I deadpanned. "You're kidding."

"They can't date. They can't get married. They can't even have an orgasm without thinking they'll burn in hell for it," she said. "Where's the fun in that?"

"I see your point," I said.

"I mean, if I want to feel psychologically terrorized, I certainly don't have to join a convent," she concluded. "I can just walk down Broadway or call up some of our relatives."

My mother's creative problem-solving, however, wasn't over just yet. A year later, as my parents' divorce settlement slogged through the courts, and as my brother and I began to better navigate the wreckage, I got a phone call from my friend Maggie, who lived just a block and a half from my mother.

"Suze, I've got sort of, well, a strange question for you," she said carefully. I'd known Maggie since we were fourteen; in high school, we'd spent entire weekends at each other's house listening to CSN&Y and eating raw cookie dough under the pretense of "baking."

"Is your mother, by any chance, a cop?" Maggie asked.

"What?"

"You're going to think I'm crazy, but I could've sworn I saw your mother standing outside Food City this morning dressed in a police uniform." Maggie wore contact lenses, and it suddenly occurred to me that she might be almost as nearsighted as I was.

"My mother in law enforcement? Yeah. Right. I don't think so," I laughed.

"I didn't think so, either," said Maggie. "But if not, I have to tell you, there's a female police officer walking around the neighborhood who looks *exactly* like her. It's really, really freaky."

A few days later, when I spoke to my mother, I mentioned this in passing. "Maggie says there's a policewoman out there who's apparently your doppelgänger, Mom. How funny is that?"

There was a pause on the other end of the line, then a sharp intake of breath.

"Oh, dammit," she said finally. "I wanted to surprise you."

"Excuse me?" I said.

"You might as well know," she sighed. "It *was* me who Maggie saw. Your mother is training to be an auxiliary policewoman."

"Excuse me?" I said again. She might as well have told me she was becoming a transvestite, a porn star, a CIA operative with the code name "Romulus."

New York City had a program, she explained, where ordinary residents could become part-time auxiliary police officers—the urban equivalent, it seemed, of a volunteer sheriff or fire department. A year earlier, she'd seen a flyer advertising it in the lobby of her building. "I figured I'd get some self-defense training. I'd get a badge and a uniform, maybe meet a few men. Most of all, though," she said, "I figured I could finally do something about our neighborhood. Between the yuppies and the crackheads, it's getting really obnoxious. You know I'm a stickler for people behaving themselves."

While auxiliary police officers didn't carry guns, she said, they did have the power to patrol the streets, issue tickets, and assist with arrests. "Friday evening, I was out on the beat with Charlene and Enrique, my two superior officers, and we busted five kids jumping a turnstile," my mother said proudly. "That's Theft of Service, or T-O-S, in police lingo. So we had this T-O-S, you see, caught the suspects right in the act, then found out they'd just robbed a drugstore. I got to frisk two of 'em, cuff 'em, and help read 'em their Miranda rights.

"Two days before that, we interrupted a drug deal. Some guy selling crack on 106th Street. Nailed him on Criminal Possession of a Controlled Substance. Third degree."

Hearing her talk like this was surreal. I tried to picture my fifty-three-year-old, petite, gray-haired mother throwing a lanky teenager up against the side of a patrol car, jamming her knee into the small of his back, whipping out a pair of handcuffs, then wrangling them onto his wrists. I tried to imagine her jumping out from behind a Dumpster in a service alley flanked by two other cops with their pistols drawn, yelling, "Freeze, motherfucker! Put your hands in the air!"

I'd never done hallucinogenic drugs before, but suddenly I had a pretty good idea of what the experience might be like.

"I was going to wait until my graduation from the police academy next week to tell you," my mother said cheerily. "That's when we get our official shields, and shake hands with the mayor. Hmm," she added vaguely. "I wonder if I shouldn't make a little party here afterward to celebrate. Maybe get an ice cream cake?"

"Mom," I said faintly. "Just tell me one thing. You're not doing this just for the handcuffs, are you? Because you know, there are mail order catalogues for that sort of thing."

After hanging up, I repeated over and over in my head, *My mother the cop. My mother the cop,* trying to get my mind around it. "Excuse me," I imagined myself saying to a drunken Romeo attempting to nuzzle me at a bar, "but I've got to call *my mother the cop* at her precinct."

"Excuse me," I imagined saying to a junk bond trader at my gym, "but *my mother the cop* has informed me that pushing people off a Lifecycle is a Class 2 misdemeanor."

Anytime my mother had put her faith in something conventional—a Norman Rockwell Thanksgiving, an interior decorator, a traditional marriage—it had failed her. What was left to rely on, really, except her own expansive imagination, her own refusal to be cowed?

The day after her graduation from the police academy, I went to her apartment with a bouquet of roses. "Don't come in," she shouted from the bedroom, as she wriggled into her uniform. "Wait on the sofa."

In the living room, I noticed, she'd rearranged the furniture. All the shutters from the wall unit had been removed. Its shelves were overrun with great, cascading pots of ivy, glossy spines of art books, decorative filigree mirrors, iridescent vases, carved wooden birds from Mexico. Overflowing with glittery treasures, it now looked like an upended jewelry box.

"Well. Here I am." My mother strode out as if she were on a catwalk, then did a slow, 360-degree turn. The clumsily cut, navy blue regulation police uniform strained across her breasts and her butt. Yet it looked strangely alluring, like a sexed-up costume decorated with buttons and patches.

My mother is a beautiful woman; from certain angles, she can look startlingly like Isabella Rossellini. But when I was growing up, I hadn't thought of her like that. She was too troubled and agitated, too unhappy with herself; she went through phases of odd haircuts, severe head scarves, unflattering clothing. In many photographs, her smile was strained, as if she'd been ordered to say "Cheese" under duress. Since she'd separated from my father, her hair had gone silver and the lines around her eyes had deepened. Yet she'd become positively gorgeous, radiant, finally free to be herself, fully unleashed in all her physical glory. Men had begun to stare after her in the street and do comedic double takes. In her policewoman's uniform, she looked adorable and formidable at the same time—a shining silver sunflower—albeit one with a nightstick and handcuffs.

"So, what do you think?" she said, pivoting again. "Is your mother a first-class kook?"

"No, not at all," I said tearfully. And I meant it, too. I was swollen with pride. "I think you look amazing."

My father had saved his own life. But my mother, I saw now, too, was engaged in rescue work of her own. Just let the world try to dismiss her. Just let the world pretend she didn't exist. She was not going to hide away in a convent, or swallow her hurt at a table by the restrooms. Oh no. If she had anything to say about it—and clearly, she did—the world was going to have to reckon with her for a good, long time to come. She would not walk the streets invisibly. She was a force to contend with. And now, she even had backup.

Chapter 13

Your Tax Dollars, Hard at Work

IN 1996, IN WHAT CAN only be described as an epidemic of bad judgment, a congresswoman offered me a job and I, in turn, accepted it.

Until that moment, the extent of my Washington experience consisted of falling into the Reflecting Pool during a protest march. While I did manage to vote—and complain to my senators on a regular basis—like most Americans, I found the words "federal government" didn't inspire patriotism in me so much as narcolepsy.

This is not to say I was disinterested in politics. In college, friends and I spent several evenings making miniature cruise missiles out of discarded toilet paper tubes. After attaching giant price tags to them, we pushed them around the local Food King in a shopping cart.

"Do you think President Reagan is a good bargain hunter?" we asked unsuspecting shoppers, before ambushing them with leaflets we'd made that cleverly estimated how many day care programs and school lunches could be funded for the price of a single MX missile. "Thirty-two million dollars for a nuclear warhead is not smart shopping."

We expected that, upon hearing our spiel, people would instantly mobilize. "One Trident missile cost sixty-four million dollars? Why, that's an outrage," they'd cry, dropping their jumbo-sized packages of Pampers and Wonder Bread in shock. "Quick, Marge. Let's leave our groceries here by the frozen foods aisle and take to the streets!"

Instead, with the ironic myopia typical of college students, we'd somehow failed to notice that two of the biggest employers in the area were defense contractors. "Almost 60 percent of my paycheck goes to military spending?" said one woman, adjusting her bra strap. "Why that's the best news I've heard all week."

As an activist, I'd gone on to build a shantytown in front of the dean's office, defend abortion clinics with a group of drag queens, and walk around dressed in a garbage bag during "Fashion Week." These, to me, seemed like far better ways to spark social change than something as dreary as running for public office. Surely, no one could be truly compelled to save the world without a performance art piece and a sing-along.

Yet, in the end, I opted to work for Congress for the same reason most people do: No one else, it seemed, would hire me.

For several years prior, I'd dwelt in the pathetic, groveling nether-world of freelance writing. As a career, this earned me only slightly more respect than if I'd been a prostitute. While people seem to understand that being, say, a coroner or a dishwasher repairman requires a level of skill, they tend to regard writing as simply an extension of talking: It's something any idiot can do if given enough paper. Worse still, given the quality of some of the books that get published, this view is not wholly unjustified.

Whenever people at cocktail parties asked, "What do you do?" and I told them, "I'm a writer," they sniggered and said, "But seriously."

Working in Washington, I figured, would finally endow me with some much needed professional credibility. I imagined myself sitting behind a vast mahogany desk flanked by an American flag and tall French windows overlooking the Capitol. Every so often, my boss would buzz me over a private intercom and ask me to deliver a national security briefing or write a speech that began, *"I, too, have a dream . . ."*

Admittedly, I'd gotten these ideas from the movie *St. Elmo's Fire,* in which Judd Nelson's character goes to work for a senator and is immediately given a private office and a level of responsibility just slightly below that of the president. If nothing else, I figured, being a communications director for a U.S. congresswoman would impress the hell out of people at cocktail parties. That alone, to me, seemed reason enough to serve my fellow countrymen.

But truth be told, I also moved to Washington due to a congenital illness. At the advanced age of thirty, it seems I'd finally contracted my family's nearly hallucinatory political idealism.

My family has always been pigheaded in its belief that politicians really *can* make a difference. Before I was born, my parents had enthusiastically supported a Democratic presidential contender named Eugene McCarthy, who inspired them so much, in fact, that in an act that could've been considered child abuse, they briefly considered naming my brother "Eugene."

As a young man, my Uncle Paul had been so moved by a politician called Stevenson that he actually did go so far as to saddle his son with the conversation-stopping middle name of "Adlai." ("Can you believe he named me after a failed presidential candidate?" my cousin groaned. "I suppose it could be worse. I could've been named after Hubert Humphrey. How much would *that* suck?")

In 1968, my Uncle Arthur had worked proudly for Bobby Kennedy and told us, teary-eyed, that during a meeting Kennedy had once doodled on his notepad lines from Shakespeare's *Henry V: We few. We happy few. We band of brothers.* In the 1970s, my Great-aunt Molly had worked just as proudly for Bella Abzug. In the 1980s, my grandmother became so smitten with Jesse Jackson that she not only campaigned for him, but taped his picture next to Patrick Swayze's in the "pantheon of hotties" she kept on her refrigerator.

Yet as a Generation Xer, the first president on my radar screen had been bulldog-faced Nixon—who, in my mind, had been guilty of not merely lying to the American people, but of preempting my favorite television cartoon, *Stop the Pigeon,* with his tedious Watergate hearings. From there on, it seemed that politicians were harbingers of either stupidity or disappointment. President Ford with his Whip Inflation Now buttons. Jimmy Carter forging peace in the Middle East yet being called a wimp because—for some ridiculous reason—he refused to nuke Iran. Reagan parroting "There you go again" and everyone deciding this qualified him as a communications genius. Even Clinton. Although he ate pussy, played the saxophone, and jogged to McDonald's—all excellent reasons to elect anyone president, in my opinion—his expediency was like a flashing red light at a railroad crossing: you simply *had* to know better.

Listening to my relatives reminisce about the leaders they'd worked for, I couldn't help but feel envious. They'd had passion, purpose, and hope, whereas my generation seemed to have missed out on everything from great psychedelics to canvassing for George McGovern.

So when, purely by accident, I met a politician who inspired me, my sheer relief was enough to allay any cynicism.

Congresswoman Minnie Glenn, as I'll call her, had a whiplash intellect, a nearly photographic memory, and the ability to speak extemporaneously about landfills without catapulting her audience into a coma. Better yet, she'd never met a glazed donut she didn't like or dirty joke she didn't feel compelled to retell. Really, she was my kind of woman.

As a writer, I was particularly compelled by Minnie's life story, which read like a modern-day variant of Abraham Lincoln's.

Born in a small Midwestern town called something like Flyswatter or Hairspittle, Minnie got pregnant at age seventeen and married her high school sweetheart the day after graduation. While her husband, Frank, worked in a factory, Minnie sold Tupperware and served chili dogs at a local diner. Earning wages instead of salaries, they raised two babies and bought bread with pennies scavenged from their sofa cushions.

But eventually, Minnie put herself through college, then law school, then ran for the statehouse. There, she made headlines by handing back a pay raise other lawmakers had secretly voted to give themselves because she felt it was "greedy and wrong." In 1994, despite pooh-poohing from her own Democratic Party, she ran for Congress as an "ethical everywoman"—and won.

She was thirty-eight years old.

This was the same year Newt Gingrich's "Republican Revolution" swept into Washington. Yet Minnie also arrived, a staunchly pro-choice, pro-union Democrat, wearing a green dress suit and high heels she'd purchased at Val-U-Village.

"Of course I'm pro-union," she joked to reporters. "My husband's a factory worker. I get into bed with labor every night."

Having met Minnie during her congressional campaign, I was impressed. With her humor, honesty, and working-class gonads, she was the type of person I longed to be myself, let alone see elected to Congress. Working for her meant a once-in-a-lifetime chance to advocate for causes I genuinely believed in. Why, together, I imagined, we could raise the minimum wage! Revive the ERA! Transform the Pentagon into a giant baby-sitting service!

One day I, too, could be like my Uncle Arthur or Aunt Molly, secure in the knowledge that at least once in my life, I'd done something of historical and political importance. "I was Minnie Glenn's communications director before she became America's first female president," I might be able to tell my children, in one of my many interminable stories about Washington.

I hadn't even set foot on Capitol Hill, yet already I was delusional.

———————

It's been said that Washington, D.C., is Hollywood for ugly people, and the first day I arrived on Capitol Hill, it did indeed look like a movie set. The lawn was strewn with cables, klieg lights, cameras. People dashed around murmuring into walkie-talkies, setting up benches and scaffolding, then dismantling them, while reporters and photographers moved around in packs. Anything that occurred there during the day could wind up on the evening news, and people were acutely conscious of this. There was a larger-than-life, stagy unreality to it all. No sooner did I step outside the cloakroom of the House chambers than I saw Newt Gingrich in the hallway wearing pancake makeup. It was like a drag show for bureaucrats.

Standing outside the Capitol building itself, however, I experienced the same overawed thrill that most people have the first time they see the Statue of Liberty or the Grand Canyon: you can't quite believe it actually exists in all its glory and not merely on some doctored-up postcard on your refrigerator.

Hip, urbane, Manhattanite *moi,* I pointed and shrieked like a hillbilly, "Wow. This looks just like it does on the money!" and, "Hey, isn't that Ted Kennedy?"

A strange kind of fever takes over when you arrive on Capitol Hill. Although most Americans would be hard-pressed to identify the vice president in a police lineup, once you work for Congress, you suddenly take pride in being able to spot Senator Fritz Hollings and Representative Nancy Pelosi by the cafeteria salad bar. What's more, you actually think this is exciting and of great interest to other people. "Hey, guess what?" you'll announce to your colleagues on your way back from the bathroom. "I just peed next to the head of the House Subcommittee on Foreign Aid!"

That first morning, oh, what a rush I got streaming up toward the Hill with legions of other staffers dressed in power suits and dresses with navy piping and pearls, everyone smelling of shampoo and ambition—carrying brand-new attaché cases and copies of *Roll Call* tucked under their arms—fierce with our own puffed-up sense of destiny and importance. After years of drinking jug wine with scruffy grad students in Birkenstocks, the high-gloss, super-enameled professionalism of Washington came as a relief to me. When I sashayed through the metal detectors of the Longworth House Office Building and the security guard said, "Good morning," I took this to mean, "My, you're impressive."

No sooner had I arrived than Minnie summoned me into her office. "Okay, we've got some serious business to discuss," she said gravely, offering me a seat. "I need to know," she said, sliding a box of Krispy Kreme donuts across the table. "Which do you think are better: jelly or glazed? Normally, I say the glazed, but now, I'm not so sure."

After we sampled one, then the other, and concluded that ultimately, more research would be required, we got down to work: we discussed her stance on the issues and the behavior of the new Republican majority in Congress ("They all vote in goose step," Minnie observed dryly). She then outlined my responsibilities as communications director. It turned out that my title was misleading; I wouldn't be directing anything.

"You're not to be my publicist or a spin doctor," said Minnie firmly. "Just my writer. I'm not interested in self-promotion. Instead, I need to you to describe what's going on in Congress using language that ordinary folks can understand."

One of the oldest jokes on Capitol Hill is that the most dangerous place to stand is between a member of Congress and a camera crew. Having been a reporter myself, I didn't relish the job of twisting the truth around into self-serving pretzels, or of having to suck up to the media and sell Minnie to them every day like a box of laundry detergent. I was thrilled to be absolved of any duties that might fall under the category of "media whore."

Yet the idea of making Congress comprehensible to "ordinary folks" sent me into a panic. Because what the hell did I know about Congress? The total sum of my knowledge consisted of the two-minute jingle "I'm Just a Bill" from *Schoolhouse Rock*. Why, I could barely distinguish between the House and the Senate, and I'd once— albeit drunkenly—confused a picture of the Capitol with that of the Vatican. From my grade school civics lessons, I hadn't retained anything beyond the Pledge of Allegiance. And in preparing for my new job, I'd been way too focused on things like buying a cool "power skirt" at T.J. Maxx and bragging to my friends to bother to learn anything about my workplace.

I was at least as much of a know-nothing as the rest of Minnie's constituents, and I felt compelled to tell her as much.

Minnie laughed. "My first day, I walked into what I thought was the bathroom and found myself in a supply closet," she said. "We're all learning the lay of the land. The fact that you're not already mired in bureaucratese is a benefit. You'll figure out Congress quickly enough."

By the end of our little meeting, I was fairly delirious. Why, everything was just beginning: my excellent Washington adventure . . . Minnie's stellar political career . . . the fight to keep the world safe from fascists and weirdos. Finally, I was doing something significant with my life: peon, no more!

Five minutes later, Vicki, Minnie's chief of staff, called a meeting.

"Tomorrow, you may have a job to come to, but you may not," she announced. "Newt Gingrich is threatening to shut down the government again."

"You're kidding," said Minnie.

"Nope. This time, though, it's not just because of the budget," Vicki said. "Apparently, he's upset because he wasn't allowed to ride near the cockpit on Air Force One."

"Oh, for fuck's sake," said Minnie, displaying the very language skills that had inspired me to work for her. She kicked off her shoes and flopped down on her couch. "This isn't the United States Congress. This is the Hatfields and the McCoys, the Capulets and Montagues, the Bloods and the Crips—except with leather office chairs and more money."

While the prospect of the federal government shutting down was unnerving to me, it wasn't nearly as unnerving, I discovered, as my new office mates.

For her legislative assistants, Minnie had hired three political go-getters whose colorful characters could easily form the basis for a comic strip. Lee was a handsome, ambling lover-boy with the molasses-like demeanor of a true Southern Gentleman. When irate constituents telephoned the office, he suavely picked up the receiver and announced, "Now, watch this, y'all. I call it, 'The Touch.'"

Then we'd listen to him coo, "Now, Mrs. Kublicki, you just calm down a minute there. That's it. Take a deep breath. Now, tell me *exactly* why you're upset about farm subsidies."

Kiran, who sat across from me, was an ambitious pre-law student whose big goal in life, he informed me, was to be able to zip around from the copy machine to the wastepaper basket then back to his desk without ever leaving his chair. "My other goal, of course, is to go to law school and become the first Indian-American Supreme Court justice," he said. "But then I thought: why not aim lower?"

Zachary was a hot-tempered workaholic who won me over instantly with his penchant for M&M's and gratuitous profanity. "I'm sorry, Mr. Ramses, but I'm going to have to put you on hold for a moment," he'd say in the middle of a phone call. Then he'd set down the receiver and yell over at Lee, "Hey, dumb-ass. You're sitting on the fucking stapler." Then he'd pick up the phone again. "I'm sorry, Mr. Ramses. Now, let me explain to you about Medicare co-pays."

Each one of these guys instantly impressed me with his ability to identify all 435 House members simply by hearing their voices over C-SPAN. Each one could master the nuances of a mind-numbing House resolution in less time than it took me to operate the copier. They could absorb and process volumes of bureaucratese faster than any computer. There was just one problem: they were, on average, twenty-three years old. When they weren't going to legislative meetings or answering constituents' detailed questions about discretionary funding, they liked to play a game in which they twisted each other's fingers back to see who would squeal first from the pain while hollering, "Had enough yet, douchebag? Who's your daddy? Who's your daddy?"

Except for Vicki and Minnie's deputy chief of staff, Edna, I was by far and away the oldest person in the office. After a lifetime of being called "kiddo" on the job, I found this profoundly disconcerting.

Worse yet, as I surveyed the cafeteria, it seemed that nobody else in the entire Longworth House Office Building looked old enough to drink legally. While the top senior staff positions in the House tended to be held by lawyers and middle-aged politicos, most of Capitol Hill was staffed by people who'd graduated from college so recently they still referred to time in terms of "last semester" and "sophomore year." Mainstays of their vocabulary were "awesome," "dickhead," "Beer Pong," and "roommate."

I had just one friend on Capitol Hill, Bruce, a communications director who worked across the hall from me. At twenty-nine, Bruce was a former journalist reinventing his career and therefore just as much of a freak as I was.

"Bruce," I groaned. "Why do I feel like I just landed on the set of MTV's *Spring Break*?"

He laughed and clasped his hands together delightedly. "Surprise," he said. "Welcome to Congress."

Unfortunately, when he explained it, it made sense: each day, members of Congress must ingest huge amounts of turgid information, craft or oppose legislation based on it, then share it in a compelling way with some 700,000 disgruntled constituents who'd sooner be out bowling. They must do this while shuttling back and forth to their district, fund-raising, attending six meetings at once, and appearing on interminable Sunday morning talk shows. Last time anyone checked, this was humanly impossible.

And so, members of Congress must hire a staff to be their surrogate eyes, ears, mouths, and brains. These staffers must be able to work up enthusiasm for congressional hearings on things like the pasteurization of cottage cheese. They must be capable of staying awake while reading "The House Subcommittee Report on Managing Bio-hazardous Waste at the Sandusky Nuclear Plant." They must be willing to work insane hours for salaries that often make baggage handling at Dulles Airport look attractive. And, since they have absolutely zero job security, they must believe it's worth forfeiting their entire personal life and financial welfare for a cool-looking business card and a job recommendation printed on congressional letterhead.

In other words, they must be twenty-two years old.

"After all, who else is stupid and ambitious enough to want that?" said Bruce.

Still, it was unsettling to realize that Congress was essentially being run by people whose parents—for the most part—were still paying their rent. And when it wasn't being run by them, it was largely in the hands of the senior staff. More often than not, these were adrenaline junkies who'd spent their entire careers a) hopping from the twilight zone of one election campaign to another, or b) slavishly serving one elected official out of some sort of demented love.

The two groups running the day-to-day operations on Capitol Hill were precisely those with the least in common with the rest of America.

"Explains a lot, doesn't it?" said Bruce.

Indeed, I hadn't been at my job a week when a legislative assistant for the House Appropriations Committee tried to slip a provision into the D.C. budget authorizing a dog run to be built next door to his apartment. Over lunch in the Longworth cafeteria, I listened to a twenty-one-year-old staffer argue: "If girls can't talk to their parents about abortion, why not put them in foster homes with parents they *can* talk to?" Another staffer—this one on the Senate Banking Committee—suggested a federal law requiring all banks to have "greeters" in their lobbies who'd wave to the customers and hand out lollipops. "This way, Americans would trust big banks more," she explained brightly.

Later that week, Kiran himself proposed a bill that authorized euthanasia for any Medicare patient over eighty. "I mean, like, why should my tax dollars go toward keeping Grandma alive when she's going to croak anyway?" he shrugged.

Given the environment we were working in, it took Zachary and me two full days to realize he was kidding.

Yet, it was not just the staff who made the Hill feel like one enormous middle school. All day long when Congress was in session, bells went off to summon the members to the chambers. As soon as they sounded, representatives scurried through the hallways, clutching notebooks and sporting distinguishing little lapel pins like members of an honors society or a fraternity. The same catty cliquishness existed among them—the same sniping, gossiping, whispering—that you'd find in any seventh grade bathroom. Names were called, tantrums were thrown. People ganged up on each other out of pettiness or sheer malice. And throughout the proceedings on the House floor, members would summon the congressional pages—glorified gofers, really—and pass notes to them. Sometimes these notes were instructions for staffers, but other times they were candy orders. In the middle of a heated debate on foreign aid, you might see a congressman beckon to a page, then hand her a note and whisper in her ear urgently. A moment later, she'd return with a bag of malt balls. Rumor had it from the Senate side that Ted Kennedy was partial to Red Hots, which caused no degree of snickering. One time, Minnie herself was filmed eating M&M's on C-SPAN.

"So, how's the new job?" my mother asked when she called. "Gosh, it must be so impressive, working with all those big shots."

Naively, I'd assumed that, being the arbiters of democracy, all members of Congress were equal. Yet it turned out that some were distinctly more equal than others. As a freshman in the minority party, Minnie was the lowest of the low in the pecking order. In the office lottery, she'd come in second-to-last out of all 435 representatives, so she'd had to settle for an office divided into two separate spaces. These spaces were conveniently located on two different floors in opposite corners of the building. This meant that anytime you needed, say, a briefing memo or a paper fastener, you had to climb a flight of stairs, then walk the equivalent of two city blocks. As a source of anaerobic exercise, it wasn't half bad, but it pretty much undermined any attempt to "make government more efficient," as Minnie had pledged to do during her campaign. Anytime she needed to talk to us, it took ten minutes to assemble for a five-minute meeting. It could've been funny, except that it got old almost immediately.

Assigned to the upstairs "annex," Kiran, Zachary, Lee, and I worked together in a space clearly designed to store brooms. Amid a jumble of file cabinets, desks, and computer wires, the four of us easily violated the fire code every day in our service to democracy.

Back in college, it had once occurred to me that my love affair with the sound of my own voice might make me an excellent lawyer. And so, for several summers, I'd worked as an intern for the New York State attorney general. The offices were located high up in the World Trade Center. The building was a gargantuan beehive of activity, and it was simply impossible to work there without coming into intimate contact with at least three million people whose tax dollars paid for my stipend each week. Xerox repairmen, corporate lawyers, secretaries, janitors, stockbrokers, dishwashers, mail carriers, travel agents—everyone piled into the elevators together to ride to the "Sky Lobby" on the forty-fourth floor, and you had no choice but to breathe in other people's armpits, choke on their overzealous cologne, and overhear dozens of enlightening conversations like:

So, did you fuck her?

What? Are you kidding me? Of course I fucked her, motherfucker. Who the fuck do you think I am? Richard fucking Simmons, you fucking motherfucker?

And:

You hear from your kid yet?

Yeah, and if he hits me up for money one more time, I swear, his mother and I are going to take a contract out on him.

And:

So then she tells me I can't exchange the dress if I don't have a receipt. So I go, "Look, bitch. The tags are still on it. You think I went to my own daughter's wedding with the tags on my dress?" And she goes, "Well, why the hell not? That's how I went to mine."

It might not have been Shakespeare, and it might not have been pretty, but it was the language of real life. And unfortunately, it was nothing we ever heard working on Capitol Hill. For a place that is ostensibly of the people, by the people, and for the people, the

Capitol is about as open and accessible as a cryogenic freezer. Kiran, Lee, Zachary, and I might have felt cut off from civilization in our office, but the truth was, we were no more removed than anyone else on the Hill.

The Capitol complex seems to have been designed by gerbils: situated on a mound above the rest of Washington, all the buildings are connected to each other by underground tunnels. Inside this subterranean complex, members have their own cafeterias, credit unions, post office, parking facilities, barber shop (which explains a lot about politicians' hair, actually), and yes, their own elevators to ride, off-limits even to staffers. It is physically possible to work in the Capitol for years and never once come into contact with either direct sunlight or actual constituents.

Of course, constituents do visit all the time, eager to meet their representatives, buy gift soaps emblazoned with the congressional seal, and get a tour of the Capitol. But except for a whining child or two, they are always, *always* on their absolute best behavior, awed and cowed by the majesty of the place. Trundling through the corridors with their camcorders and fanny packs—or dressed poignantly in their Eagle Scout uniforms and military medals—they speak in hushed tones as they beamingly present their representatives with handcrafted commemorative plaques and pennants from their local basketball team. "Now, Skylar, now, Tiffany," they prompt their children. "What do you say when you shake the congressman's hand?" All this civility is fine and good, but it only contributes to the artificiality of the atmosphere. After all, if everybody behaved in real life the way they do when they visit the Capitol, we wouldn't need a Congress in the first place.

My second day on the job, Vicki called a staff meeting while Minnie was away "in committee." Vicki was a sallow, no-nonsense woman with about as much warmth and charisma as a metronome.

Ushering me into a chair before the rest of the staff, she said, "I want to discuss your attitude. It seems some people in the office have a problem with it."

I had been on the job exactly one day.

"Excuse me?" I said.

"See, that's exactly what I'm talking about," Vicki said, frowning. "Now some people—I don't want to say who—have complained that you think you're better than they are."

As a newcomer, I'd spent most of the previous day filling out paperwork, figuring out the code for the Xerox machine, and struggling to log on to the computer network. Later in the afternoon, I'd dribbled Diet Pepsi down the front of my blouse and sopped it up ineffectively with paper napkins. How this qualified as diva behavior was beyond me.

When I said as much to Vicki, she replied, "See, there's that attitude again. If you're going to be on this staff, you're going to have to become a team player."

Then she turned to the guys, who all seemed to be absorbed in staring at their shoelaces. "I don't want any of you helping her out. Don't give her briefings. Don't show her the library. Don't share any information with her. Understand? Let her find her own way around Congress."

Kiran raised his hand. "I'm sorry, but if we can't work with her, how is she supposed to become a 'team player'?"

Vicki gave him a look that could fuse metal. "Don't you start, either," she said.

When the four of us were back upstairs, I said, "Was she kidding?"

"Afraid not," said Zachary.

"I'm sorry," I said. "But exactly what fucking 'attitude problem' do I have?"

Zachary shook his head. "You don't. It's Vicki," he said. "Vicki has a problem with you."

"After one day?"

"'Vicki has a problem with everyone," Lee sighed.

"What about Edna?" I asked. As the deputy chief of staff, Edna was the person we were supposed to go to if we had problems with Vicki.

"Edna has a problem with everyone, too," said Lee.

"Look," Zachary said, "we didn't want to tell you this right away, because you just got here. But you know that Vicki and Edna are Minnie's best friends, right?"

This I knew. I'd met both women during Minnie's congressional campaign. The three of us seemed to have gotten along well, in fact; Edna and I had even made several important donut runs together.

"And you know that Vicki and Edna are also lovers?" Zachary said.

This I also knew. It was no secret to anyone that they were essentially an old married couple. They even dressed alike. On the campaign, they'd seemed to have a penchant for Bermuda shorts and gum-soled boat shoes. No one could ever accuse them of being slick Washington operatives.

"Usually, you have a chief of staff *and* a deputy so that if employees have a problem with one, they can go to the other," said Zachary. "But we can't do that here, because the chief of staff and the deputy are live-in girlfriends. And we can't complain to Minnie about them either, because they're her best friends."

"And they don't trust any of us, and they don't like any of us," said Kiran. "Even me. And I'm adorable."

"Every day, the whole staff will meet with Minnie and agree to sponsor some piece of legislation, or create some sort of filing system or whatever," said Lee. "But then Vicki and Edna go home, talk it over, and decide alone between themselves and Minnie to do things completely differently."

"Then they yell at us for not following orders properly," said Kiran.

"We have no power in this office. We're treated like suspects," said Zachary. "All of us are fucking miserable. Every evening, when we appear to be working late? We're printing out our résumés."

"Yep. This office is totally fucked," Kiran declared, almost proudly.

I sat down, stunned. "But Minnie seems so great," I said.

"Minnie is great. Minnie is amazing," said Zachary. "Minnie is the only reason any of us stick around."

"But Minnie is almost never here," said Lee. "She's always running back to the district to stay connected to the voters."

"So we get left with the two evil stepmothers downstairs," said Zachary.

"Sorry we had to tell you this so soon," said Kiran. "But it seems that Vicki already has a problem with you. And no offense, but after one day, that's kind of a record in this office."

That night, my mother called again. "So? How'd your second day go?"

"Well, the chief of staff informed me she doesn't like my attitude. Her girlfriend is the deputy chief of staff, so I have no one else to go to, and I found out all my colleagues are miserable and looking for other jobs," I said. "Other than that, I guess it went fine."

On the Hill, it seems, every politician carries with them the circumstances of their election. It haunts them like a trauma, like a childhood of abuse. Even if they're not conscious of it, they remember where every campaign check and endorsement came from, and they never forget their enemies. While they have one eye on their reelection, they inevitably have the other on their back.

When Minnie ran for Congress as the self-made wife of a factory worker, she had few established players in her corner. A lot of politicians have a vast army of power brokers backing them: big businesses, alumni associations, interest groups, trade associations: more than a few candidates actually run for office with a sense of entitlement.

By contrast, when Minnie declared she was running for Congress, even though she was ahead in the polls, the head of the Democratic Party in her own district tried to bully her out of running.

"The unions here don't want a skirt representing them," he told her bluntly. "Go to Washington and mark my words: you'll get no support from us, and your husband will leave you."

Until the fund-raising group Emily's List stepped in, most of the support Minnie received was grassroots: a coffee klatch here, a PTA there. Meanwhile, opponents from her own party literally went through her trash, looking for anything personal she might have scribbled on statehouse letterhead so they could claim she abused the privileges of her public office.

As Minnie's campaign struggled to kick into high gear, Vicki and Edna were moving to the Sunbelt. When Minnie called them in tears one evening at their motel, they literally turned their U-Haul around and returned to the Midwest. After that, they pretty much lived at campaign headquarters, straightening out Minnie's budget, running to the printers for extra bumper stickers, organizing chicken dinner fund-raisers. During Minnie's moments of exhaustion and insecurity at two o'clock in the morning, it was Vicki and Edna who sent out for pizza, held her hand, and told her bad jokes. Their loyalty was bulletproof.

So it was no surprise to me that Minnie wanted them beside her in the foxholes of Washington. Managerially, it was a terrible decision, of course. But as I sat in the Hawk 'n' Dove after work, watching boyish Hill staffers in suspenders smoke cigars and slap each other on the back shouting, "Dude, that Contract with America is awesome!" I knew I'd probably have done the same thing.

And Minnie was hardly alone. I quickly learned of two other freshman members who'd hired their best friends, too. In the viper pit of Washington—where your enemies pay good money to "negative research firms" to dig up dirt on you, where any misstep can land you before a phalanx of television cameras, and where your own young, ambitious staffers are often using their jobs as springboards to higher places—hiring trusted friends doesn't strike some people as unethical but as a sheer necessity if they ever want to get a good night's sleep.

While my office mates complained about their powerlessness in the office, I, as a writer, was pretty much used to it. Editors almost never took my suggestions, and after I wrote the articles they assigned me, they went ahead and cut them up any way they wanted, then waited until the next vernal equinox to pay me. Unlike my office mates, who had dreams of law school, White House jobs, or running for public office themselves, the only reasons I'd taken the job with Minnie were to impress people at cocktail parties, live out some high-minded ideals, and bore the hell out of my progeny. Once Vicki and Edna realized that I was playing for their team exclusively, I figured they'd get off my back. Until then, I just concentrated on my work.

The first week, Minnie telephoned me from the House floor. "I'm speaking in ten minutes," she said. "Can you find me a pithy quote about power and responsibility that I can use to spice up my remarks?"

Since we didn't have Internet access yet, I flipped open our one quotation book. In no time, I found a brilliant line.

There was just one small problem.

It was by Richard Nixon.

Then I found second great quote.

This one was by Machiavelli.

Although Machiavelli has some huge fans on Capitol Hill, I suspected he wasn't quite the person Minnie wanted to be heard quoting on the House floor.

The third quote I found was the best yet: a real gem, short, powerful, and eloquent.

Unfortunately, this one was attributed to Adolf Hitler.

"So what?" Kiran cried. "Minnie can just say, 'As a politician once said . . .' She doesn't have to name names. Who's going to know she's quoting Hitler?"

Zachary looked at Kiran in amazement. "Only every fucking Nazi, Klansman, and Aryan Nation yahoo in the entire country, you fucking moron."

"Plus," said Lee diplomatically, "I could see where some Jews and World War Two veterans might recognize it and get a little upset."

Minnie called me back. "Did you find anything yet? Whatever you do, make sure it's nonpartisan."

In the end, the best I could find was a quote by Harry Truman, whom even the Republicans seemed enamored with. Even so, we got an irate phone call afterward from a constituent who wanted to know why Minnie had been on C-SPAN quoting "that degenerate fag novelist." Apparently, the caller had confused President Truman with Truman Capote.

These were the type of people we were dealing with back in the district. Every day, we got bags full of letters, many of which had all the cheerfulness and penmanship of ransom notes. It seemed that anyone who had enough time to write their congressperson was almost, by definition, someone with way too much free time. We heard disproportionately from retired people, schoolchildren, conspiracy theorists, and the criminally insane. While the schoolchildren's letters were charming, we rarely answered them since children don't vote. The others tended to consist of laundry lists of misery. People would write demanding that Minnie do something about the industrial incinerator next door to their property, the potholes in their driveway, their children's dilapidated schools, the pornography at their local video store, the noise emanating from the airport, the lack of affordable housing, and the high cost of health insurance. They would then conclude their letters by writing, "But above all else, I want you to lower my taxes. The government sucks. It'll be a cold day in hell before I vote for any of you lying, thieving bastards."

We'd have to log these letters in a database and respond with a form letter, thanking them "for sharing your valuable opinion with the congresswoman."

Since Minnie had instructed me to "communicate to constituents on their level," I tried to figure out exactly what this "level" was. While I made sure to slog through the *Congressional Record,* the *Congressional Quarterly,* and *Roll Call* each day in order to understand what was going on in Congress, I spent the remainder of my time boning up on those things that seemed to be of far greater interest to our constituents: namely, soap operas. I then followed up with a healthy dose of *Ricki Lake, Geraldo,* and *Sally Jesse Raphael,* then an intensive reading of the *National Enquirer, TV Guide,* and *People* magazine, before finally finishing off with a perusal of the Fingerhut catalogue.

For the first month or two, this strategy seemed to work. I not only figured out the difference between things like mandatory and discretionary spending, but how to explain them to voters in clear, simple, language. (*Mandatory spending is a fixed, regular expense— like your rent or car payments. Discretionary spending is what you decide to buy with whatever's left of your paycheck.*) However, the more I began to think like our constituents, the less I cared about House legislation and the more I became invested in what was going on between Alan and Monica Quartermaine on *General Hospital.* While I still couldn't name the head of the House Ways and Means Committee or explain how a filibuster worked, I did learn everything there was to know about Kathie Lee Gifford's new spring sportswear line, the hidden dangers of liposuction, and how a kitten, a vacuum cleaner, and a parakeet could make for one uproariously wacky home video. In less than three months, I went from being a know-nothing to a total moron.

———

Ironically, while working on the Hill is never easy, I found that it was particularly difficult working for somebody who'd been elected to Congress largely because of her contempt for it.

One of the first things Minnie did upon arriving in Washington was to pledge that neither she nor her staff would accept any gifts or perks. At the time, both the House and the Senate were debating a gift ban that limited the freebies Congress could accept from outsiders, but Minnie wasn't waiting. When the nurses' union offered to take her to lunch, she declined. When direct mail firms sent her boxes of candy, she mailed them right back. When schoolchildren sent her cookies, she donated them to a local hospital. She was scrupulous. A free junket to Disney World, a round of golf at Pebble Beach, or a steak lunch at the Palm? No thank you. Other members might scarf at the congressional trough, but *she* was not for sale.

Our entire staff was extremely proud of this. Our boss was demonstrating the very strength of character that had inspired us to work for her. We felt righteous. We felt privileged. We felt profoundly just.

That is, until the Häagen-Dazs lobby arrived.

You didn't know there was a Häagen-Dazs lobby? Me neither. Apparently, it's actually a lobby for dairy subsidies or sugar subsidies or some such thing, but I never learned exactly what because as soon as the lobbyists began wheeling little ice cream carts through the hallways of Longworth and happily handing out as many free chocolate-coated ice cream bars as anyone could carry, they were besieged by staffers. "Ice cream, ice cream!" legislative assistants shrieked to their colleagues. All along the corridors, you could hear staffers yelling, "Gotta go!" then hanging up on constituents in mid-sentence in order to dash out of their offices and chase after the ice cream cart. "OhmyGod. They have a flavor called Dark Belgian Chocolate," somebody squealed.

"Hey, I'll trade someone Vanilla with Almonds for a Sorbet and Cream!"

"Let me in! Coming through! I'm an ice cream *specialist!* This is an emergency!" yelled another, barreling into the fray.

The scene was savage. It was hysterical. It brought a whole new level to the term "feeding frenzy." And Kiran, Lee, Zachary, and I had every intention of joining it.

"Not so fast," said Vicki, bodily barring the door. "You know the policy. No freebies."

"But, IT'S ICE CREAM," we fairly wailed.

"I made a promise," said Minnie matter-of-factly.

"Have you no heart, woman?" cried Lee, as we watched the entire office across the hall load up on frozen novelties.

"Minnie, for fuck's sake," cried Zachary. "For the love of God, let us eat an ice cream bar."

"Nothing doing," chuckled Minnie.

"But Minnie, think of it this way: If I was the average voter," I said, "frankly, I'd be more inclined to vote for you if I knew you were bought and paid for by the ice cream industry."

"Nice try," said Minnie, leaning against the door frame.

"You know, this is a violation of our civil rights," said Kiran. "What happened to 'life, liberty, and the pursuit of happiness'?"

"What happened to you getting back to work?" said Vicki. "That's it, people, move it upstairs."

Just then Bruce, my cohort from across the hall, came in with his arms full of ice cream bars. "Hey, guys?" he said. "You don't happen to have any spare room in your freezer, do you? Ours is full-up."

Back in the annex, Zachary picked up a dictionary and hurled it against the wall.

"I don't fucking believe it," he said. "Minnie hires her two best friends—a lesbian couple—pays them a combined salary that's equal to her own—but won't let her staff eat a free goddamn ice cream because she's afraid *that* might cause a scandal back in the district? What kind of fucking drugs is *she* taking?"

Salaries were increasingly becoming a sore point with us. When Minnie had been in the statehouse, she'd won people's hearts by returning her pay raise to the taxpayers each month. Now, she hoped to score points with voters by returning most of her congressional budget to them as well. This required her to run her office as cheaply as possible.

While attempts were made to limit our office supplies—often, it was easier to borrow a pen from another office than to requisition one from the politburo Edna had set up—the best way to trim costs, of course, was to pay the staff as little as possible.

Hill salaries are notoriously low. They are also a matter of public record, published yearly in a dense little government book. After Zachary got ahold of a copy, we often took turns reading aloud from it to see where we stacked up. Virtually all our friends in other offices, we discovered, were earning more than we were in comparable positions.

Worse yet, they knew this. Everybody on the Hill did. Because all the other staffers spent their lunch hours exactly like we did—looking up everybody else's salaries to see how theirs compared and which poor bastards got paid the least. "You guys work for Minnie Glenn?" they'd hoot whenever they met us at Hill happy hours. "Our condolences. Please. Allow us to buy the next round."

What galled us most, however, was that while we were all paid on the low end for our positions, Vicki and Edna were paid roughly the average for theirs. Living together, they enjoyed a combined income equal to Minnie's.

Meanwhile, Kiran began house-painting with his cousins on weekends to make ends meet, while the newest legislative assistant, Tim, started deejaying at college parties after-hours. Ironically, any time my phone bills were higher than expected, I found myself trolling for freelance writing assignments all over again. To keep from defaulting on his student loans, Lee moved back in with his sister, agreeing to baby-sit her two kids in exchange for free rent, thereby earning himself the degrading new nickname around the office of "Nanny Man."

After putting in a full day on the Hill, almost all of us wound up working some sort of improvised "second shift." Subsisting on five hours' sleep, we'd then stumble back into the office each morning to help Minnie fight for all the hardworking, underpaid Americans she cared so much about.

Occasionally, Edna, at a loss for something to do, would come upstairs to the annex, putter about, and describe to us the meals she and Vicki had eaten at their favorite four-star restaurant in Georgetown.

"Really, you guys should treat yourselves to Citronelle," she said. "If you order only appetizers and desserts, you can easily get away for under $75."

"You know," Kiran remarked once she'd gone back downstairs, "it's a good thing we all have such a great sense of humor. Otherwise, something like this could get really demoralizing."

That summer, Minnie was chosen by the party leadership to address the Democratic convention; her two-minute speech would be broadcast live during prime time. It was an enormous coup, and Tim, Lee, Zachary, and I went to Kiran's house to watch it together on TV. The mood was festive—copious amounts of popcorn got tossed into the air—but when Minnie came on, we all became strangely silent. Minnie's hair had been styled beautifully, her makeup had been professionally applied, and it was clear that some of the spin doctors had also gotten ahold of her, because she gave a rousing rah-rah speech far less critical and policy-oriented than the one she'd been preparing. But then, midway through, she lapsed into her own language, delivering catchphrases of hers that we were all so familiar with, we recited them along with her as she spoke.

"Too many Americans work too hard for too little," she declared before the cheering conventioneers. "Too many Americans are holding down two or three jobs just to make ends meet."

"Yeah," Lee, Tim, and Kiran shouted mirthlessly at the screen. "Like your staff!"

Growing up leftie, I'd been surrounded by friends and relatives who believed "the personal is political." My friend Allison could barely buy a box of Raisin Bran without leafing through her copy of *Shopping for a Better World* to make sure she wasn't inadvertently clubbing baby seals to death in the process. Stupidly, naively, I'd believed that a person with humane political views would be a humane person to work for—and that female bosses would treat women employees better in the workplace because we were all "in this together."

Yet it probably comes as a shock to no one but me that on Capitol Hill—as perhaps everywhere else—a huge disconnect exists between political ideology and personal conduct. A member of Congress could actually be a fantastic boss, despite the fact that he believed all welfare mothers should be sterilized—while working for someone like Minnie, who felt compassion for every spotted owl, transgendered teenager, and autoworker on the planet, could be an act of masochism. "Sisterhood," I realized glumly, was often a myth, too. Vicki and Edna no doubt considered themselves feminists, yet virtually every young woman I knew who worked for them in D.C. left the office in tears. Edna routinely bad-mouthed them to the female office manager back in the district, while Vicki occasionally rounded up Zachary, Kiran, and Lee for chummy golf games, leaving me and Natasha, the new receptionist, to open the mail and answer the phones. "I'm not excluding you," Vicki would say acerbically. "It's not my fault you two don't play softball or golf."

"Each congressional office is its very own dysfunctional family," Bruce said when I came to his office enraged.

And it was true. Word got around the Hill quickly about which congressional offices were a dream to work in and which ones were nightmares. Minnie's was quickly earning a reputation as the latter. Bruce himself worked in a dream. His boss, a mellow Northern Californian, was perfectly in sync with his largely vegan, hemp-wearing district. Indeed, he won his House seat each term by something like 70 percent of the vote. Occasionally, a student from UC Santa Cruz might call the office and complain that the school's mascot—a dancing cartoon Banana Slug—had frozen up on the congressman's Web site again and couldn't they possibly upgrade their software? But that was just about as disgruntled as his constituents ever got.

In true California style, before Bruce's boss hired anyone, he had them "hang" with him in the office for a few days to "test their dynamic" with the other staffers. As a result, his staff got along so well they often stayed late just for the fun of it and came in over the weekends to eat potlucks together. Every time I stopped by to borrow a pen or have a small nervous breakdown, they all seemed to be sitting on the congressman's couch, brainstorming bipartisan environmental legislation while one of them idly strummed a guitar.

"Oh, Susie, you're just in time for our Arbor Day celebration," the chief of staff would say cheerily, holding up a cake plate. "Care for a chocolate leaf cookie?"

The four of us from the annex used any opportunity we could to stop in and linger awhile, soaking up all their positive good vibes and sunny, California energy before reluctantly returning to our gulag across the hall.

It was an election year, and Minnie had begun spending more and more time back in her district. Whenever she returned to Washington, she was preoccupied and inaccessible. Rushing immediately into her chamber, she spent most of the day in closed-door meetings with Vicki and Edna. The atmosphere became increasingly exclusionary and punitive; it was like working for three cliquish seventh grade girls. Accordingly, the rest of us regressed. Whenever Minnie finally did emerge to mingle with the rest of the staff, we fawned around her like insecure children, making wisecracks and performing stupid tricks for her, vying for her attention and approval.

One of my ambitions was fulfilled, however. For the first time in my life, people were impressed with me at cocktail parties. "Oh, look at the little gold eagle on your business card," they squealed. But by then, it was only too apparent to me that the miseries of working for a congressperson were the same as any other job, if not worse. The same pettiness, poor morale, and lousy management existed on the Hill that existed in offices throughout America. In this way, I supposed, Congress was a truly democratic institution.

I, of course, had done little to help myself, and my own situation quickly deteriorated. One day, Edna would announce I was to do nothing but log constituent mail into our database and double-check the punctuation in letters we sent out. Then Vicki would yell at me, "I thought you were supposed to be Minnie's writer. Why aren't you writing?"

Edna went back to the district. Yet every time I faxed my work to her to approve, she claimed never to have received it. Although I could send it twelve times over the course of the day, and hold a dozen fax confirmations in my hand, Edna would insist, "Nope. Haven't got it. Funny. Everybody else's faxes have come through."

Then Vicki would plunk a stack of *Congressional Quarterly*s on my desk. "You've been here how many months and still don't know the basics?" she said. "I'd advise you to start reading." Two days later, she'd call me downstairs. "I'm not going to name names. But certain staffers are complaining that all you do is sit at your desk all day and read."

At my past jobs, I'd experienced a whole range of emotions. Paranoia, however, had never been one of them. Although I was pretty sure I was being set up to fail, my confidence had fallen so far below sea level I couldn't trust my own judgment anymore, and so I spent a lot of time in a highly productive state of paralysis, staring out the window.

"Oh yeah. Vicki and Edna are fucking with you, big-time," Zachary confirmed. "They've been trying to sabotage you since the day you walked in here. They didn't like that Minnie hired you without consulting them."

Had I been more experienced in office warfare, I might have strategized cunning ways to defend myself and retaliate. Instead, not throwing up each day soon became my idea of a major achievement. All my life, I'd read about other people's professional successes in magazine articles entitled: "Who'da Thunk: My Boss Now Works for Me!" But where were all the stories about office fuck-ups, I wanted to know? About employees with sadistic and persecuting managers? Where was the advice for people like me, who developed acid reflux as soon as they arrived at their office each morning?

A horrendous job is like a chronic illness, a rotting tooth. It infects everything in your life; your world constricts and collapses into the toxic, throbbing ache of it. You can't go to a café, walk your dog, or go away for a weekend without a constant, low-grade sense of dread: *Augh. Work.* Soon, I was waking up every morning feeling poisoned. Hitching a ride to the Hill with another communications director named Jeannie, who was equally miserable, we practiced deep breathing together to subdue our churning stomachs. Then, after receiving either my daily chastisement from Vicki or silent treatment from Edna, I spent every free moment I had job hunting with Zachary, helping Kiran with his law school essays, and crying in the nurse's office. So much for my moment of professional glory.

The nurse, whom I secretly christened "The Angel," put a cool compress on my head. "I have to tell you, I've been on Capitol Hill for years," she said sympathetically. "It is an incredibly punishing place for young staffers. There is so much backstabbing and nastiness. Bright young people are just devastated all the time in this environment. To be honest, I'm grateful my own children don't work here."

She wrote down an address and handed it to me. "People have been so traumatized working here that a special counseling office has been set up for Hill employees," she said gently. "Why don't you make an appointment?"

The Hill counseling office was actually not on the Hill, but a good quarter of a mile away in a low-slung office building across a small field and a series of access roads. Had it been any farther away from the Capitol, it would've been in Virginia. Stranger still, there was no sign on the door; I half expected a little peephole to slide open and a voice demanding a password. Indeed, when I knocked, a panicked voice cried out, "Just a minute, please," followed by a series of thumps. A moment later, a young woman answered the door breathlessly.

"Sorry to make you wait," she said, "but with each client, we have to clear out the waiting room in order to protect them."

Protect them? From what, I wanted to ask. *Fallout?* But then, I supposed, this was exactly right.

Having grown up as I did, I couldn't understand why most Americans regarded therapy as something to be embarrassed about. People often claim you'd have to have your head examined to live in New York City, and we New Yorkers tend to agree. In Manhattan, everybody is in therapy. In fact, we're suspicious of people who aren't. Whenever we're dating someone who's never been to a therapist, our friends invariably caution, "Uh Oh. Watch out. He'll be carrying *baggage*." Walking down the street in Manhattan—I kid you not—I have actually overheard somebody saying: "So I said to my therapist, 'But what about *my* needs?'"

In Washington, however, it's generally assumed that if a politician—or if anyone who even works for a politician—has ever been in therapy, it is an enormous liability. No doubt, their enemies can use it against them to claim they're mentally unfit. Only we Manhattanites, it seems, would probably be *more* likely to vote for a politician because they'd been on the couch. "Hey, *I've* been to a shrink," candidates could brag to us. "It's my opponent who still has *issues*."

On Capitol Hill, the one counseling service set up to help staffers was cloaked in secrecy and shame. Going there every week felt like visiting a speakeasy or back-alley abortionist.

"That's it," I told my mother on the phone. "It's one thing to drive people crazy. It's another to make them ashamed of it. I'm outta there."

Minnie did win reelection, and two days passed before the staff back in Washington received e-mails thanking us for our hard work throughout the term. The next week, Vicki and Edna returned to the Capitol and sat me down alone in Minnie's office. They handed me a job evaluation that made me sound only slightly less heinous than Saddam Hussein. It accused me of gross incompetence, lousy people skills, poor writing abilities, an abuse of phone privileges, and, of course, an "attitude problem." While they insisted it was a standard congressional evaluation form, it looked to me like Edna had whipped it up on her computer the night before; I had to restrain myself from pointing out a typo.

"You can resign if you'd like," Vicki offered, "or finish out the year on probation."

"Any questions?" said Edna.

"Yes," I said. "This is the worst job evaluation I've ever seen in my life. Why aren't you firing me?"

Vicki and Edna looked at each other. After a moment, Vicki said grudgingly, "Well, Minnie doesn't want to fire you. If nothing else, you've been loyal."

It suddenly occurred to me that it was likely Minnie hadn't even seen the job evaluation at all.

Vicki gave me a week to decide whether I wanted to stay "on probation" or resign. But by then, mercifully, my months of job hunting with Zachary had finally paid off; that same day, I was offered a job in the Communications Department at a trade association starting right after New Year's. There, people earned decent salaries, promoted worthy causes, and nobody made you run the gauntlet for an extra ballpoint pen. It wasn't nearly as sexy or glamorous as the Hill, but the atmosphere was exceedingly kind. This, I'd come to realize, was more important than anything else in a workplace.

Best yet, my future boss wanted to have coffee with me. "But unfortunately, I can't do it this afternoon," she explained over the phone, "I've got a therapy appointment that I absolutely can't miss."

I've relished few things more than giving Vicki and Edna my two weeks' notice; as I told them how *truly* devastated I'd be not to work with them another year, it seemed as though bars from Tchaikovsky's *1812* Overture were reverberating through the office, and I had to restrain myself from leaping up on the desk and doing the "Nah-nah-neh" butt-wiggling victory dance I'd perfected when I was four.

Soon after, Vicki and Edna returned to the district for Christmas, leaving Lee, Kiran, Zachary, and me alone in Washington to close out the term. Now that she was no longer a first-term congresswoman, Minnie was literally moving up in the world. Having fared much better in the office lottery this time around, she had secured a large office on the top floor of Longworth. It opened up onto the roof, which provided a vast terrace of sorts from where you could see the Capitol Dome, the tip of the Washington Monument, and the gentle swale of the mall.

It fell to us to oversee the move, and we spent the last few days before Christmas romping giddily around the piles of furniture and unopened boxes. A few offices on our new hall had draped garlands of tinsel over their door frames, but most everyone had gone home to their districts for the holidays. There was absolutely nothing for us to do. Kiran briefly went into a panic because, after a year of obsessing about his law school essay, he'd finally mailed it out, only to discover that he'd written about wanting to go into "pubic" service instead of "public." We got a lot of mileage teasing him about that one, until an early acceptance letter arrived. Lee boasted about his latest girlfriend. Zachary invented a new game that involved a "welt scale." Everyone congratulated me on getting a new job.

My last day in the office, a package arrived. It was a five-pound box of chocolates sent to Minnie as a Christmas present from a supporter. Yet amid all the boxes and packing materials, Zachary somehow lost the return envelope. We had no idea who'd sent it.

"Shit," he cried. "Minnie is going to have a heart attack when she finds out we can't return it. What the hell are we going to do?"

We all looked at each other.

As we tore into the trays of nougats and butter cremes, a young reporter for the *Baltimore Sun* knocked on our door.

"I'm sorry to bother you," she said. A photographer skulked behind her, fiddling with his Visitors Press badge. "But I was sent to interview Hill staffers about their experiences. The Maryland offices have closed already. Mind if I interview you guys instead?"

We looked at the reporter, then at the half-eaten box of chocolates sitting on the couch next to us. It was even more forbidden to talk to reporters without Vicki's approval than it was to accept gifts from constituents.

"Well, you know," Lee reasoned, "we're already going to hell."

Zachary looked at the reporter, then at the photographer. "If we agree to be interviewed, can we get our picture in the paper, too?" he asked.

"Sure," she said.

I held out the box. "Chocolates, anyone?"

In between mouthfuls of candy, we answered her questions and posed on the couch. After she left, the three of us, heady with sugar and transgressiveness, climbed out onto the roof and looked out at the Capitol Dome, rising monumentally before us in the bracing December sunshine. It really was something to behold, *still*.

For my last day, I'd brought a disposable camera and asked each of the guys to pose with me in front of the Dome as part of my last, official Capitol Hill memory. As I stood there with them, I thought of the first day when I'd arrived, how awed I'd been, how hopeful and excited I'd felt when Minnie and I had eaten donuts together in her office. It occurred to me then that I'd revered Minnie for her humanness, yet in the end, I'd faulted her for it, too. Like most Americans, I'd wanted a "Normal Everyperson" on Capitol Hill, then felt betrayed when the person I'd supported had actually behaved like one—when she'd wound up exercising the same flawed behavior and poor judgment that the rest of us always did.

I stood before the Capitol—first with Zachary, then with Lee—and blinked into the sunlight as they each took turns with the camera.

When we were done, Lee gave me a squeeze. "I'm going to miss you," he said.

"Aw, I'll miss you guys, too," I said.

"No, I mean I'll *miss* you," Lee grinned. "When you were standing there next to me just now, I got a touch of your boob."

Chapter 14

Hypocrite in a Pouffy White Dress

AS I REACHED my thirties, a strange thing happened—a lot of my friends actually thought it was a good idea to start getting married. Orchestrating weddings similar in size and scope to the invasion of Normandy, they suddenly began obsessing about floral centerpieces and disposable cameras. Yet the amount of fun I had at their weddings never had anything to do with the monogrammed napkin rings they'd chosen or their "signature cocktails." Rather, it always depended upon one thing *only*: whether or not I happened to be getting laid at the time. If I was single, it didn't matter if they served lobster tails at a wedding, decorated the reception hall with ice swans spitting grain alcohol, or gave me a Tiffany silver picture frame as a party favor. If I felt lonely and pathetic, I watched the beautiful bride walk down the aisle amid clouds of rose petals and thought only one thing: *I am going to die alone, surrounded by seventeen cats.*

And yet, even when the Amazing Bob and I got engaged, I remained supremely ambivalent about marriage myself. Never mind that the media constantly depicts women in their thirties as husband-hungry hysterics. As a child of divorce, I harbored no illusions that walking down the aisle led to happiness and fulfillment. If anything, marriage seemed to me like the one thing you could do to inevitably bring yourself closer to needing alimony. What's more, I wasn't convinced that marriage was all that good for women, period.

When I was younger, I'd leave the war zone of my own household and wander through my friends' living rooms, admiring the little framed pictures scattered around their pianos and end tables. "Wow. Who's that?" I'd ask, pointing to photos of young women who looked like starlets in pedal pushers, taffeta cocktail dresses, shiny graduation robes.

"Oh, that's my mom," my friends would say dismissively, "before she met my dad."

Invariably, the carefree, dazzling young women in the photographs looked nothing like the haggard, irritated, sexless mothers I saw forever unloading groceries in the kitchen, soaking their feet in Epsom salts, and snapping at my friends to "get that goddamn Yahtzee set off of the sofa."

Lying awake at night, staring at my clock radio, I worried that once I got married, I would become one of those exhausted, invisible women obliterated by the demands of her family. After I became first a Wife, then a Mother, my career would disintegrate like fireworks and I'd quickly be reduced to nothing but a pair of giant, lactating mammaries. Crying children would swing from my neck like albatrosses as I stumbled around the kitchen, bovine in a bathrobe, holding a frying pan and a breast pump. Soon I'd be wearing drugstore bifocals, Isotoner slippers, and sweaters decorated with knitted sheep, and even my husband would start calling me "Mom." When he talked about me to other people, he'd behave as if he were addressing a grand jury: "My wife here," he'd say, rolling his eyes, "thinks we should drive around with snow tires until April."

"Why can't we be like Jean-Paul Sartre and Simone de Beauvoir?" I often moaned to Bob. "You know, just remain two lovers who spend the rest of their lives together arguing at a café in Paris."

Yet eventually, both my overwhelming love for him and the desire for joint health insurance won out. "We're going to have a beautiful life together," Bob and I agreed the night we got engaged. "Our marriage will be ours to live in our own way, and we'll plan our wedding exclusively on our own terms, nobody else's."

Okay. You can now put down this book and commence laughing.

―――――――

As a newspaper journalist, I'd had to maintain objectivity while interviewing all sorts of sexist, ideological yahoos. Working on Capitol Hill, I'd been forced to reevaluate my assumptions about sisterhood. But as a feminist, nothing was as daunting to me as getting engaged. Because as soon as Bob slipped the ring onto my finger, it was as if we were instantly catapulted back into 1957. Virtually overnight, people stopped treating us like individuals and began relating to us instead as a traditional Bride and Groom—sex roles as shallow and reductive as the symbols on public restrooms.

"Ohmygod, you're engaged," my feminist girlfriends squealed, lunging for my hand. "Let's see the ring!"

"Hoo boy, welcome to the club," said our guy friends, slapping Bob meatily on the back. "Kiss your freedom goodbye, bud."

Our friends were hardly what you'd call reactionaries. In fact, they were mostly a hodge-podge of tofu-eating political activists, artists, scientists, social workers, massage therapists, lawyers, and astrologers. Yet oddly, they kept referring to our wedding as *my* "Big Day" alone, in which Bob had little more significance than a door knob. What's more, like the rest of the world, they seemed to assume that our wedding would be the one legitimate opportunity I'd ever have to dress up, boss people around, and act out all my narcissistic and exhibitionistic impulses, when—as far as I was concerned—that was precisely what my everyday life was for.

The ring had barely been on my finger a week when the onslaught of bridal magazines began mysteriously arriving in my mailbox. They weren't so much magazines as "wedding porn," each one loaded with six hundred pages designed to get me hot and drooling over hand blenders, hair ornaments, and dresses that could easily double as slip-covers.

"The flowers you choose for your wedding reception," one article began, "will be the most important flowers of your life."

"Oh. Please," I groaned to Bob. "Spare me the frou-frou bullshit."

Neither of us, we agreed, wanted a traditional wedding. The whole premise struck us as regressive, degrading: The groom was practically straight-jacketed in a tuxedo, then led around like a man on death row, while the bride was dressed up like an enormous doll and encouraged to live out every fantasy she'd ever had as a five-year-old in order to enter into the most adult commitment of her life. This hardly seemed to us like an intelligent way to kick off a marriage.

"I don't want any icky, Freudian, father-daughter waltzes," I told Bob. "And no insipid bridesmaids' dresses, either. I love my friends too much to make them dress up like giant eggplants. And no sadistic bouquet toss. I mean, why do that to people?"

"Agreed," said Bob. "Let's just keep it small, simple, and funky."

"What do you say we just hire a deejay, an ice cream truck, a bartender, and be done with it?"

"There you go," said Bob. "You just planned our entire wedding in three minutes. See, that wasn't hard at all."

"Really, I don't know why couples get so bent out of shape over this," I sniffed. "Some people are such drama queens."

———

Stunningly, of course, Bob and I had somehow managed to miss the fact that weddings are giant Rorschach tests onto which everyone around you projects their fears, fantasies, and expectations—many of which they've been cultivating since the day you were born. The moment we began planning our small, simple, funky wedding, the telephone started ringing.

I heard you're not having bridesmaids. How can you possibly have a wedding without bridesmaids?

You know, you can never go wrong with prime rib.

Polkas are always nice for the elderly generation.

"Listen," said my father, "do you really want to spend the equivalent of a down payment for a party that lasts only four hours? Why don't you guys do something cheaper and laid-back and just get married at an old Southern roadhouse somewhere? I mean, D.C. is close to Virginia, isn't it?"

"An 'old Southern roadhouse'?" I said. "Why, that's a great idea, Dad. I'm sure the locals down in Killjew, Virginia, would just love to host a Yankee interfaith wedding ceremony."

"It's just a suggestion," said my father. "Bob could wear a Stetson. We could all dance the Texas Two-Step. Serving barbecue would certainly be a lot less expensive than a sit-down dinner in New York."

"And if we could arrange to have the Klan chase us out of town before dessert, I bet we could save a bundle on the wedding cake," I said.

After hanging up, I called my brother in a panic. "John," I asked, "what drugs is Dad on? He actually suggested throwing our wedding at a Southern roadhouse and having Bob walk down the aisle in a cowboy hat. Does he have us confused with some other family he has?"

"Suze," my brother said after a minute. "I've got only one piece of advice for you: Elope."

———————

Somehow, Bob and I had also overlooked the fact that even if all you wanted was an ice cream truck, a bartender, and a deejay, you still needed a place to put them. And if you decided it might be nice to have some photographs of the day—photographs that did not scalp anyone, or feature detailed close-ups of your uncle's thumb—it was best to hire a photographer. And then, as my mother diplomatically pointed out, if relatives were going to travel across the country to witness your marriage, it was probably polite to feed them more than a Fudgsicle and a glass of champagne. And surely, you couldn't expect older folks to balance a plate on their hand all night: they had to sit somewhere. And since you were going to have tables anyway, would it really kill you to put out a few flowers to brighten things up?

By the end of the month, Bob and I had sixteen rotating appointments with photographers, florists, wedding halls, deejays, and caterers. The only upside to this was that most of the vendors we interviewed made any crazy and annoying relatives look reasonable by comparison.

"Okay. This is how you're going to do your wedding," a photographer named Blaine—no first name, no last name, "just Blaine please"—informed us. Just Blaine Please, I noticed, wore a voluminous silk shirt tucked into a pair of tight Armani jeans, giving him the distinct look of a homosexual pirate.

"You Jewish?" said Blaine, leading us through a hallway lined alternately with black-and-white wedding photos and stagy self-portraits of himself wearing chaps. "Yes? No? *Partially?* Well then, immediately after the ceremony, go into the hora. Don't even have the guests walk into the reception area. *Dance* them in. Do you understand what I'm saying? *Dance* them in with that Jewish sort of bunny hop you guys always do. Then, do that hoist-the-bride-up-on-the-chair bit, and then, before anyone's even sat down, immediately wheel out the wedding cake and start cutting it. Do you hear what I'm saying? Cut the cake right then and there, before they've even brought the salad out. That way, your makeup will still be fresh and all your guests will still look interested. And that way, if for some strange reason, God forbid, I have to go and photograph a second wedding that same night, you'll still have plenty of Blaine originals of all the best moments."

"Was he kidding?" Bob said as we walked, shell-shocked, to the parking lot. "What's a 'Jewish sort of bunny hop'?"

The next photographer, Mildred, was everything Blaine was not. Unkempt, gentle, and obese, she arrived at my apartment dressed in a paisley muumuu with a portfolio tucked under one armpit and an enormous pastrami sandwich beneath the other. No sooner was she seated at my kitchen table than she unwrapped the sandwich and offered us sections.

"I hope you don't mind if I eat while we talk, but I have this strange blood disorder," she laughed. "If I don't eat protein every one or two hours, I tend to pass out. I mean, like, *boom.* Right down on the floor like a redwood. Craziest thing. You've never seen anything like it."

Determined to resist the orgiastic consumerism that passed itself off as a premarital requirement, Bob and I refused to register for gifts. It struck us as greedy and presumptuous somehow: *Hi. We're getting married. Now here's the blender we'd like you to buy for us.* But then, Bob happened to mention this at a dinner party at our friend Lucy's.

"I have only two words to describe what happens to couples who don't register," Lucy said flatly. "String art."

"I have only four words," said Andrea, also a newlywed. "Orange plastic salad bowl."

"You can't think of it as being greedy," Brian advised, as he got up to refill our wineglasses—beautiful glasses which, Lucy pointed out, they'd registered for. "You have to think of it as insurance against bad taste. It's something you do preemptively to make sure you don't wind up with cartons full of shit."

"Look," said Andrea. "If you really have the masochistic urge to let your guests select their own gifts, I'll be happy to give you the salt shakers shaped like lawn trolls that Peter and I received."

"It's like the Borg on *Star Trek,*" Bob observed in the car ride home afterward. "Resistance is futile. You will assimilate."

"So that's our choice?" I said. "Register—or receive sixteen salt shakers shaped like lawn trolls?"

A week later, when we arrived at a bridal registry office, we were greeted by Mrs. Marscapone, an older, well-coiffed woman with the officious air of a headmistress. As our "personal registry consultant," Mrs. Marscapone came around to my side of the desk, put her arm protectively around my shoulder, and presented me with a clipboard.

"Here you go," she said proudly, as if it was something I'd earned. "This lists every item we have on this floor, as well as in Bedding, Linens, and the Electronics Department." With an expert flourish, she flipped through the sheets attached to the clipboard. "These are just checklists, guidelines to help couples register. You see?" she pointed to a list that read *Serving bowl, creamer, gravy boat.*

Gravy boat? I thought. *Now that I'm getting married, I'm supposed to register for a gravy boat?* Just the thought of it made me feel eligible for Social Security. I looked down the list. *Butter dish,* it said. *Chafing dish. Punch bowl.* Who actually used these things? The only place I'd ever seen them was at my grandparents'. Was I supposed to buy all this stuff and save it for when I was reincarnated as a society wife or a Republican?

Casual china, the list read, followed by *formal china.* I considered asking if "casual china" was called that because it slept around a lot, then looked at Mrs. Marscapone and decided against it. When two lesbian friends of mine had a commitment ceremony in New York City, they'd registered for sex toys at an erotic boutique called Eve's Garden. Their registry had been remarkably different. *Two-headed dildo,* it had read. *Hitachi Magic Wand vibrator. Ribbed latex strap-on. Size: medium. Color: magenta (but lilac OK too).* I wondered if it was too late to change stores.

"Don't be afraid to dream a little," Mrs. Marscapone told me grandly. "Remember, *you're* the bride. This is *your* day. People want to buy you expensive, high-quality presents. So if you've always dreamed of owning a bread maker, now's the time! Register for a bread maker! You want a hand blender? Register for a hand blender! You want a Krups food processor with mini-bowl attachment? Register for a Krups food processor with mini-bowl attachment!"

Before I could even think of asking, "What if I want a two-headed dildo?" Mrs. Marscapone turned to Bob. "Here," she said perfunctorily. "You get the gun."

The "gun" turned out to be a bar code scanner, thoughtfully designed to make the holder believe they were carrying not a price-checker, but a piece of high-tech weaponry.

Once we were properly armed in accordance with our sex role stereotypes, Mrs. Marscapone steered us out of the office toward a sign reading "Dishware."

"Happy registering," she called after us as we staggered toward a forest of dinner plates.

The selection was overwhelming, and the lists on the clipboard somehow made it worse. *Serving forks, fondue pots, toaster ovens.* What were we supposed to do with all of this stuff? And where were we supposed to put it? Bob and I each lived in compact, one bedroom apartments that, on a good day, could double as "before" pictures in an IKEA catalogue. We were living apart not because we were old-fashioned, but simply because we'd gotten too busy planning our goddamn wedding to find the time to move in together. Between the two of us, we had roughly enough storage space for a colander and a pair of salad tongs.

"You know," I said to Bob, as we eyed the enormous stacks of gourmet kitchen appliances, "for the price of a bread machine, a convection oven, and a Cuisinart, we could probably hire a maid to do these things for us instead."

In the aisles of flatware, the sample place settings gleamed seductively beneath the halogen spotlights, and each one had a name conjured up by someone to suggest grandeur or exoticism: *Cobalt. Chantilly. Artemis.* We did need flatware. Bob's stuff had been purchased at a garage sale—no two pieces of it matched—and mine had had an unfortunate run-in with a garbage disposal. Scanning the displays, I picked up a curvaceous dinner fork from the *Ganges* design collection. "Hey, Bob," I called out. "You like this fork?"

Bob came over and examined the fork. Unlike me, he seemed unconcerned with what it looked like but rather with how much food the tines could hold.

"Yeah, it's okay," he said finally. "Sure. I could live with these forks."

"For the rest of your life?"

Bob dropped the fork.

"Yeah, I pretty much had the same reaction when I thought about it that way," I said as he crawled under the display case to retrieve it.

For the next forty-five minutes, we walked around Housewares in a state of paralysis, virtually unable to register for anything. We found enough stuff that we liked—some blue, ceramic dishes, a geometric sushi set—but we just weren't sure we liked them enough to commit to looking at them for the rest of our lives.

We did come across some wine goblets we loved, but at $30 apiece, they seemed slightly ridiculous.

"That's good," said Bob. "We'll use the world's finest crystal to drink the cheap shit we buy at Sam's Club."

Still, Mrs. Marscapone's "Venus/Mars" strategy began to pay off, because soon Bob became itchy to try out the scanning gun. "Then again," he suggested, "maybe I should just scan a few of them in, you know, just to see how it works."

After three hours at the department store, we registered for exactly one set of wineglasses and a pizza cutter.

Choosing each other as spouses had been fairly easy. The dinnerware, however, was proving a bitch.

I must say that during the whole planning process, our families were amazing. The bridal magazines had prepared me for the worst, running articles with titles like "Managing Your Mother" and "Sisters Who Sabotage." Yet after the initial flurry of advice, both families respectfully backed off. No one called to quiz us about expenses or emotionally blackmail us into adding people to our minuscule guest list.

We attributed our parents' restraint to their unique maturity and wisdom. But truth was, they were simply too stunned to say anything. The only detail we'd bothered to share with anyone was that we'd arranged to have our wedding ceremony performed by one of our nearest and dearest friends, Carolyn. Carolyn just happened to be a Wiccan priestess from Berkeley, California. She was a lesbian

Wiccan priestess, to be exact, seeing as we'd met her through her lover, Cecilie, a friend of mine from college, and all four of us had become extremely close.

"A lesbian Wiccan priestess?" my churchgoing, Catholic future in-laws said when we told them. "You don't say."

"A lesbian Wiccan priestess?" my father said. "What's she going to wear for the ceremony? Leather?"

"A lesbian Wiccan priestess?" said my mother. "Hmm. Anyone I know?"

Yet since Carolyn lived in Berkeley, she wasn't licensed to perform marriages in D.C. We had to scramble to find some phenomenally open-minded clergy to co-officiate. Blessedly, we came across a rabbi named David.

"Let me get this straight," he said. "You're a non-practicing Jew and a 'recovering' Catholic and you'd like me to perform an inter-faith wedding ceremony with a lesbian Wiccan priestess?" He sat back for a moment and stroked his beard pensively. "Well, Jewish law does not list 'sheer curiosity' as a reason to do so, but it's as good as any I can come up with."

Both Carolyn and Cecilie loved the idea.

"It's like the basis for a sitcom," Cecilie exclaimed. *The Rabbi and the Witch.* Can you just picture it? OhmyGod. I'm hearing a theme song. *The Rabbi and the Witch!* she sang. *"The Rabbi and the Witch! He keeps Shabbas, she worships the goddess. They'll have you in a stitch! The Rabbi and the Witch!"*

Although Bob and I worried that this unique, possibly-Saturday-morning-cartoon-series wedding ceremony might alienate our fami-lies, it actually united them in utter confusion. It also seemed to compel them not to ask any more questions. Apparently, they agreed it was simply best not to know.

Back when my friend Lucy had been planning her nuptials, she and her fiancé had instituted a policy they called "Wedding-Free

Wednesdays," which meant that for one night a week they were forbidden to discuss anything wedding-related. At the time, Bob and I snickered over this. Now, it was starting to look like a stroke of genius.

All our free time was soon consumed writing checks, making elaborate lists, faxing, e-mailing, and bickering over liquor, parking arrangements, and even the song we'd walk down the aisle to. (I wanted the Rolling Stones' "[I Can't Get No] Satisfaction," while Bob opted for "Should I Stay or Should I Go" by the Clash.) No detail, we discovered, was too stupid to obsess over. Soon, like the zillion other engaged couples we'd vowed never to be like, we began to think that once our wedding was over, we'd be ready to spend our honeymoon in a mental institution.

"Guess what I got to help calm us both down?" Bob said one night when he came home. "I'll give you a hint. It begins with a 'P.'"

"Prozac?"

"No. Porn!" he exclaimed gleefully, unveiling an unmarked videotape.

"You just can't wait until your bachelor party, can you?" I said, shaking my head.

"It's 'couples porn,' see?" he said, pointing to the Day-Glo sticker on the spine reading "His 'n' Hers." "It's made to appeal to both sensibilities."

"You mean horny *and* sleepy?"

After sending out for pizza and cutting it with the pizza cutter we'd already received from our registry, we loaded the videotape into the VCR and settled back for an evening of fine adult entertainment. As soon as the requisite 1970s synthesizer music kicked in, the title of the movie flashed onscreen across a pair of enormous breasts. *To Have and to Hold*, it read.

"Ha ha," said Bob.

"Ha ha, indeed," I said.

But a few minutes after the opening scene began, we realized why this movie was labeled "for couples." Its premise was that—I am not making this up—an engaged couple, Traci and Brad, have a huge series of fights over their upcoming wedding. This compels both of them, of course, to storm out of the house and have sex with other people.

Yet for a good ten minutes before any sex occurs, Traci and Brad argue in elaborate detail about their wedding band, the seating plan, the menu, and her mother.

"Okay," said Bob. "Why am I not finding this relaxing?"

"I know," I said, while before us, Traci finally began having sex with one of the bridesmaids at her wedding shower. "All I can think about while I'm watching this is 'Where did she register? Is that serving platter they're on top of from Villeroy and Boch?'"

––––––

Yet the biggest issue, by far, was The Dress. Quite simply, I refused to wear one—at least not a traditional white one. My plan was to be "the Anti-Bride" and walk down the aisle in scarlet or black.

More than anything else, big frothy wedding dresses struck me as silly and infantilizing, as leftovers from the Eisenhower administration, the couture of future homemakers and Cinderella wannabes. They were the epitome of every value I rejected and of everything I did not want to be. To join Bob in matrimony, it struck me as foolhardy, even dangerous, to present myself to him as a fantasy, to walk down the aisle with any pretenses to living in a fairy tale.

"Let's face it. I'm neither royalty nor a virgin. Who would I be kidding?" I told Lucy. "In a traditional wedding gown, I'd just be a hypocrite in a pouffy white dress."

Truth be told, I also rejected the idea of a traditional wedding gown because I couldn't stand to shop for one. I couldn't bear spending weeks, if not months, trying on dresses that were supposed to make every woman look beautiful but that would undoubtedly confirm that I was fundamentally, chromosomally *yech*.

Clothes shopping, for me, has always been an act of masochism. As every woman knows, the garment industry will routinely cut some size 8s that are more like 6s, and others that are more like 10s. With my hourglass figure, I'm invariably two different sizes on the top and the bottom, thereby quadrupling the equation. After fifteen minutes in a dressing room, all my humor and perspective invariably fly out the window. Buttons don't close. Fabric pulls across my upper back. Waistbands hula-hoop around my hips, and I'm reduced to a jelly of self-hatred and despair. Never mind that children are starving to death in Africa: *I am an un-dressable freak!*

You would think that when you're shopping for your "dress of a lifetime," bridal stores would bend over backwards to alleviate such agonies. Yet amazingly, many exclusive wedding boutiques will not even let you try on dresses in anything but their "stock size." This means they hand you a sample dress in size 8, and you're supposed to decide if you want it judging from the "idea" you get of yourself in it.

Any woman who is not built like a surfboard knows it's impossible to gauge what a dress will look like without trying it on properly first. Big breasts or hips change the drape and distribution of material: you can't select a style based on hypotheticals. The idea of paying thousands of dollars for a dress that I couldn't even try on enraged me. I would have none of it.

My friends, I assumed, would understand this only too well. Most of my girlfriends had tales about shopping for bras and bathing suits that rivaled only "gym class stories" for their agony and pathos. Yet when I told them of my intention to walk down the aisle in red or black, they were apoplectic.

"Oh no," Desa cried. "But you'll never get to wear a wedding dress again in your life!"

"Try to think about how you'll feel twenty years from now," said Stefie. "Trust me. You don't want to be like those people in the 60s who got married in hot pants and clogs and now feel like idiots whenever they open their wedding album."

"Just try one on first before you reject it," Lucy pleaded.

Grudgingly, I dragged myself to David's Bridal, a chain store in a strip mall that subscribes to the revolutionary idea of actually stocking wedding dresses in different sizes so that women in different sizes can actually try them on. My plan was to simply confirm that I'd look ridiculous before heading up to a vintage clothing store in New York called Trash and Vaudeville to pick up something campy or punk.

I did everything all the wedding books instructed me not to. I arrived at David's Bridal alone, without an appointment, and with absolutely no idea of what would look good on me, other than, perhaps, an enormous paper bag.

A saleslady, Annette, led me back to the dressing room and set me up in a cubby with the few, plain dresses I'd reluctantly selected. "Let me get you some foundation garments," she called out. "What size bra do you wear?"

When I told her, the entire dressing room came to a standstill. Okay: so I have large breasts. That does happen to women, occasionally. But one of the mothers-of-the-brides trying on a suit stopped in mid-twirl before the mirror.

"OhmyGod. *That's* your size?" she exclaimed, staring at me over the rim of her glasses. "If I were you, I would have surgery."

I wish I could say this was the first time anyone ever said something so awful to me. But it wasn't. Unfortunately, women feel compelled to remark about my breasts all the time in dressing rooms. It's another reason I hate shopping.

My first impulse, of course, was to reply, "I wish you would have surgery. Have someone sew your mouth shut."

But instead, I said, "Really? You'd cut up your body just to fit into a dress? What's wrong with you?" Then I whirled around, yanked the curtain shut across my cubicle in defiance—and burst into tears.

Annette, the saleslady, had seen the whole thing. When she came back into my area laden with plus-sized bustiers, I was weeping quietly and telling her that I was sick of feeling like a mutant and this is exactly why I didn't want to shop for a wedding dress in the first place and what was wrong with a bride in a red plastic rain poncho anyway?

"There now," Annette said, giving me a conspiratorial squeeze. "Don't listen to that lady. Some people have no sense. We're going to make you look beautiful."

This seemed hard to believe, given that my face was now what might charitably be described as a mucus farm. But I leaned over the bustier (performing the old "drop 'n' prop" as I called it) while Annette hooked it across my back. Then I tried on the first dress.

Since the only white wedding gown I'd ever liked had been the one worn by Carolyn Bessette Kennedy, I wriggled into a series of plain, spaghetti-strapped white columns. Unfortunately, as I quickly discovered, in order to look good in a dress like Carolyn Bessette Kennedy's, you essentially had to be built like Carolyn Bessette Kennedy. Studying myself in variations of her dress, the only word that came to mind was "bratwurst."

I tried on a beaded, silvery-satin sheath that made me look like a female impersonator, and another with a flouncy lace bolero jacket that made me look like a French prostitute on the Place Pigalle.

"Okay, that's it," I told Annette. "Hideousness confirmed. Visit over."

"Hm," said Annette, studying my figure and pretending not to have heard. "Let's try something different. Just for variety's sake."

Then she hoisted me into a big, pouffy, ivory-satin dress by Oleg Cassini—a dress with a Battenberg lace train long enough to carpet a legion hall, a voluminous, sweeping skirt, beaded, sequined lace-capped sleeves, and a lace sweetheart neckline that revealed a décolletage underneath. It was confectionary, princessy, glittering. It was exactly the type of dress that I had sworn on a stack of *Ms.* magazines that I would never, ever wear.

It looked spectacular on me.

My mind might have been that of a twenty-first-century feminist, but my body was that of a nineteenth-century Victorian, and the dress seemed to have been custom-made for my proportions. It curved where I curved; it went in where I went in. It accentuated my height, it emphasized the smallness of my waist, it lengthened my neck, it lifted my breasts slightly and balanced them with my hips. Granted, it made breathing nearly impossible, but this was not because of the cut, but rather because I simply could not believe what I looked like.

When Annette sidled over to me and whispered coyly, "Would you like to try on a tiara with that?" a gurgle escaped from the back of my throat that sounded distinctly like "goo."

"I'll take that as a yes. Come here," she smiled, motioning to the three-way mirror in the center of the room. "Let's get you on the pedestal, too."

Flabbergasted, I climbed up on the pedestal, the dress fanning out around me. "Here we go," said Annette, pinning the tiara to my head, then turning me toward my reflection.

I couldn't help it. I almost started to weep. I looked beautiful. More beautiful than I had ever seen myself look in my entire life. I looked queenly, glorious, uncompromised. The dress swept around me as if I were a great work of art carved from marble, as if I had emerged from the ocean on a half-shell, heralded by angels.

For the next four hours, I stood in front of the mirror, zombielike, refusing to take off the dress. Occasionally, Annette would come over and check up on me, "How you doing up there? Still liking that dress, huh? Well, you just let me know if you need a glass of water or something."

All around me, women came in, tried on dresses, twirled before the mirror, then left, while I stood there, catatonic in their midst.

"That girl by the mirror, is she all right?" I overheard one of the other customers whisper to Annette. "I don't think she's moved in over an hour."

"Oh, she's doing just fine," Annette assured her with a chuckle. "Just a little bride shock, is all."

What can I say? I was having a total ideological meltdown right there in the middle of David's Bridal salon. Because this was not what I was supposed to look like. This was not who I was supposed to be. This dress was symbolic of everything I'd railed against, everything I feared and fought again. Putting it on hurtled me closer and closer to becoming Superbride, Susie Homemaker, Giant Mammary Mom.

I was supposed to be the Anti-Bride, goddamn it! I was not some insipid girlie-girl dolled up like a parade float. But in that dress, with the tiara, I was intoxicated with myself. I felt gorgeous, indomitable. And I loved it. And I hated myself for loving it. Yet I couldn't stand to take it off.

And as I stood there, something else occurred to me: why did it take so long to have this experience? Every woman should have this experience—and not only *if* or *when* she gets married. Every woman should see herself looking uniquely breathtaking, in something tailored to celebrate her body, so that she is better able to appreciate her own beauty and better equipped to withstand the ideals of our narrow-waisted, narrow-minded culture.

When men shop at ordinary department stores, they are treated like brides all the time. I've watched a salesman literally get down on his knees in a dressing room to pin the cuffs on a pair of off-the-rack slacks Bob was trying on. I've seen salesmen fawn over my brother, adjusting the sleeves on a sports jacket. I've heard them tell my father, "Let me get you the single-breasted version. That will look better on you."

Men's stores seem determined to make every schmucky guy who walks through their doors feel catered to, powerful, supremely attractive. At the time that I was planning my wedding, in fact, a commercial for a popular menswear chain featured the owner assuring his customers, "You're going to like the way you look. I guarantee it."

When was the last time women heard that from a salesperson? Most clothing stores only inflame our insecurities and our sense of limitation. "If you have wide hips, don't wear stripes," we're instructed. "Designers don't make that in your size." "At your age, you can no longer get away with a hemline like that." Even the bridal boutiques, while telling women that this is "our special time," implicitly punish anyone who can't fit their sample size.

David's Bridal, I thought. What a bizarrely feminist place: a froufrou heaven staffed by women dedicated to making sure that other women look astonishing. In the dressing room, I saw three-hundred-pound blondes, wiry black women, Asian brides with asymmetrical haircuts, voluptuous Hispanic girls, acne-splattered bridesmaids, birdlike middle-aged women saying, "So what if this will be husband Number Three? This time, I'm doing it right." And every woman was treated like royalty. Yes, they have sizes 2 to 32. Yes, they have all price ranges. Yes, they will alter if for you. Yes, they will make you look beautiful. For you—*you*, my dear—are a goddess.

Shortly after 6:30 that evening, Annette came over to me. "Listen, I hate to do this to you, but we're closing the store for the night."

Panicked, I only then realized what I should have done hours before. Whipping out my cell phone, I started frantically calling my girlfriends and leaving incoherent messages on their answering machines, sounding, finally, like the hysterical five-year-old the bridal industry had been encouraging me to act like all along:

"Quick! It's an emergency," I cried. "I'm at David's Bridal! And they put me in this dress! And then they put me on a pedestal! And then they put a tiara on my head! And now I want to stay this way for the rest of my life!"

Lucy called back almost immediately. "Put the saleslady on," she commanded like a platoon leader. "I'm logging on to the David's Bridal Web site."

I handed Annette the phone. I heard her say, "Oleg Cassini. A-line. Keep scrolling down. Now click. That's it, with the lacy train . . . oh, yes. It does look gorgeous on her. I should know. I've been watching her wear it for the past four hours."

Eventually, with Lucy talking to me on the cell phone and Annette holding my hand in the dressing room, the two of them managed to coax me down off what I'd come to think of as "my" pedestal. Slowly, I changed back into my street clothes, but not before I'd put the dress on hold, called my mother, and arranged for the two of us to return the next day. You weren't supposed to buy the first wedding dress you fell in love with, but the truth was, I doubted my mental health—or anyone else's—could withstand another shopping trip.

That evening, I returned to Bob's apartment as if a tragedy had occurred.

"What's wrong? What happened?" he said with alarm.

"I found a wedding dress!" I sobbed, flinging myself down on his futon.

Bob looked at my heaving form on the bed before him. "I'm sorry," he said. "But isn't that supposed to be a good thing?"

"But it's BIG. And WHITE. And LACY. AND I LOOK LIKE A BRIDE!" I cried.

"Okay. I think I'm missing something here," he said. "I thought you were a bride."

"Well, technically, yes, but I'm not supposed to LOOK like one! I'm supposed to be the Anti-Bride! I'm supposed to be a renegade. I'M SUPPOSED TO BE SUBVERSIVE," I wailed.

Bob sat down beside me. "Honey," he said after a moment. "Don't take this the wrong way but: You? Dressed in a big, white, traditional wedding dress? If you ask me, that's about as subversive as you can get."

"Really?" I sniffled.

"If you want to shock people and defy all expectations," he said, "frankly, I can't think of a better way to do it."

I rolled over and gazed at him, tears streaking down my cheeks and pooling in my ears. My fiancé had an intense, brooding face, a landscape of complicated thought. That is, until he smiled. Then, his face became a circus marquee lighting up, boyish and gleeful, and you couldn't help grinning back at it. Looking at him, I saw his profound goodness, his poignant strength, his refusal to be cowed by either convention or rebelliousness.

Decades earlier, on the afternoon that my mother and my father had announced they were engaged, both their families had inexplicably declared war on each other. Battles were pitched over who paid for liquor at the wedding, who paid for the flowers, who could invite an extra cousin. By the time my parents finally got married, an invisible line seemed to have been drawn down the center of the chapel. My mother's family sat on one side in frigid silence, my father's on the other. It was like a wedding with the Berlin Wall plunked down the middle of it. In the photographs, my poor parents look miserable. They were only kids at the time. Trying to build a life together on such a fractured foundation, in the face of such volcanic animosity, why, they'd hardly stood a chance.

The decision to pledge your life to someone is such an enormous leap of faith. You grab each other's hand and jump, hoping you'll manage to navigate together whatever life hurls at you. It's crucial to be good to each other, to feel supported and endorsed.

Lying on the futon, looking at Bob, I saw a man who would not fault me for my own contradictions, but rather, see their humor and encourage me to live with them.

If I married him in a big, pouffy white dress, he'd appreciate equally the irony and the beauty of it. We would stand before our lesbian Wiccan priestess and our highly elastic rabbi, surrounded by our innermost circle of family and friends. Michelle would be there, plus Jill, Vanessa, Jeff, Maggie—all my childhood friends who'd seen me through so much of my life. It would feel like the grand finale of some great, epic musical, but also like a lavish, opening overture to one. I would stand there shimmering, regal and self-assured, because the wedding gown, like Bob, fit me uniquely—because it, like him, brought out my best qualities in spite of myself. Adorned in that dress, I'd go on to become who I wanted to be, regardless. I would let hope vanquish fear. I would grasp Bob's hand tightly. I would say clearly, "I do."

Chapter 15

Speak at the Tuna

BEFORE I MET my husband, the Amazing Bob, I dated a guy who dreamed of living in the suburbs of Cleveland. He painted pictures for me of big, family barbecues we'd have in our backyard and of trips we'd take to Disney World. As he waxed rhapsodic about his own suburban childhood—in which his mother spent hours in the kitchen preparing twice-baked potatoes and homemade chocolate cake—it became clear what my role in his scenario would become. When I told him I didn't want to spend my life driving kids around in a minivan, he put his arm around me reassuringly.

"Don't worry, hon," he said, squeezing my shoulder. "You can always car-pool."

The first time I met Bob, I made a point of asking him where he ultimately wanted to live. *Please say "a city,"* I prayed. *And please, by a city, don't mean Cleveland.*

I shouldn't have worried. His answer was even better than I could've imagined.

"Where do I dream of living?" Bob said. "Abroad, I guess."

When I was in elementary school, I spent every Saturday night transfixed before the TV watching that paragon of romantic propaganda, *The Love Boat,* followed by the equally preposterous *Fantasy Island.*

"Love—exciting and new!" I'd sing along to the lounge-music-y theme song of the first show, before shouting and pointing, "Look, boss. Zee plane! Zee plane!" along with Herve Villechaize during the opening sequence of the second. Both TV programs had a nearly criminal effect on my imagination, but one episode of *The Love Boat* in particular made a lasting impression. Its story line featured a sophisticated older couple (Shelley Winters and Bob Goulet, perhaps?) who'd spent their entire married life traveling the world. For three days on the Lido Deck, they regaled Julie, Doc, and Gopher with tales of their foreign adventures.

The husband would say things like, "Once, when we were riding yaks in Kathmandu—" His wife would interrupt, "Remember, dear? That was right after we had dinner in Monte Carlo with the Aga Khan." Showing off their snapshots of Florence and Cairo, they modestly referred to themselves as "citizens of the world."

Never mind that these characters had been cooked up to resuscitate the careers of C-list movie actresses and struggling soap opera personalities. Watching them, I felt a bolt of recognition and desire: *that* was how I wanted to live. Adventurously. Wildly. Like a character in a great novel. When I grew up, I vowed, I'd travel the world. I'd ride camels across the Sahara and drink absinthe in Parisian cafés. I'd take up residency in exotic-sounding cities like Sparta and Perth. My husband and I would celebrate our wedding anniversaries with three-day Princess cruises to Puerto Vallarta. Our glamorous, international lifestyle would be devoid of ring-around-the-collar, PTA meetings, and all the other banalities adults seemed to worry about.

It was a childhood dream that far outlasted my tutu. A few months after we were married, Bob came home from work and said, "So. How'd you like to move to Switzerland?"

There was a temporary posting in Geneva, he explained, that his boss was encouraging him to take. If I could arrange a sabbatical from my job, we could spend a year or two living out our fantasies, then paying for them in Swiss francs.

Hearing the news, I took a few steps backward. "You want us to move to Geneva?" I said. I then proceeded to do what people often do when they realize a lifelong dream is about to come true: I had a full-blown anxiety attack.

Stupidly, belatedly, it dawned on me that for all the years I'd said I'd wanted to live abroad, what I'd really meant was *live abroad in London or Paris*. What the hell did I know about Geneva? Not much, except that it had something to do with the treatment of war prisoners, which hardly sounded promising. A huge disconnect existed between bragging to people that I "lived abroad," and actually moving to a foreign country, which was enormously migratory and difficult.

Yet Switzerland was not exactly a "hardship post." A nurse I'd known had spent three years in the Amazon rain forest caring for indigenous tribes; in her e-mails home, she'd described how rats ran up the ropes of her hammock each night to bite her while she slept. Switzerland, by contrast, had laws forbidding people to flush their toilets after 10:00 P.M. lest the sound of the plumbing wake up the neighbors. Moreover, it had the highest per capita chocolate consumption of any population on earth. If that alone wasn't a reason to move someplace, what the hell was?

I then thought of Ernest Hemingway, Katherine Mansfield, Truman Capote: so many great writers had lived abroad in Europe, it practically seemed like a rite of passage. If we moved to Geneva and I ever managed to fulfill my delusions of literary grandeur, critics could refer to this time in my life as "Her Switzerland Period." How cool would that be? *Her years in Geneva,* I imagined my biography reading, *proved to be enormously inspiring for her—not only literarily, but also in terms of dark chocolate truffles.*

"Okay, let's do it," I said to Bob resignedly. "I mean, it's not like we have anything better to do, right?"

"There you go," he laughed. "That's the spirit."

In the months following our wedding, life had thrown us a few proverbial curveballs. Several of our family members had undergone major surgery, and the September 11 attacks had literally hit us where we lived. For weeks after 9/11, I'd staggered around Washington like a mental patient, traumatized and paranoid. I couldn't eat, sleep, write, or concentrate. Amazingly, people told me I'd never looked better in my life.

"Oh my God," they cried. "You've lost so much weight. You look fabulous! How on earth did you do it?"

We had to resume living, I knew—and living courageously. Bob and I would move to a foreign city we'd never been to before, where we knew no one, where we had no place to live, and where, from all reports, a pound of ground beef and a box of macaroni could easily set you back $146,000.

Oddly, many of our friends didn't understand the appeal of this.

"Why on earth would you want to move to a country where it's dark all the time and everyone's an alcoholic?" they said. "Why move to a place whose entire culture consists of ABBA and meatballs?"

They'd confused Switzerland with Sweden, but we didn't bother to point this out. Geneva was smack-dab in the center of Europe. It was possible to wake up there each morning, then go to France for lunch and a former Axis power for dinner. No doubt, in Switzerland, we'd live in a quaint little cuckoo-clock house overflowing with geraniums, then take off each weekend for some incredibly thrilling international destination. If our friends ever knew this, we assumed they'd commit hari-kari out of jealousy.

The day our Swiss adventure finally began, Bob's new boss, Shiv, picked us up at the Geneva airport and installed us downtown in a modern, concrete residential hotel called Studio House, where Bob and I would have to live until we found ourselves an apartment.

The narrow corridors smelled of fried onions and sizzling meat. As we passed doors to other studios, we could hear televisions blaring from inside, couples arguing in indistinguishable languages, babies crying shrilly. A barefoot man in a batik robe stood in a doorway, eating a plate of curry. The hotel was a holding pen for transients and foreigners—a category which, I realized suddenly, Bob and I now fell into.

Shiv set down our suitcases. "I hope this is all right," he said, gesturing to the small living area that looked like a dentist's waiting room. The bed was in an alcove partitioned by a rubberized curtain. The room smelled of vinyl, of cigarettes.

"It's fine. It's great," said Bob, nodding. "We really appreciate this."

"Okay then," said Shiv, clearing his throat. "Come by the office tomorrow, and we'll get your residency permits in order."

Residency permits. Right now, technically, we were aliens. Watching Shiv leave, I felt a jolt of panic. *Please, don't go!* I wanted to dash after him, shouting, *Don't abandon us here!*

Blearily, Bob and I plunked down on the miniature couch. For a while, we just sat there, listening to the purr of the hotel's ventilation system and the unrelenting growl of traffic. The name of street we were on translated to the Route of Acacias, but I was already mentally rechristening it as the Route of Little Fucking Motorcycles because it was overrun with mopeds, scooters, Vespas, Harley-Davidson wannabes, and dirt bikes, every single one of which sounded like a turbocharged leaf-blower.

Ambulances whooped by. People disembarked from hissing city buses, women in high heels pushed strollers over the pavement—*click, click. click.* An entire world was thriving beyond our window, thoroughly indifferent to us. There was nothing for us to do, nowhere to go. Back home—we kept checking our watches, subtracting six hours, mentally transporting ourselves back to Washington—everyone was asleep. We were in uncharted territory, beyond any radar, suspended between worlds.

"I guess this is it," Bob said after a moment.

"Yep," I said. "Here we are." *Internationals. Expats. Citizens of the World.*

Surveying the modular European light fixtures, the incompatible wall sockets, the 1970s plastic furniture, I suddenly wondered: Did Hemingway ever have to stay in a residence hotel like this? Did F. Scott Fitzgerald and Zelda ever feel so disoriented and out-of-place when they first arrived overseas? Probably not, I surmised, if only because they'd had the foresight to stay drunk all the time. Funny how glamorous stories about people going abroad always conveniently seemed to leave out this part—the unnerving schizophrenia of arrival—the panic you can feel in a strange city when you realize: whoa. This is it. You're not going home next week with a bagful of snow globes to hand out at the office.

Cleveland, I thought anxiously. Cleveland was suddenly looking pretty good to me.

———————

Geneva is in the French-speaking sector of Switzerland. As luck would have it, I'd studied French for years in school, visited Paris twice, and made out with several Frenchmen, all of which, I assumed, qualified me as bilingual. No doubt, plenty of Swiss citizens would be happy to engage me in lengthy discussions about "Totour and Tristan, the two wooden soldiers" who I'd studied ad nauseam in grade school, then listen raptly as I informed them that "whenever Pierre and Simone go to the market, they purchase a pair of shoes, a cauliflower, and a small brown monkey." Drawing upon the French literature I'd read in my high school Advanced Placement class, I could then impress the hell out of them by concluding each conversation with a quote by the existentialist philosopher Jean-Paul Sartre, *L'enfer, c'est les autres.*

L'enfer, c'est les autres translates to "hell is others," and it was an idea, I saw quickly, that the Swiss were only too willing to agree with after listening to my French for five minutes. For all my schooling, I hadn't the foggiest idea how to say such basic, things as "lightbulb," "extension cord," and "Can you please help me? My husband is stuck in the bathroom."

Our first day at Studio House, Bob accidentally locked himself in the toilet. As I ran downstairs to find the concierge, it occurred to me that Madame Bovary had never needed a locksmith. Seized by linguistic stage fright, the only thing I could manage to say was, *"la clef, il ne travaille pas,"* which roughly translates into "the key, it is not doing its work" creating the distinct impression of a key slacking off and lounging around a pool with a daiquiri when it was supposed to be manning a cash register and answering telephones.

Stupid things I'd never given a second thought to in the States—buying a carton of skim milk, operating an intercom system—soon took on a whole new level of exoticism and frustration as I attempted to do them in French. Determined to adhere to the old "When in Rome" adage, I spent my days butchering the French language with the dexterity of a fry cook, routinely asking the local grocer if he had any "low energy yogurt" and if it was possible to "disgust the cheese" before buying it.

The first item we purchased in Geneva was a cell phone, and I walked around quite proud of myself for recording our personal voice mail greeting in French. The English speakers who left us messages were genuinely impressed. "My, aren't we *parlez-vousing français* like a native," they remarked.

But it was the Swiss-French themselves who seemed truly moved by my fluency. Before they left a message, they invariably preceded it with an appreciative laugh. "Bonjour, Suzanne," they sang out, charmed.

"See," I bragged to Bob triumphantly. "Fifteen years of French weren't a waste after all. In just two weeks, I'm totally acculturated."

The next day, a Swiss woman I'd met at the Geneva Welcome Center stopped me in a café. "I have to tell you, your answering machine message is just so adorable," she said, lightly touching my arm. "Everyone at the center thinks it's the funniest thing they've ever heard." It turned out my voice mail message was instructing callers to "please speak at the tuna."

Hoping to improve our vocabulary, Bob and I surfed the television channels for an English program with French subtitles. We found exactly one. *The Jerry Springer Show.* After watching this every night for a week, we learned how to say two whole sentences in French: "You slept with my sister, you big fat whore" and "Don't you call me a pimp, you lying bitch."

Incredibly, I'd somehow assumed that as a white American, all I'd need to do to blend in in Switzerland was to speak French. Yet everything I did, I soon discovered, marked me as a foreigner.

Europeans are by nature more reserved than Americans. Crowded into hilltop villages and ancient, ingrown cities—and having spent much of the last two thousand years attacking, raping, and pillaging one another—they are not inclined to greet each other by bellowing, "Show me the love, Big Fella!" or to say goodbye by cheering, "Okay, everyone! Group hug!" They would never dream of walking around in a sweatshirt reading "Ask Me About My Grandchildren" or of sending a national television show a videotape of themselves driving a golf cart headlong into a swimming pool by accident.

With my big, confident strides, I discovered, I walked distinctly like an American. Draping my arms across the back of a couch and sprawling luxuriantly, I sat like an American. I talked loudly, like an American, and laughed loudly, like an American. Effervescing with self-revelation, I was more than happy to crack jokes at my own expense, like an American, informing everyone in great detail about my latest hilarious drugstore snafu or dining faux pas.

As a New Yorker, I'd always considered myself more sophisticated and urbane than the rest of America, whom I'd once referred to as "the yokels across the Hudson." But once I was in Geneva, I saw that I, too, was a yokel.

I didn't understand that the city's "no smoking" signs were only meant to be ironic. Compared to the French-Swiss women—who'd don bustiers, Fendi boots, and pancake makeup simply to buy a box of laundry detergent—I dressed like a bumpkin suffering from depression. Compared to the French, my cynicism was superficial. Compared to even the Italians, my friendliness was outsized. Compared to the Scandinavians, my politics were reactionary. Compared to virtually everyone in Europe, I was naive, buoyant, and annoyingly transparent in my desire to be liked. No matter what I did, everything about me was quintessentially American. On the streets of Geneva, I was an enormous, star-spangled, overzealous puppy.

Growing up as I had, you'd think I'd have gotten used to feeling like a misfit. But in America, even misfits get their own television shows. In Geneva, if I entered a neighborhood store and said, *"Bonjour, madame,"* I immediately felt invisible. As I stood there, awaiting acknowledgment, the shopkeeper's eyebrow would arch, then her lips would purse, and in an instant, her entire face would be like a crab retreating into its shell: Oh, a *foreigner.*

In the mildest, most pampered way possible, I was experiencing the degradations and frostiness that immigrants, minorities, and refugees have experienced throughout history. I was constantly aware of people speaking in a sort of code around me—exchanging knowing glances and gestures that were impossible to interpret except for the fact that they were definitely not saying: *My, this young stranger is lovely. Let's make her feel as welcome as possible.*

More than once, I'd see prices listed in a local salon or photocopying service, only to be presented with a much higher bill afterward. When I questioned it, I always received an impatient, rapid-fire explanation by the cashier: did Madame not know that those prices did not apply to the services she'd requested?

Each time this happened, I thought shamefully of all the times in the States when a cab driver had asked me, "Repeat please the address?" or a busboy at Ruby Tuesday's had smiled uncomprehendingly when I'd asked him for a napkin. Each time, I'd been huffy with them, my tone ripe with frustration: *Christ. Can't you people speak English?* Now, I was both the cab driver and the busboy.

As the saying goes, payback is a bitch.

Yet the biggest challenge Bob and I faced was housing. In Geneva, apartments are in notoriously short supply, and the rental process is like a Miss America contest for real estate. You have to apply for each apartment; landlords then review all the applications to decide whom if anyone, they'd like to rent to.

When employees for private companies are transferred to Geneva, they're given hefty housing allowances and the services of relocation agencies. Bob, however, was working for a nonprofit agency. The only relocation expert we had at our disposal was me.

Armed with classified ads downloaded from the Internet, I tromped all over the city feeling like a world-class idiot. When I came across places that were actually available, I was invariably lost within a pack of other desperate apartment hunters. My French repeatedly failed me. Trying to ask the proprietor if the rent included heating, I asked him instead if it came with "unemployment." Once I realized my error, I then inquired if the rent included "shoes."

"WE ARE NEVER GOING TO FIND AN APARTMENT," I yelled at Bob when he arrived home from his second day at the office. "WE ARE GOING TO WIND UP LIVING IN A FUCK-ING PUP TENT IN THE PARK."

"A pup tent in the park," Bob said with a sigh. "And you know this after exactly two days?"

Every day that week, Bob came home to discover he'd married not a citizen of the world but a lunatic. As I prepared frozen ravioli on our hot plate, I ranted to him how I'd seen fourteen apartments that day, and each one was either more hideous or more unobtainable than the next.

When Bob replied helpfully, "But you saw fourteen places. So there *are* some apartments out there, no?" I immediately began yelling at him, "HAVE YOU NOT LISTENED TO A SINGLE WORD I'VE SAID? PUP TENT! PUP TENT! PUP TENT!"

A real estate agent had told me that getting an apartment in Geneva depended upon relationships, upon "knowing someone."

All the other apartments hunters, I sobbed to Bob, were Swiss. They were rich. They had relocation experts taking them around in a Smart Car. What did I have? A bus pass and an accent that, judging from people's faces, made me sound like the French-speaking equivalent of Latka Gravas on *Taxi*.

Ernest Hemingway, I continued, had probably never had to tour an apartment decorated from floor to ceiling in burgundy bathroom tiles. Henry James, as far as I knew, had never had to come up with the French phrase for "How come this place is missing a kitchen?" Why, Gertrude Stein and Alice B. Toklas lived in France during World War Two as two *Jewish lesbians,* and yet, I cried, you never heard about *them* going insane trying to find a one-bedroom with a working toilet.

What the hell were we doing here? Why on earth did we ever think this would be fun? Why hadn't we just stayed in America, where everything was familiar, and people knew and loved us? Why weren't we living someplace convenient, full of Cracker Barrel restaurants and narcotizing strip malls? Someplace homey, and middlebrow, where we didn't need a goddamn French-English dictionary just to figure out how to operate a washing machine?

"Why did moving abroad seem so much easier for everyone else?" I cried. "They never talked about this stuff on the goddamn *Love Boat*."

———

When I eventually calmed down, however, I realized that while I didn't have money or connections, I did have one thing going for me that probably no other apartment hunter in Geneva had: utter shamelessness. As a native New Yorker, a former child outcast, a wannabe gonzo journalist, and an aspiring slut, I'd developed a near-immunity to embarrassment. Totally lacking any sense of social propriety, I would to talk to just about anyone. If apartment hunting in Geneva depended upon relationships and engaging people, well then, I decided, I'd treat it not as an apartment search, but an apartment *seduction*.

The next day, my first appointment was to see a one-bedroom not far from Bob's office. The landlady, a Madame Duvalier, wore a leopard print dress and chain-smoked as she climbed nimbly up the stairs in high heels to show me an attic apartment. With an old slate roof and tar-papered balcony, it was a place guaranteed to feel like a pizza oven.

Still, revving up my engines, I complimented her on her earrings. Jewelry is an excellent icebreaker among women; every piece inevitably tells a story. Madame Duvalier's earrings, it turned out, were a gift from her second husband. When I complimented her on her brooch as well, she informed me that it came from her third husband. Her necklace, she volunteered, was from her fourth. Husbands were clearly a "thing" with Madame Duvalier. "Oh," I said politely. "How many have you had so far?"

"Six," Madame Duvalier said airily. "And each one of them was a piece of shit."

"Men, Their Infinite Shortcomings, and How to Exploit Them," turned out to be a pet topic of Madame Duvalier's. For the next forty-five minutes, I listened to her bad-mouth her ex-husbands, explain the intricacies of Swiss marital law, and extol the virtues of surveillance cameras. The only conversation required on my part was feigned comprehension. *"Vraiment?"* I nodded. Really?

My next appointment was for a two bedroom in the heart of downtown. The apartment itself was the epitome of old Europe: it had high ceilings, transoms, elegant moldings, and not a single closet. The owner who greeted me at the door was wearing rope sandals and holding a trumpet. With his floppy hair and poignant acne, he could not have been older than twenty.

"Bonjour, my name is Jacques," he said in French. Then he added, in English, "Oh. You're American? Then please, call me Miles." From the way he said this, it was clear he'd secretly been testing this out in his head for years. Saying it out loud, he seemed shocked by his own audacity.

Jacques/Miles, it turned out, was showing the apartment for his parents, who had obviously been gone for a while because every room was a landslide of CDs, jazz books, sheet music, and strategically discarded plates full of pizza crusts. Jazz was playing on a boom box in the kitchen. "Oh, Herbie Hancock," I remarked, trying desperately to make conversation. "My mother went to college with him."

Upon hearing this, Jacques/Miles looked stunned, as if Herbie Hancock himself had materialized right there in front of the refrigerator. "*Vraiment?*" he cried. Really?

"*Oui,*" I nodded. And it was true. My mother had actually gone to college with Herbie Hancock.

"Did your mother ever speak to him?" Jacques/Miles fairly begged.

"Of course," I said.

Then, seeing the reverence on his face and sensing my advantage, I couldn't help it. Before I knew it, I was creating the writer's equivalent of a jazz riff: it began plaintively enough, with a few opening notes of truth, before quickly giving way to full-blown improvisation.

My mother had, in fact, attended a small land grant college in the Midwest during the Eisenhower administration. Although the school had a reputation for liberalism, its farm-raised students routinely sang earnest songs about "taking Jesus as your savior" and "the darkies picking cotton" before saying grace each night in the dining hall. Herbie Hancock had been the only black student on campus; my mother had been the only New York Jew. Their "friendship," I gathered, was based not on actual conversations, but on fleeting looks of sympathy and mutually acknowledged dread across the green.

Since it was hard to convey all of this to Jacques/Miles in French, however, I simply told him that my mother and Herbie Hancock had been extremely close. Why, if I remembered correctly, she'd listened to him compose several of his earliest pieces. And of course, I added, she always did regret turning down his marriage proposal.

"Herbie Hancock asked your mother to marry him?" Jacques/Miles exclaimed.

"Well, practically," I said.

"*C'est incroyable!*" Jacques/Miles cried ecstatically. Then, looking at me as if I were a jazz deity myself, he yanked a frozen pizza out of the refrigerator and said, "Please, you will stay for lunch, no?"

The next apartment was in a modern high-rise that might as well have been in Cincinnati, yet it was quiet with floor-to-ceiling windows overlooking the lake. The current tenant was a dapper Italian businessman named Vincenzo. "Oh, you're Italian?" I said. I then felt compelled to share with him every Italian phrase I'd ever memorized. *Good morning*, I parroted. *Thank you. I'd like to make a reservation. Where is the Vatican? Where is the toilet? Toothbrush. Motor scooter. Don't touch that. He's not my husband, he's my little brother, you idiot.* After exhausting this repertoire, I proceeded to recite a list of my favorite gelato flavors.

To my great relief, Vincenzo spoke fluent English and not a word of French. Unfortunately, it turned out that he himself was not the owner of the apartment; he was only a renter.

"But you know, there's this amazing American woman next door," he said. "She's also a writer. Beautiful woman. She's eighty, but she looks sixty and she knows the landlady. Would you like to meet her?"

Any polite, decent person would've said, "Oh, no. I couldn't possibly disturb a stranger in her home." Instead, I followed Vincenzo across the hall, asking, "You really think she'll pull some strings for me?"

An hour later, Ruth and I were still sitting in her kitchen, drinking gimlets and discussing art, literature, and politics. Amazingly, Ruth herself had been born and raised in New York City—in the same neighborhood, in fact, as my grandmother. Her father had been a rabbi, and during the 1950s, Ruth had spent summers working with the activist folk singer Pete Seeger, whom my parents had revered as a deity. Now, her living room was strewn with the same novels I was reading and with stacks of *New Yorker* magazines. Like my grandmother, she had a penchant for hard liquor and dirty jokes, as well as for referring to certain politicians as "shitheads." Among the four hundred thousand people in Geneva, I'd managed to find the only one to whom I could've possibly been related.

"What are the chances of this?" Ruth marveled. "My God, you're like my long-lost little *bubehluh*." Then she cupped my chin in her hands and smiled. "You do know what a *bubehluh* is, don't you?"

By the time I arrived back at Studio House, it was nearly 8:00 P.M.

"Where were you?" asked Bob, as I wobbled in grandly, reeking of gin.

"Apartment hunting," I said, flopping merrily onto the couch. "Yee-ha."

"You're in a freakishly good mood," said Bob. "Did you have any luck, or are you just drunk?"

"I started off the day with a husband collector who spent forty-five minutes educating me about Swiss divorce law," I said. "Then, I had frozen pizza with a twenty-year-old trumpet player after telling him that my mother was engaged to Herbie Hancock. I spent the afternoon reciting Italian ice cream flavors to an Italian in Italian. Then, I drank three gin gimlets with an eighty-year-old former leftie from Brooklyn."

I kicked off my shoes with a flourish. "If that doesn't get us an apartment here," I sighed, "we might as well just go home."

The next week, we learned that we'd been approved for all three apartments.

Suddenly, we not only had a place to live, but a choice. Hearing the news, I shouted, "NOT JUST ONE BUT THREE! THREE! COUNT THEM!" Then I started leaping around the studio, squealing: "I DID IT! I WON I WON I WON!" Because, did I forget to mention? Apartment hunting was a contest: whoever landed the most apartments, I believed, won.

Instead of falling at my feet in awe and gratitude, however, Bob just said wearily, "I told you it would work out. Did we really have to go through all that melodrama?"

We decided to rent the one-bedroom next door to Ruth. Once we had a place to live, I was finally able to calm down. For the first time since we'd stepped off the plane, I felt something akin to genuine peace and excitement. With our "legitimation cards" from the Swiss government, a signed lease, and our annoying little cell phone in hand, we had finally, truly arrived.

Since I couldn't begin my own work until our personal effects arrived from Washington, I found myself with three blank weeks of calendar pages spread before me. Finally, I was an unransomed Woman of the World, living abroad, with nothing but adventure at her disposal. I could take a high-speed train to Paris or Zurich. I could tour the local art galleries, visit the Olympic Museum in Lausanne, even ride a funicular in the Alps. Yet one cultural experience clearly eclipsed all others in its immediacy and importance. I was, after all, a girl who'd once emptied an entire one-pound bag of M&M's into her grandmother's silk evening bag, then eaten every one of them.

"Fuck the museums," I said to Bob. "The guidebook says there are chocolate makers here who give private tours of their facilities."

The owner of the *chocolaterie* seemed surprised when I showed up alone.

"I thought you said you were a group," she said. "We only do group tours, madame."

"Oh, but I am a group," I insisted. "Trust me."

As the woman led me to the back of the shop, she eyed me suspiciously. In order to appear more Swiss, I'd dressed for the occasion in a slinky black sheath, a stylish white linen coat, full makeup, and high heels. It was nine o'clock in the morning. I was dressed like this to stand in a kitchen, surrounded by three harried chocolate makers in chocolate-spattered aprons.

They looked at me like, *"Quoi?"* (Translation: What?)

When most people are in an awkward situation, their impulse is to clam up and be as deferential as possible. I, however, feel immediately compelled to start talking. I prattle away, a veritable fountain of logorrhea. And of course, this virtually guarantees that the situation will only become ten times more awkward than it already is.

Seeing the confounded looks on the chocolate makers' faces, I wasted no time digging myself a hole. *"Bonjour,"* I said brightly. *"Je suis Madame Gilman, et . . ."* I suddenly felt compelled to justify my existence to them—always a dangerous thing. *"Et j'ai une grande passion pour le chocolat!"* I proclaimed. I'm Mrs. Gilman, and I have a grand passion for chocolate. Yep, that is exactly what I said. And as soon as those words were out of my mouth, I wanted to stick my head in the chocolate machine and kill myself.

This time, the look of contempt from the chocolate makers needed no translation: I was possibly the biggest asshole to set foot in Geneva since the Duke of Savoy had tried to invade it back in 1602. I knew I had to say something quickly to modify my bombastic and ridiculous entrance. Not knowing what else to do, how else to salvage my reputation, I lied. I told them that I was a schoolteacher. Back home in America, I explained, my students loved a book called *Charlie and the Chocolate Factory.* And I figured that since I was in Switzerland, I should see how chocolates were made just so that I could tell my students about it.

"So I'm here, you see, for the little children," I said bathetically. "The little children of America."

Which was partially true, I supposed, in so much that I was there for my own little inner American child.

There is still some justice left in this world because the chocolate makers of Switzerland, at least, still revere the public schoolteachers of America. As soon as they heard my explanation, their tone changed completely. "Oh, you are a professor," they said admiringly, then got very busy giving me a tour of the kitchen and showing me photo albums of their work. It became clear that I was standing amid the Michelangelos of chocolate. They crafted actual sculptures out of chocolate: Grecian urns, Easter tableaus, chocolate soccer fields, chocolate violins, chocolate bears, chocolate penguins skiing down chocolate mountains on tiny chocolate skis.

They ran the chocolate machine for me so I could watch them coat dark truffles and imprint them each painstakingly by hand with a little, filigreed thimble. They showed me the kilos of pure chocolate they melted down in an enormous vat that made the entire room an olfactory orgasm. They showed me trays upon trays of fresh chocolate-dipped fruits, truffles, and hazelnut creme.

Finally, the master chocolate maker said, "I'm afraid that's the end of the tour, madame." Peeling off his rubber gloves, he then gestured toward the racks of hundreds of newly crafted chocolates. "But please," he urged. "Be our guest. Eat whatever you like."

Eat whatever you like.

Hearing these words was like having a seizure. Because of course, by that point, I wanted to eat EVERYTHING. More than that, I wanted to BE everything—I wanted to plunge my hands into the vat of liquid milk chocolate and rub it all over myself, then lift it up and pour it over my head and COAT MYSELF ENTIRELY IN CHOCOLATE and roll around the floor in the cocoa dusting myself like a giant truffle. I was in a delirium—I was a chocolate pervert surrounded by chocolate pornography—I could easily have had an orgy of one in that kitchen—CHOCOLATE, CHOCOLATE— EVERYWHERE. ME AND THE CHOCOLATE, FINALLY, AS ONE!!!!

But I had to keep myself in check. Because I'd told everyone that I was a *teacher*. I thought of Mrs. Mutnick back in kindergarten, who'd charitably believed that I was changing my name to "Sapphire." I thought of Mrs. Goldsmith in sixth grade, who'd encouraged me to audition for the Christmas pageant. How could I besmirch such a much abused and underappreciated profession by behaving like a complete pig in their name?

Demurely, painfully, I shook my head. "I couldn't possibly," I said, waving away the trays. Then, trying to change the subject as quickly as possible, I said miserably, "The bunnies. They, too, are milk chocolate, *non?*"

After I left, I felt stunned. It was hard to remember the last time I'd said no to anything—let alone anything covered in milk chocolate. Had I really just turned down an all-you-can-eat buffet? What was happening to me? Who was this person? Not knowing what else do to with myself, I walked through the narrow streets toward the waterfront.

Silhouetted by mountains, Geneva sits at the mouth of a large, glacial lake. Bisected by rivers, laced with bridges, the city has an expansive, breezy, maritime feel. Boats bob in its marinas, and a spectacular man-made geyser shoots up hundreds of feet in the air. Known as the Jet d'Eau, this is the symbolic landmark of Geneva— the liquid equivalent of the Empire State Building or the Washington Monument—the city's prized contribution to the eternal "who can build a bigger penis" contest that seems to go on between civilizations.

For a long time, I stood on the Mont Blanc Bridge, which links the two banks of the city across the Rhône. The night before, slightly homesick, I'd bought a phone card at the train station and telephoned friends back home. Lucy had just had a baby; for as long as I'd known her, she'd wanted a family. My friend Desa, meanwhile, was busy starting her own business, which she'd been talking about since college. It felt slightly strange talking to them when I was sitting in a residence hotel in Geneva, in what might as well have been an alternative universe, where I was taking such a different, untrammeled path. But as we talked, our inverse experiences sounded strangely, eerily similar.

"I had no idea that having a baby would be anything like this," Lucy told me. "Nobody ever tells you how truly frightening and difficult it is. Sometimes, I feel so completely frustrated and helpless."

"Every day," Desa said, "I tell myself, 'Remember, you've always wanted to be your own boss. Think about where you'll be in five years.' But each morning, I wake up in a cold sweat."

"Until now," said Lucy, "I only really thought of the big picture. You know, how wonderful it would be to have a child. And it is. But the day-to-day reality is baby-poop, breast pumps, and smelly diapers. Whoops, gotta go. Case in point: Precious here just spit up all over the sofa."

My friends and I had reached the age when we had the great, good fortune to be living out some of the dreams we'd had when we were young. Now, we were discovering the truly hard part: the realities.

Having a new baby made you psychotic with exhaustion and self-doubt. Professional success could make you delirious with insomnia and anxiety. Living abroad rendered you lonely and infantilized. And no matter what road you took, you still had to brush your teeth every morning, pay your bills, do your damn laundry, worry about taxes, check your breasts for cancer, argue with your loved ones about whether to defrost the refrigerator. Nobody, after all, it seemed, was exempt from banality.

"Those bastards," Desa and I laughed over the phone. "What happened to all those perfect 'happily ever afters' they promised us?"

Moments of pure bliss were often accidental. Getting something you'd consciously worked toward, on the other hand, was often far more emotionally complicated. Fulfilling an ambition was an experience that could oscillate wildly between terror and exhilaration, helplessness and fulfillment, anxiety and mind-numbing boredom.

But squinting across the water, I felt for that one instant that everything was right with my world. What would my seven-year-old self think, I wondered, if she could see me here in Switzerland, surrounded by mountains, old clock towers, and a lake even bigger than the one she'd swum in every summer? She'd probably be pissed, I realized. She'd be pissed that I'd turned down the opportunity to stuff my face with as much free chocolate as humanly possible. In her eyes, I'd be deranged.

Oh, well.

Since coming to Geneva, I'd invented a little game with myself, in which I calculated the time back in New York City, then imagined what the people I knew might be doing. Back in Manhattan, it was early morning now, just the verge of rush hour. The sky would be suffused with light from the east; as the sun rose, it would cut through the spaces between the buildings and striate the pavement with dramatic, dusty slats of gold. Downtown, garbage trucks would be grinding away on their rounds, the subways would be filling up, storekeepers throwing pails of water out onto the sidewalk. Vendors along lower Broadway would be setting up stands, kicking out the legs on card tables to display I ♥ NY T-shirts, one hooded guy on the corner acting as a lookout. My father would be getting to work early to prepare some briefs; he'd be stepping off the elevator and walking to his office on the forty-eighth floor in a building that overlooked Ground Zero. From his window, the Statue of Liberty would also be visible, standing sentry in the pearlized Hudson.

Suddenly, my gaze switched from this reverie to the reality of the Jet d'Eau, now spraying water across the lake in great parabolas. Geneva was a U.N. headquarters. On the bridge behind me, Indian women in saris walked leisurely by. A French cycling team barreled past. Teenagers skulked across in their oversized pants, their bumper-car sneakers. (Teenagers everywhere: *they* looked the same.) On the shore, two Arab women in hijabs stood with their husbands, tossing bread crumbs to the swans. A little blond boy raced across the bridge on a Razor scooter while his very pregnant mother waddled behind him frantically shouting at him in French to slow down and wait by the light. WAIT BY THE LIGHT. Rows of United Nations flags on either side of the bridge flapped wildly in the wind, the silk of them straining, flailing, seeming to dance. On the street in front of the Hôtel des Bergues, a truck suddenly backfired, and for a moment, everyone flinched, then exhaled. Looking across the right bank, I could see the office building where Bob was working, struggling with a hopelessly slow computer, his face poignant in its frustrated concentration, a cup of cold coffee abandoned by his keyboard. The sun seemed to burnish my skin, the wind raked through my hair. I felt weightless, exhilarated. This was it. I was doing something I'd dreamed of. I was living in the middle of the world, and all of us were in it together, each one of us extraordinary and yet, really, no different from each other. I flung my arms back and for a minute, it felt like I could levitate. Then I laughed, loudly, like an American. Like a defiant bride. Like a seven-year-old girl with a rhinestone earring clipped to her nose. I had absolutely no idea what would happen next. But then, I suppose, no one ever does.

About the Author

Susan Jane Gilman is the author of *Kiss My Tiara: How to Rule the World as a SmartMouth Goddess*. She has written commentary for *The New York Times, The Los Angeles Times,* and *Ms.* magazine, among others, and her fiction and essays have received several literary awards. Though she has lived most recently in Geneva, Switzerland, and Washington, D.C., she remains, eternally, a child of New York.

Kiss My Tiara

HOW TO RULE THE WORLD AS A
SMARTMOUTH GODDESS

by Susan Jane Gilman

A Cynthia Heimel for a new generation, Susan Jane
Gilman serves up uncommon wisdom and practical
advice on everything from sex to politics, from turning shopping skills into a power tool to using man-
catching techniques for salary negotiations. Here
are the smart rules for smart women of all cultures,
sexualities, and sizes. Irreverent, provocative, hip—
and always funny—this guide to power and attitude
offers women an intelligent alternative to the negative messages we hear every day from magazines,
television, and relatives.

"Hilariously sarcastic . . . It's worth it just
to hear the way Gilman debunks myths."

—*MS.*

"Don't you just love it when there's a wickedly
smart BRAIN behind a wickedly smart MOUTH?
Kiss My Tiara is dee-licious."

—JILL CONNER BROWNE,
THE SWEET POTATO QUEEN'S BOOK OF LOVE